ROMANCES OF THE FRENCH REVOLUTION. By G. LENOTRE, Author of 'The Flight of Marie Antoinette,' etc. Translated by FREDERIC LEES (*Officier de l'Instruction Publique*).

In two vols. Demy 8vo. Fully illustrated. Price 20s. *net.*

AFTER WATERLOO. REMINISCENCES OF EUROPEAN TRAVEL FROM 1815-1819. By Major W. E. FRYE. Edited by Dr. SALOMON REINACH (*Membre de l'Institut*).

One vol. Demy 8vo. Price 15s. *net.*

THE REVOLT OF THE 'POTEMKIN.' REMINISCENCES OF CONSTANTINE FELDMANN.

Crown 8vo. Price 6s. *net.*

LONDON: WILLIAM HEINEMANN
21 BEDFORD STREET, W.C.

RECOLLECTIONS OF A SPINSTER AUNT

EDITED BY

S. SOPHIA BEALE
AUTHOR OF 'A HANDBOOK TO THE LOUVRE,' ETC.

LONDON
WILLIAM HEINEMANN
1908

Copyright, London and the United States of America

CONTENTS

CHAPTER	PAGE
I. FOREWORD	1
II. CHILDHOOD	6
III. BETTY AND NANCY	26
IV. CONCERNING CHURCHES	52
V. SWIMMING	66
VI. A HARVEST HOME	77
VII. POOR THOMAS	88
VIII. THE DEN	109
IX. ART AND ART STUDENTS	125
X. THE DEN	148
XI. THE MYSTERY OF A LONDON STREET	172
XII. RHEINLAND	192
XIII. PARIS	213
XIV. THE FRANCO-GERMAN WAR	241
XV. ACTORS AND ACTRESSES	272

CONTENTS

CHAPTER							PAGE
XVI. OBER-AMMERGAU	.	.	.	.	.	288
XVII. PARIS	.	.	.	.	.	302
XVIII. BATH	.	.	.	.	.	322
XIX. MISS GARIBALDI	.	.	.	.	.	330
XX. BAYREUTH	.	.	.	.	.	343

RECOLLECTIONS OF A SPINSTER AUNT

CHAPTER I

FOREWORD

'Why not?'

'But would any one care to read such a book? You know Aunt Jane was never acquainted with any distinguished folk. Would it be interesting, think you?'

'I do not see why it should not be. If she never knew any celebrities personally, she must have seen many people and a vast number of interesting things and places; and just think for a moment of the changes which have taken place during the last fifty years; and change is not the only development. Things were quieter, and people less hurried in the middle of the "wonderful century"—and what a really marvellous century it was! The world was more conventional, more fussy, and prudish; but on the other hand, it had time to think. Now all is rush; there are plenty of ideas floating about, and possibly the big brains are as good; moreover, their owners may develop their ideas as well, or better than their forerunners were apt to do. But the small people fly from one subject to another, and have no time to think nor to meditate; and as for concentration of thought or calm contemplation, it is as much out of fashion as snuff-taking and toddy-drinking. Why not try the book?'

'But query, can I find the necessary middleman, a publisher?'

'Why, surely that cannot be difficult, considering the absolute rubbish which gets thrown upon the market, presumably to be bought or read, possibly both?'

'You are right, good Friend, as regards the printing of much rubbish, and no doubt a good deal of it is read; but we know no more of the relationship of those who write to those who print the aforesaid rubbish, than we do of the relationship between the Guardians of our various Unions, and the provision and coal merchants whose tenders are accepted. The world is made up of mysteries, and not the least extraordinary are the whys and wherefores that select one book for publication and doom another to oblivion; it is as if a disagreeable little demon pursued some brain-workers, authors, painters, sculptors, music-men, and the like, and, preceding the agents carrying the works, whispered into the Middleman's ear the advice of Pilate's wife.'

This conversation took place while the speakers

were walking along that exquisite moorland of Dorsetshire which overlooks Poole Harbour, the Venice of England. Do not laugh; but look over that space of water at half-tides, and in imagination, if you have any, people the sandbanks with a series of campanili, substitute stout piles for the weakly little sticks of our harbour, and raise the background of hills into seven thousand or eight thousand feet snow-capped mountains, 'that misty band' of which Ruskin speaks; and have you not something, a little scrap of Nature, that reminds you of the Venetian lagoons? with the addition of colour—the heather, the bracken, and here and there in summer, masses of rhododendrons growing wild. And then the effects of light and shade upon the water; it is all most beautiful, though Poole itself can scarcely claim to be even a very poor relation of the Queen of the Sea.

As to the subject of our conversation, it referred to a scheme for putting together some old letters and an incomplete diary written by a spinster aunt. The letters were sent to a cousin in the country, our old aunt being a Londoner. Was it likely, was it even possible that the diary of an insignificant member of society, and her letters to a commonplace friend, could be of any interest to the general public? Yet, on the other hand, the diary of an artistic uncle, found, years ago, in the same ox-skin-covered trunk as these letters, had appeared in an early number of the late Harry

Quilter's interesting *Universal Review*, under the title of 'An Old-World Diary,' and had met with a certain amount of appreciation.

There was also in the box another bundle of letters tied up with a blue ribbon, and bearing the Jamaica postmark upon the folded letter paper. The handwriting was evidently a man's (you could not mistake a woman's writing in the thirties and forties of the last century); the composition was somewhat sentimental, unmistakably that of a lover, but also of an old friend. These I put aside to burn, deciding that we had had of late years a sufficient instalment of love-letters, for unless they be written by celebrities, proving that all the world's akin and the intellectuals as silly under certain conditions as their commonplace brethren, such effusions are apt to pall upon the mind. But the remainder of the letters and the scraps of diary being considered of sufficient interest by an unbiassed reader who sat in judgment upon them, it was determined to arrange them in order to afford a sort of disjointed account of my old aunt's childhood and early life.

She came upon the stage in the Victorian age, when women wore cottage bonnets, short skirts with one flounce, and shoes with sandals in fine weather, and clogs in wet, the latter having superseded pattens as more seemly. They were wooden-soled things, with a hinge under the instep and a leather toe-cap, as clumsy as the pattens, but not quite so difficult to walk in, as the latter rested upon a circle of iron under the centre of the foot upon which the wearer had to balance herself.

One of the earliest letters was written when the aunt was eight or nine years of age. The family had gone to Herne Bay one summer, when that watering-place consisted of merely half a dozen cottages with few or no visitors.

RECOLLECTIONS OF

CHAPTER II

CHILDHOOD

May 10*th* 1847.

MY DEAR COUSIN MARY

We came heer yesterday, and this morning we had our first barth in the see it was so funy. We got in the barthing machine and it jogged down the beech into the see i was so fritenned and it is horrid going into the water The rope did not brake but nurse thought it wood Then we undrest and stud on the steps. and then down came a grene curtane and we only saw the see like a room it was so cold as we stud on the steps and then the curtane was lifted up and an ugly old woman drest in blue came in under the curtane she had such lots of cloths on she was so fat and a shiny cap on her hed and she looked something like the Diver at the Pollyteknik and i began to cry. and then she said don't cry, Deerey, and she took hold of me with both her hands and held me in her arms and then throwed me into the water 3 times and every time i kickt her so and skremed and the water got into my eyes which was as bad as the sope at home in the hot water and i went on

A SPINSTER AUNT

skreming all the time Mama wiped me for she rubed me so hard i was so cold and i don't like the see it is wurse than that big bath at home were Papa yust to put me in when i was little he tride everything to make me like it but i always kickt and the see is quit as cold You remember when i had a little frog on a piece of wood in the bath but that never made me like going in but i liked playing with mister froggy from the outside he looked so prety sitting on the wood he was quit wee and grene. I am going to play now so gud by

Your afecshonate cosin,   BA.

May 20 1847

MY DEAR MARY

Do you beleve this Mamma says when i was a very little gurl she took me one day to hungerfud markit to buy a fat chiken and wile she was talking to the man i was out side the shop and i puled a little pigs tale out and she found me suking it how cud a tale be puled out of a pig but the others always tese me now and call out who stole the pigs tale we came hear by the bote it was called Father Thames and some of the pepel were so sik but i wasent and it was ole Brandy Ball who drove the hakney coch to the river were we got the bote there was plenty of room for us all its so big i like bilding karsels in

RECOLLECTIONS OF

the sand and we put stones all along the parths up to the karsel and i hav got a spade and a pale and i wish you was hear and Nipper sends his luve and i am your afecshonate cosin Ba. Mama has a big sugar loaf today and we are going to cut it up with nippers.

Janery 7 1848

MY DEAR MARY

We had a party last nite and a big cake not so big as those at the shop in the Strand wich we went to see the other day. One had a karsel on it, and another a big ship with barly sugar masts and ropes. Ours was as big as a chairs seat and had white sugar flowers on the top and it was so good we had caracters and Edward and Evey wer the king and queen and they cut the cake did I tell you about the big party Mamma had at Christmas. I did not like it much because I had to walk all round the room and shake hands and say good nite to every boddy I was so glad wen I got away but what do you think I did one night I walked down stairs and into the drawing room in my nite gown all asleep and they were dancing Bekky carried me up again before I went to bed they all sat round the room and one lady sang a song and another lady played the harp at the same time. She looked like the pickture books and they said she was prety but I don't think so

A SPINSTER AUNT

she had long mittens and a big thing on her head like a Turk and she was too old to be prety I am sure she was 40.

Your afecshonate   BA-JANIE.

P.S.—Fanny and Ellen took me to the Pantheon to buy wax to make flowers its a luvly place and there are parots and cockatus, and we went one nite to the Sury Gardens to see the Sige of Badderjoz all fireworks and soljers. I want to go agane. Mama says its like Voxhorl wen she was yung. and Ranneler They were both gardens but are shut up now. But we saw a play and Madam Celeste—O she does scream so. I like the horses at Aslys much better they dance and do all sorts of things and I have been in the Thams tunel it drips so and smells of earth.

April 8 1848

MY DEAR MARY

There is to be a great meeting of Chartists the day after tomorrow on Kenington Common. every one is very excited and peple are being made into speshal cunstabels. Leo is one not Papa because he is a docter and has not time and if any one is shot he will have to bind them up. Papa is going to take me to see the cannons tomorrow so good bye. I am Your afecshonate BA.

RECOLLECTIONS OF

April 9 1848.

MY DEAR MARY.

We went to the Common this morning but there was nothing to see. Papa talked to a polliceman and he said there were some big guns in some of the back yards and gardens so we came home to tea and every body thinks they will fight tomorrow out there on the Common.

I am your afecshonate cousin   BA.

Septembur 11 1848

MY DEAR MARY

We are going to Briteton tomorrow wont it be fun. I will write more there.

Septembur 12

Here we are at Brighton I dident spell it properly yesterday and I have seen the chain pier and the Pavillon but the jolly part was coming down in the train we were in an open carrage the thurd class and as we were very early at the station we got seats with our backs to the engin and so we were out of the wind but some times the sparks flu about and one woman got a hole burnt in her shawl. there was no lid to our carrage like some of them had resting on 4 posts at the corners. I should not like to go in these carrages in winter

Your afecshonate cousin   BA.

A SPINSTER AUNT

At this time, 1848 or 1849, my aunt seems to have begun writing her diary. The first entry must have been, I think in 1849, early in the year—but it is not dated.—Ed.]

I am going to keep a diary mamma says that it is the best word or I might say journal, and I shall copy it for you sometimes or send it to you and you can send it back. Mr. Whitmore is made doctor to the opera and he says he will send us some tickets sometimes I shall like that

---

My dear Mary

Mamma took me to see the opera last night and it was so lovely it was the lady of the lake Madame Grici was the lady Ellen I think she was called and Madame Albony was her lover Malcolm and he came down the hills with his Highlanders and they had plaid sashes over muslin gowns I mean Ellen and the ladies had. It was so lovely and I hope Mr. Whitmore will send us some more tickets.

I am your affectionate Ba.

The Diary

—— 1849. We went last night to see Don Giovanny and we had a lovely box on the grand tere. of corse we were late because we had to dress and we were in such a hurry Signor Tamburini was don G. and Madame Persianni was in it and Mario and Madame Grisi Don Giovanny and Zerlina she is a peasant girl had such fun running about after each other in one of the senes and then Mazetto came and ran about too and he was so cross and Zerlina screamed he was called Signor Ronconi. they all sang italian so I could not understand what they said. donna Ann and don Attavio don means Mr. you know, were very sad people but their servant Leporeller is great fun and he has a great long strip of paper with a lot of names on it and he undoes it and then they all laugh. Don G. gives a large party and they all come to it and don Attavio and his wife and another lady sit down on 3 chairs. there are only 3 chairs in the room. Some of the people at the party had lovely dresses but those 3 were all in black. I love the music and the end is so funny. A lot of little black and red boys with tales like cows come up the trap doors and dance round Don Giovanny. and then fire comes up and I was so frightened but Mamma said it was not real fire and the imps Mamma calls them so tried to hold don Giovanny and a statue comes in with a stiff arm sticking out and he catches hold of don Giovanny and he carnt get away and then they all go down trap doors. O it was fun. the conductor is so handsome his name is Coster and he wears white kid gloves and holds a white stick.

A SPINSTER AUNT

June 28 1850

MY DEAR MARY

Last night we went to Covent Garden and heard the Prophet, a lovely opera with beautiful costumes. The Prophet is a sort of priest or bishop and he has a mother who was Madame Viardot Garcia; the Prophet was Herr Tamberlick. But something happened which was quite new. The dancing scene is meant to be skating and it was just begun when every one ran about in a very excited way. We were in a small box up at the top of the theatre opposite the royal box and all of a sudden every one stood up and cheered and made a great noise. Then we saw the Queen and Prince Albert come into the box, and they came to the front and bowed and looked very pleased. And then Madame Grisi rushed on the stage in evening dress from her box, she was not acting, and all the singers sang *God save the Queen*. It was a wonderful sight as there had been a drawing room in the afternoon and every body was covered with diamonds and dressed very smart. It was very funny to see Madame Grisi standing by all the skaters and old-fashioned people in her evening dress. The reason of it was, Papa went out and asked the box keeper what had happened, and he said a man[1] had thrown a stick at the Queen when she was driving in the Park, but it did not hurt her. So after

[1] An ex-officer named Pate.—ED.

they had sung *God save the Queen*, the opera went on.

Last week we saw the Hugernots. Its all about Protestants and Catholicks in Paris and there is a lot of killing. Madame Grisi and Signor Mario were lovely when they sang a duet, and then he jumps out of the window, although she tries to hold him. But the old servant has such a loud voice and sings so many hymns I don't like him much, for he seems to be always scolding some one. Its so funny to see the Queen of France riding about Paris streets all alone on a white horse. I wonder if she really did. The chorus called the Benedictine *is* lovely; it means blessing the swords. The stage is full of men and soldiers and monks and priests and princes and they all stand and sing holding up their swords, and then they all run up to the prompter's box. And then they turn round and walk quietly back like the archery ladies and when they get to the back of the scene they turn round and run to the prompter and sing again with their swords up. I don't know why they bless their swords twice. Mamma said that was what they were doing when they held up their swords.

I don't care for dancing even on the skates, but some people do very much and I was reading yesterday about 4 very celebrated dancers years ago in a ballet called the Seasons. They were called Taglioni, Cerito, Carlotta Grisi and Fanny

A SPINSTER AUNT

Elsler and the person who wrote about them talks such nonsense I think you will laugh at him. You know a ballet is a sort of play where they act but do not speak or sing. The book is called *the Mirror of Fashion* and it was written in 1838. And this is what he says. 'You will see in a few minutes the most divine dancer Taglioni.' Fancy a divine dancer! no one would write like that now! 'Her form and motion suggest the most exquisite images of beauty. She sets us dreaming rather than reasoning—and carries us into a world of spiritual Fancies, out of the world of Thoughts. In Taglioni there is an aërial simplicity, a purity of taste, and an involuntary grace, that contrast strikingly with the voluptuous energy, the poetical license, and startling grandeur of the Elsler—the dove and the eagle are not more opposite. The step and mien of Taglioni are as soft and touching as the beatific visions of some of our old saints. Fortunate for the anchorites that such visions vanished with their sleep! Had the angels, that visited their slumbers, lingered in their cells in such shapes, the world would have lost some of their fine treatises on dogmatic theology and ghostly inflictions.' I don't know what all that means, do you? I don't see how dancers can be like angels as they wear very short petticoats and show their legs and angels wear long gowns which don't stick out and cover them all up except their feet and no shoes, and dancers wear satin shoes. I saw lots of angels at the National Gallery one day [when Miss Jolly took us all. And here is some more about the dancers which Mr. Rose, Papa's French friend said was *quite true* about them. 'Taglioni's elasticity is even more remarkable than that of the Elslers. She floats like a blush of light before our eyes; we cannot perceive the subtle means by which she contrives, as it were, to disdain the earth, and to deliberate her charming motions into the air. The dance is an acted Poem, sparkling with images, which, reduced to words, would resemble the brilliant conceits of Carew and Suckling.' I found them out in the Dicktionary and they were poets a long time ago, but I don't know who he means is conceited, do you? 'She relieves the office of wings, without their encumbrance. Her sweetness and gentleness have a wooing tone, which breathes from her with no more external appearance than the aroma from flowers; and she sometimes seems to fade away like a gossamer caressed by the winds.' The Dicktionary says gossamer means the down of plants. 'Whichever way she turns there is an expression of beauty, a figure which, could it be fixed in any of its phases, could convey an embodied sentiment to the imagination. Theresa Elsler suggests at once the motion of one of the Titanesque Graces.' (That's a sort of prayer.) 'Her proud crest seems to aspire to the clouds,

A SPINSTER AUNT

which dissolve before the dainty majesty of her brow. Fanny Elsler is the miniature of this fine reality, with a multitude of smaller beauties that play round her like a halo.' (Thats a red circle round the sun or moon.) The scale of her execution is reduced, but her style is the same, glittering with more minute and dazzling points, that would be lost in the loftier stature of her sister. Their series of brilliant measures, attempted by others, would be no more than feats of gymnastic skill; but by them they are achieved with a feeling of inexpressible beauty. Their intertwining action is a triumph of art. The incessant variety of their motions,—the novelty that constantly grows up out of their steps, which have a blinding lustre in their rapidity—fill the eyes with flashing rays, like the perpetual circles that chase each other in some of the freaks of the *phantasma.*' I wish I could find out what that means, its not in my Dicktionary. 'The slightest speck of resting-place suffices to sustain their gyrations' (that's the act of turning anything about) 'and they almost seem to realize the fabulous capacity of the Angels crowding upon the point of a needle.' How could they? they are like women and as big. 'In the dance of the Elslers there is a strict rhythm' (that's something to do with music) 'which at once charms and captivates the ear. They ascend and descend, advance and retreat, soar and flutter, with the punctuality of notes delivered in accurate time. When their feet press the ground, they may be said to express music from their touch. But the peculiarity of the Taglioni is that you can only describe her through the emotions she causes. You cannot separate her from them. She has something of the effect of a tradition from the East; invested with spells and inspired with Fairy gifts—a legend of miracles to which you willingly subscribe.' There, I don't understand it all but isent it rubbish? How can you subscribe for miracles? Can you find out what Phantasma means I carnt and when I asked Mamma she said if I found it out in the Dicktionary myself I should remember it better, but its not in the Dicktionary. I thought you would like to know what a ballet is like, as you have never seen one. I've only seen the skating one in the Prophet, but Papa said *they* did not dance like Taglioni. I call it ugly and silly to see a woman standing on her toes with her petticoats all sticking straight out and then turning round and round like a humming top.

Your affectionate cousin BA.

November 10, 1850

MY DEAR MARY

We went to see the Lord Mayor's Show today at the Bacon's house in the Strand. There were lots of bands and men on horse back in armour like Richard I and the Black Prince at the Tower of London. I think it was them we saw at the Tower. But the procesion was not half so pretty as the water part we saw before. The barges all gold and blue and red, and the men in scarlet coats and the flags were all *so* pretty and there was no mud. There was lots of mud yesterday and all the crowds looked so dirty and they pushed about so and it was foggy and rained a little.

I have been to see a lot of plays lately with Papa. He takes me to the Haymarket theatre at half price after dinner as he likes commedies We go at 9 and theres plenty of room. I saw the School for Scandal and the Gamester thats a crying piece, and the Rivals and the Hunchback and She stoops to Conquer. I like that best its such fun where Tony Lumpkin takes the old lady and drives her round and round the garden in her coach and drives it into the pond, and she thinks hes a highway robber!

We went down to Woolwich by the steamer on tuesday and a lot of barges passed us full of straw and all their big red sails up. O they are *lovely* and painted bright green and they are so close to the water it washes over there sides. Then we walked to Abbey Wood and picked lovely flowers, primroses and orchises and violets and lots of things (Papa and me I mean) and then over Woolwich Common where there-s gorse like Hampstead Heath. Did I tell you we went one day to Greenwich Fair where we saw a clown called Billy Buttons riding a spotted horse like the wooden ones the wrong way and holding on by the horses tale. It *was* funny and everyone laughed so. I like the steamers better than the top of the omnibus which we go to the Welch Harp on. We go to Kilburne Gate and then walk and we find lots of flowers there to in the fields and by the water. Papa likes the front seat because he can talk to the coachman and he says he likes to here what all sorts of people think about things and he nurses me. There is only room for 4 people outside. The inside is horrid all shut up and its so funny to see the conductor standing on a little pece of wood at the back, a sort of shelf and he holds on by putting his arm through a strap and he holds up the other arm and shouts, 'Kilburne, Kilburne come along mam, sixpence all the way' then he stops and runs back and pulls the lady along and stuffs her in and slams the door and begins to shout again 'Kilburne, sixpence all the way,' like the butchers in Newport Market and the milliners in Cranborne alley who run at people passing and hold up bonnets and shout 'buy, buy, only 5 shillings.'

Next time you come to London Papa says he will take us to the Pollyteknick where we see the Diver go down into a large well all dressed and with pipes going into his clothes for air and we are to go in the diving bell. It has a great hole

A SPINSTER AUNT

in the bottom and you sit all round and no water comes in because its full of air. Its such a nice place with little moddels of docks and boats and the dock gates open and the boats go through and there are magic lantern pictures of the snakes and frogs in the water we drink And you are to go to Burford's Panorammer too. thats *lovely*. We saw Rome and Venice and Switzerland. You stand on a sort of open balcony and the pictures go all round and then you go up stairs and see another picture. The bottom one is the biggest and the top one the smallest. O I do love them and I want to travel like the Hamiltons and see the *real* places, dont you? Heres a long letter.

I am your affectionate cousin BA.

P.S.—I forgot there is another place we are going to the Unitted Service Museum in Scotland Yard were you will see a friggate full sail and all the ropes quite a big ship not as big as the boys one at Greenwich.

P.S.—I forgot to tell you we saw such a *lovely* play what they call a burlesk or Extravagantser called the King of the Peacocks. Madame Vestris came on a beautiful car covered with peacock's tail fethers all spread out and all the stage was peacocks fethers. She sat in front of the car and looked something like a peacock with this great lot of feathers just like a real bird spreads his tale in the sun. She is very beautiful but Papa says she is old and painted up to look young with ruge and powder and some one said she kept the stuff on always. it must be very uncomfortable but as she was a great beauty she does not like getting old. Mamma saw her when she was a child at the Adelade Gallery and she was called the Infant Saffo who Papa says was a Greek poet and she sang beautifully. I mean Madame Vestris did and now she has married an actor who is younger than she is, such a funny actor, Charles Matthews.

January 5. 1851.

I did not send you the letter about King Charming because we had a splendid idea of acting it and I waited to see what Miss Jolly would say. Well she says Yes, only no gentlemen are to come except the girls' fathers. It is to be here and I have been again to see it and Lionel is going to help and so will Ellen but they won't act. Maud Allen is to be the silly King and Julia the Queen because she is much taller than Maud and Alice the bad fairy because we don't like her and Susy will be King Charming and Sarah will be the Princess. I have two parts, the good Fairy and the Lord Chamberlain because he sings a song, and he wears a turban and baggy trousers and I wear a beard and mustarche. The car will be the old arm chair drawn by frogs—

A SPINSTER AUNT

large green frogs with red sealing wax eyes and as we have so much to do I will say good bye.

Your affectionate cousin BA.

January 30. 1851.

MY DEAR MARY

I wish you could have seen the play. A lot of people came and they thought it was lovely; there was a big pie and blackbirds jumped up on springs when the crust was taken off. Susy looked so pretty as King Charming and when she fell behind the boxes in the greenhouse and the green Tarlatan cage came up and the parrot every one clapped so: he was changed into the bird you know. I was all right when I came on in a big cloke like an old woman, but when the cloke was tumbled off and I appeared as the Fairy Asuzena I was so frightened I forgot the words. But I did not mind when I was the Turk in a turban and a beard and moustachos and black eyebrows. Every one laughed so when I sang the song;

> ' Come down the back stairs, come down with me.
> Come „ „ „ „ , of the door I've the key,
> „ „ „ „ „ , and let nobody see,
> And come as if you were not coming to me.'

I thought Lily would have had a fit she laughed so. Mrs. Oliver and her sisters were here and George and Henry and Fanny and a lot of the girls' friends. O it was fun and we want to do it again. O I forgot to tell you how pretty the end was. Marianna and all the little girls dressed in white with little paper wings stuck about the greenhouse behind the plants as fairies.

Thats all I can write today.

Your affectionate cousin Ba.

June. thursday 1851

My dear Mary

We have been to see the great Exhibition It is very pretty, but I don't like it as well as the Colesseum. We went there one evening and walked about Switzerland, over bridges, wooden ones and there's a waterfall. And then you go to a Greek temple which is a ruin the same size as the real Partenon, it only has 6 columns. Then up stairs there is a panoramer of London. You stand on St. Pauls and its daylight. And then the houses are all lighted up and it comes on to rain and all the people put up their umbrellas. It is nice. I remain your affectionate

Ba.

[No date. Probably 1852.—Ed.]

My dear Mary

We saw the great Globe today its put on Leicester square and the Statue is buried underneath. Its very funny to walk inside the earth

A SPINSTER AUNT

instead of outside it. And we went one day, no night, to the Egiptan Hall to see a moving Panoramer of America—and theres a prayery on fire and all the people running away. I will write more one day.

[A note is put at the bottom of this letter in a different handwriting: 'It seems that Ba had the measles and so could not finish her letter,' but there is no name.

After these letters there seems to be a gap in the correspondence that may be accounted for by my aunt Jane going to school in Germany soon after the opening of the Great Exhibition of 1851.—Ed.]

RECOLLECTIONS OF

CHAPTER III

BETTY AND NANCY

19th November 1852. We went yesterday to see the Duke's funeral. We were on Ludgate Hill but Papa and Ellen were in St. Pauls. It was a beautiful sight but the car was very ugly and heavy and it almost ran away in St. James St. the best part was the soldiers such a lot of horse soldiers and the muffled drums played the dead march. We saw the lying in state at Chelsea barracks too but I dont like the crowds and getting up so early in the morning we had breakfast at 5 oclock as we had to walk to the city and get in our places before 8 as the barriers were shut.

June 12*th* 1854 The Cristal Palace was opened the day before yesterday.

[This is followed by a letter with no date but the year 1855, so it was probably written some months after the opening of the Palace.—ED.]

A SPINSTER AUNT

We have got season tickets. It is a delightful place, the courts are so well arranged by Mr. Digby Wyatt and Owen Jones. You can walk about the Alhambra and listen to the fountain in the Court of the Lions and admire all the beautiful plaster work of the Arab artists; then you pass out by the colonnade of Sphinxes and enter the Egyptian temple of Karnak; and there are the great Memnon Statues with their hands on their knees just as if they were the real ones sitting on the banks of the Nile. Then across the nave are the Medieval Courts, lovely casts of our Cathedral porches and cloisters; and all this without packing trunks or the trouble and expense of a journey. Surely this Palace of Art will be a great educator, though I must fain say that I met no one in my perambulations; most people (and there were many, being a Saturday) preferring to prance up and down the nave bowing, and gossiping with their friends. People are so stupid and care absolutely nothing about art, nor for nature either for that matter for no one walks in the exquisitely beautiful grounds. How many of the hundreds of folks who cross the London bridges ever look at the beautiful effects of the sky? Or how many observe the exquisite cloud pictures which are to be seen over and over again in walking up Oxford St. on a winter's afternoon? Who cares for the soft silver grey fog effects in London?[1] Even

[1] Fogs in London fifty years ago were rarely yellow.—ED.

people in the country rarely appreciate nature. The men ploughing a field are blind to the lovely colouring of autumn trees, and the hunting and shooting folk, though they pretend to admire nature, race about too eagerly and watch the birds too earnestly to have time to admire the woods in their winter dress. The old fashioned sporting man tramping the country with his spaniel may have been a nature lover, but even he cared nothing for the beauty of the rising bird, the movement and the colouring of the Pheasant's plumage; the sportsman's passion is the display of skilfulness in killing something. I once found a nature loving Hodge. It was a still autumn day during a flooded season. The meadows were inundated, and the river had even invaded the cottages the day before. I was watching and admiring the soft grey of the bare trees reflected in the water, the sunny glow piercing the mist, and I involuntarily said, 'How beautiful!' An old man, a farm labourer, passing, replied, 'Truly ma'am, it *is* beautiful.' But that man was one in a hundred.

Diary, 18*th May* 1855. We saw the Queen give the medals to the Crimean soldiers to-day at the Crystal Palace. It was a sad sight to see so many men on crutches, lame, armless and otherwise wounded. The Queen pinned the medals on to the coat of each man, and addressed him by name, and spoke a few words to many of them.

[The next entry has no date.]—We saw the Naval Review the other day. We were on one of the big ships, and the Queen in her yacht passed down between the two lines of ships. It was a lovely sight, but unfortunately I was soon obliged to lie down on the deck and saw very little and when the firing began the noise was awful, and the smoke prevented our seeing anything. We were staying at Sea View and one day when the *Queen*, the *Caledonia*, and the *Agamemnon* sailed out from Spithead it was so pretty—all the ships full sail; it was like one of Turner's pictures.

—— 1855. Went to the Crystal Palace to see the Royalties. The Empress is very beautiful and walking with Prince Albert they were a very handsome couple. One could not help contrasting the Sovereigns with their Consorts. Louis Napoléon is frightful, and of course our Queen is not the elegant woman that the French Empress is. But oh! her crinoline! It must have been four yards in circumference; the Queen is much more sensible in her costume. The Empress is most elegant, but probably a vain woman and fond of dress; whether she is more than beautiful we do not know; however she seems to be very popular in Paris, but I wonder how she could marry such an unscrupulous adventurer—murderer one might say for the Coup d'Etat was an atrocious business It was not warfare, but massacre pure, or rather impure, and simple, and it always seems to me so extraordinary that our people, high and low should have whitewashed the Emperor so completely. People say he is a good friend to us! But it's only because it pays him to be within the halo of British prestige and respectability. Perhaps also he wishes to make friends here in case he should be obliged some day to come over like Louis Philippe, a Mr. Smith in a cab! Who knows? '*L'Empire c'est la Paix*,' but it was born in blood. One would like to know what the Queen and Prince *really* think about their dear guests. One can imagine no two women more unlike in every way than the Empress and the Queen. These are Papa's opinions.

—— 1855.

MY DEAR MARY

I have been turning over some notes of my mother's about Betty, the Grandfather's old servant and her family, and perhaps as you cannot go out this cold weather you may like to hear the fragmentary story! Betty's name appears in the family Bible soon after the birth of the

A SPINSTER AUNT

eldest grandchild; 'Betty Whimshurst died aged 70 at the old house in Millbank after having lived in our family's service 31 years, during which time she behaved most faithfully.' How different those old servants were to those of the present day! Betty was a quaint soul and many were the quaint sayings of this faithful one who thought it quite unfitting for the daughters of her Master to go to France and 'Furrin plazes,' for 'Furriners have no respect for age, and there was no end of bats and other insects there John said. But if Miss will marry a furrin man, she must put up with them and all sorts of nasty ways.'

Betty's home was a queer little village of one street and one shop large and roomy, with the usual rural contents of groceries, haberdashery, boots and bacon. It was a corner house with a door at the angle, so that on each side over the windows were the names of the owner and of the wares he sold; but the words were so placed that they read:

TEA   GREASE   MEN
FAMILY   GREASE   GROCER

At the opposite side of the street was the church, St. Cuthbert, and over against it the hanging lamp of the principal inn, on the glass of which one read the landlord's name:

GREEN
FLY
PROPRIETOR

while higher up the street the stranger saw by day and night upon another and larger lamp what appeared to be the curious attractions of the rival hostlery:

MOIST
BEDS

and strange though it may appear to the general public, Mr. Peter Moist never would admit that the local manner of placing the words could possibly be unpleasantly suggestive. 'If folks did think my beds was damp, there was the warmin' pan.' The village did not like its ways to be discussed and criticised by the Philistine.

And these were not the only illuminations, for Dr. Duggin also had his lamp, a fine red bull's eye illustrative of his importance over mere innkeepers, and just round the corner was the one parochial oil suspension—so my Mother said.

The village was a typical Sleepy Hollow for it lay in a hole and was intersected by little streams. It was one of those places where a living seems to be mainly derived as far as the men are concerned, from standing about pipe-smoking, with their hands in their pockets. So my mother said.

The women worked somewhat harder for they generally had a baby in their arms which presumably had to be put to sleep and comforted in many small ways, and a bigger child almost invariably clung to their skirts. They also, stood about the streets a good deal but mostly in their doorways;

but now and then, in a casual sort of manner, they did a little washing,—'We know,' their friends would remark, 'what sort of a husband that means.' Cleanliness and tidiness were not quite unknown in the village, and thrift was practised by one or two of the older couples who remembered the far-gone sail-making days; but the general tendency of the villagers was the true Dorset disposition to let things slide. During haymaking and harvest, work was pretty brisk; but at other times the great industry seemed to be running up an account at Master Grease', and Master Moist's establishments, and the 'Fox and Hounds.' Then in the more aristocratic circles much trotting to and fro was accomplished. The Doctor's lady, living in the house on the Green, wanted a word with the Rector's wife about 'those wretched little twins that were born last night.' But in crossing the field to the Rectory, she happened to see Captain Perkes (R.N. retired) in his garden, inspecting his peaches, so she just stepped aside to say a pleasant 'Good morning'; and then Mrs. Captain Perkes took the opportunity of asking her dearest friend Mrs. Doctor Duggin if she could account for the damson cheese being less solid than usual this season; and then they went into the house to inspect the cheese; and then the nursery had to be visited and the dear children had to be kissed; and finally passing the Captain's study, what could Mrs. Doctor Duggin do but tell the Captain (he had returned from the peach inspection) all about the uproarious meeting last night at the Board, when one of the Guardians absolutely proposed that the children's winter frocks should be made high with long sleeves. 'Just fancy the expense and such nonsense coddling pauper children like that and unfitting them for their proper position!' By this time it was half past twelve of the clock, and the Doctor being given to punctuality, Mrs. Duggin was obliged to return and leave her visit to the Rectory until the afternoon.

'The Shop's' owner Master Thomas Grease was the second husband of Betty's aunt, and by marrying the widow of Silas Whimshurst, Thomas naturally came into possession of all Silas' worldly goods and chattels including a little land and 'the Shop.' The aunt was a quaint personage when Betty was young, but very proud of 'the Shop' and its large and various stock of goods. Was it not created by the wisdom of 'poor Silas'? and was not 'poor Silas' the best of husbands to his adoring and adorable Keziah? 'Generally,' I remember my mother saying, 'what you wanted was just sold out.' Shirt buttons of useful sizes were scarce, 'they expected them in every day,' and one wondered at the huge sizes of villagers' feet, for sixes were the smallest attainable measures for women's boots and shoes. On one historic occasion when the black elastic desired was pro-

A SPINSTER AUNT

duced, it seemed to have lost its natural quality of stretchableness, and this being pointed out to the good lady, she remarked with her usual urbanity: 'Some ladies prefer elastic which does not stretch over much.' Betty's opinion upon 'the Shop' was that they must put up with what it produced, for in those days all the goods had to come over to the village by carrier, which was expensive and slow.

Mrs. Grease was also a near relation of Madam Malaprop—'It was the presperation and the 'air which had discoloured a lady's fur tippet.' She also had a wonderful specimen of a servant girl named Nancy, who later on came to live with us. She was a tower of strength, but her nerves had unfortunately been shaken by an accident; she having been thrown off the top of a stage coach which was being driven by a drunken Jehu. She was not much hurt, but an old lady passenger had her arm broken and Nancy fainted away at the sight. So frightened was she, that on coming to, she cried out that she must go and look for the severed limb in the neighbouring churchyard; and rushing through the breach in the wall made by the falling coach, poor Nancy was only prevented from having another fit of hysterics by the guard threatening her with partial immersion at the village pump.

But Nancy was also a very humane person. She deemed it cruel to let a flea struggle in the hand basin into which she dropped him upon the rare occasions when such an insect was found during the bed-making process; she preferred 'to cut off his head with a handy pair of scissors.' But they were 'nasty beasts,' and she 'thought it must be true what the Vicar's lady once told her, that they had at least twelve at a confinement, for they did multiply so fast'; but Mistress said 'that was second sight of the Vicar's lady.'

Nancy was in many respects delightful company, and when she expressed her opinion upon certain members of the family she was exceedingly entertaining. Her estimate of Aunt Ann was 'that she was one of those people who was made with something left out; like the eggs in the pudding or the barm in the dough.' And not only was Nancy original in her ideas and discourse, but her appearance added quaintness to her manner of speech. Short and slim with what most people would call a pleasant face, she was seriousness itself as regards expression. She was as wanting in any conscious sense of humour, as the Old Masters themselves when they depicted their Saints in those queer grotesque attitudes which we all know so well. She was excessively neat in her attire; a short skirt and very strong laced shoes with outrageously thick soles. Oh! the noise she made stumping all over the house! She wore a large white apron with a bib and a cap with a thick frill round it, an article of head-gear

A SPINSTER AUNT

that was a constant source of trouble both to Nancy and her Mistress, for it always had a tendency to lop over on one side: 'Mistress does fuss me so and fash herself about my cap; but if it *is* all awry, its better to have a crooked cap than a crooked heart.' She was full of the quaintest sayings, and she travestied the King's English with the most unconscious simplicity. On one occasion when a most diabolical murder had been committed by an Austrian woman, she 'did not wonder for her part, that the woman could knock down a big man, for those Ostrich women were as strong as elephants'; and upon her Mistress' birthday she 'brought in a brace of cartridges with the Doctor's compliments, and they were high enough to roast at once.' Nancy was wonderful in her travesties of words. She saw a demsteration in Trafalgar Square one day, and a woman had a 'paroxcikim' in the crowd, 'a sort of fit,' she explained. And then the 'huckabacks' who hold the candles at them high church plazes. Perhaps the finest of Nancy's sayings was an explanation of a Greek vase as 'what the Greeks put their hashes in.'

On that celebrated occasion when we children were going to Herne Bay, our first seaside outing, Nancy was invited to accompany us. It was, as you remember, in those primitive times when the little town boasted of one policeman, a ricketty pier, and a tower holding a clock which galloped and lost time alternately like the voices of school children. The journey was made by water from London Bridge with pleasurable or other results to the passengers according to their capacity for enduring irregular movements of the body. Poor Nancy was not in the happiest mood; she did not like the 'nasty fidgety boat wobbling about like an india rubber ball in a washing tub,' and upon landing she surpassed herself in her various comments upon men or rather women who 'let,' and the various things provided by the same. She inspected the lodgings and interviewed the landladies with much detail; and it was only after ringing many bells and mounting many stairs, that we at last sat down upon our own horsehair sofa. Lodgings as well as servants have changed since the early years of the century, and slaveys have given place to good high-priced generals. Also the sofa with weak springs, the two armchairs on which you could only sit at the extreme front edge, and the six other horsehair seats hard and high, from which children whose legs would only dangle, were sure to slide down under the table,—all these accessories of seaside lodgings have disappeared with the slaveys and given place to Tottenham Court Road 'suites' which reign in their stead. The only possessions of the old lodging houses over which I would drop a tear were the china poodles, the Chloes and Colins, and now and then an ill-used Worcester teapot or Chippen-

A SPINSTER AUNT

dale chair whose burial-places have been the dustbins or the shops of dealers in works of art. I wish these persons had carried off the 'Moonlights' and 'Sunsets' of our summer apartments last year —'pictures in oil all done by hand, Ma'am, I assure you,' and had given them decent burial in the dustbin, or cremation in the garden.

I should like you to have seen Nancy's expression when she was asked if the general arrangements of the most promising lodgings were to her liking. 'Yes, the rooms for lodgings are tolerably clean, and there are plenty of feather beds to soften those shameful pollyasses.' But her satisfaction was somewhat tempered after a few days' residence in Rose Cottage, for she found a 'terrible scarcity of the Grace of God in the house,' although the mutton leg did return to our table a sufficient number of times—cold, broiled, deviled, and hashed. This was of course a saving virtue in our Nancy's eyes, and the future of Mr. and Mrs. Roberts might not be so bad as if the remainder of each joint had found its way into Mrs. R's stock-pot.

Nancy's religious opinions were very matter of fact. I am sure she had never seen any print of Orcagna's 'Last Judgement,' and our National Gallery then possessed little of that literal kind of sacred art; but she firmly believed in the horns, hoofs, and *et ceteras* of a certain Personage, as she herself 'had seen Him many and many a time, when she was young.' But her nature was so kindly, she was so full of such delightful inconsistences, that she made excuses, good or bad, for every one she loved and served; and once when she was quite old, she was overheard to say to a district visitor, 'I don't know, Ma'am, what to think about *him*, for it is so long since I have met him that I cannot say; but I do know that as the tree falls so it is gathered up by some one.' Hence her objection to theatres, 'you might die there.' Though even here she was deliciously inconsistent, for she travestied the legend of St. Cuthbert: 'I believe if we does our duty, it don't matter when the last day comes, and I shall go on peeling my potatoes all the same like one of them saints Miss Jane is so fond of talking about, even if I did hear the trumpet.'

Nancy's religion, or rather her church-going, was of the old-fashioned kind; Sunday 11 and 6.30; week-days, Wednesday and Friday evenings. More than that was terribly 'Papish,' and we were frequently told that our crooked road, *via* Puseyism could only lead 'she knew where.' She firmly believed in the fashionable Prophet who fixed the Millenium for the forties or fifties at latest; but she objected strongly to the ways of some of our friends, who, believing as she did, went to routs, and made gowns and tippets for festive occasions, while calmly telling the rest of us that there being only one straight way, and one gate, we having chosen the others, could not help sharing the fate of the poor lost souls to be seen on the tympani of the Romanesque churches. Where Nancy had seen any engraving of these imaginative works of art I know not; but she used to talk most graphically of the weighing of souls and the tortures of the damned, and the strange monster with the enormous jaws; but she always placed those she loved among the doubtfuls for whom the Recording Angel waited while the scale was even, hoping for the discovery of one good deed that would turn it at the last moment. Needless to say, Nancy at all events found evidence of some generous action; whether or not the Angel was equally successful we had no means of discovering. Dear old Nancy, it is long since she laid down her potato peeling, and faded away to the land where no 'taxes' are required to fix down carpets which are disturbed by 'gushes of wind.'

But you must be tired of our Nancy, or if not, you must certainly be aweary of me and my pen. So good bye, dear Cousin.

Ever your affectionate, BA, no longer, for it's time to drop the silly old name.

[No date.—ED.]

DEAR MARY

You remember the statue in Leicester Square

was buried under the great globe. It's come up again, and the other night some young men, medical students people said, got into the square, (half the railings are broken down), and painted red spots all over the horse and put a broom into the hands of the king (I think it is George I.) and a fool's cap on his head. Papa says it ought to be made into a public garden, but the parish people won't pay for it. The square now is full of rubbish—like a dust hole. If Papa had his way, all the squares would be open to the public as they are in Paris—and in the German towns also I believe.

---

26 January 1858

My dearest Mary

What think you? You know we go to Marlborough House to work off our devotion to Turner. I am doing 'Caligula's Palace' now, but the light is abominable. However that is not what I am going to write about; but a portion of a great event in England's history, the marriage of the little Princess and future Queen of Prussia. We saw her 'go away' yesterday from the garden wall, (don't take that literally as written!) so you may imagine Turner played second fiddle for even his most enthusiastic worshippers, Marian Harrison, and your present unworthy scribe. The guardians very kindly took out some of the high chairs and we clambered up, and sat upon them or the wall. It snowed off and on, the weather's way of showing its sympathy! but the Prince and Princess were in an open carriage. Fritz is a handsome fellow, a good deal older than his little wife, who looks a mere child, and was yesterday, a decidedly tearful looking child. Can one wonder? It seems so sad that she should leave home so young to enter upon an absolutely new life all alone and away from her own people and her own country; and withal to enter a formal German Court full and overflowing with old-world stiffness and etiquette, and not even an English lady or maid with her—so they say. There was an immense crowd all down the Mall, and need I say there was also the usual dog, and the usual brutal howling of the crowd as the poor creature tore along the road frightened almost to maddening point. Also the usual mail cart, cheered as we were once, E. and I, when we hung on at the back of a post cart to escape from the crowd! The passing of the dog and the cart were the only festive moments, and dislodged the pent-up feelings of the people, for every one seemed to feel the intense *tristesse* of the occasion, and many were the tears shed by the sympathetic crowds. 'Poor child,' I heard one woman say, 'how she will miss her Ma, and I reckon her Ma will miss her a goodish bit.' The cheering of course was tremendous, and not a soul but felt what one man spake: 'God bless her, and may her husband be good to her!'

     Your affectionate Cousin JANE.

---

         31 *January* 1858

What think you, dear Mary, of the big ship being launched at last—the *Leviathan*; so next time we sing Psalm 104 we shall not have our thoughts diverted to *her*. 'There go the ships, and there is that Leviathan,' which stuck fast for a couple of months, refusing to oblige the launching people, 'charm they never so wisely.'

[An undated letter follows; probably in the excitement of writing the news, my aunt forgot to date it.—ED.]

Mary! what *do* you think, I saw the Queen open Parliament to-day! Uncle sent me up a ticket for the House itself.

You remember I went into the Gallery last year, but that was only to see the procession pass; to-day I heard the speech read. It was a long affair as we had to go early, and we must have waited about two hours, but it was amusing to see the Peers and Peeresses, and Gold Sticks and Judges walking about. Such a squeeze on the woolsack, I thought every minute a judge would be pushed off wig and all! Their wigs are lovely, but don't you think a savage, used to a spare amount of clothing, would think it very droll to see several respectable old gentlemen in red gowns and enormous heads of hair (wigs) huddled up all round one backless seat? The peers in their robes are not impressive—Englishmen have no notion how to wear unusual clothes with dignity; they seem to pull the robes on anyhow, mostly in a crooked slovenly fashion like a mere trumpery boy undergraduate. Why don't the Peers and Peeresses wear their crowns?—I suppose they only do at coronations; but if they did, they would probably only look like ill-dressed fifth-rate actors.

The Peeresses, of course, were gorgeous; all ladies in evening dress and mostly covered with diamonds; but such a function requires artificial light. Why not have it in the evening? No, that would not do for the outside part. When the trumpets sounded in the Gallery we all took off our wraps. Ada went with me; evening dress at mid-day is something like a French wedding. The doors each side of the throne opened and in came the procession. First the Heralds, lovely people in tabards, (a sort of dalmatic) made of the Royal standard. It all seemed so unreal—the sword-bearer, the cap of maintenance, the crown on a cushion—it was just like a play, only the actors seemed less at their ease—it is not every day that they have to walk about in trains carrying strange ornaments upon cushions! Suddenly up starts every one, and the woolsack gentlemen seemed relieved to have a little more space. Enter the Queen and Prince Albert. The Queen mounts the throne; the beautiful Duchess[1] arranges her train, Prince Albert takes his lower seat, my Lord Chancellor presents H.M. with a roll—the speech; and then all is silence broken by a penetrating melodious voice, soft and clear, which thrills through the house. A few minutes and pouf! all is over. The train is picked up by bearers, Prince A. steps down, the Queen joins him and they are gone! You wait an instant expecting them all to return and bow right and left as on the artificial stage; but no, the outside cheering tells you 'tis all over, and the hurly-burly begins, and every one scrambles to get away to lunch! Ah! I forgot one incident, the pause after the entrance of the Queen and the excessive silence; you could 'hear a pin drop.' Suddenly, a rush as of a herd of buffalos—tearing, struggling, pushing each other in most unmannerly fashion to arrive in front at the Bar. After a pause, the buffalos (H.M.'s Faithful Commons) stand still, and the Queen addresses the crammed house. How queer all these customs of an old country are! customs and ceremonies which began probably with dignity

---

[1] Wife of the 2nd Duke of Sutherland.

and solemnity, and have evolved into formality, and very often, apparently senseless ceremonial verging upon the comic. And yet, it would be a pity to reform it all into a paw-shaking by gentlemen in evening dress, as at the White House, Washington. I could not help feeling sorry for Prince A. Were it not for unreasonable jealousies, and malice prepense, I suppose he would have been made King Consort. A Queen in the same position is Queen Consort and sits on a throne under the same canopy as the King; why should not the Q.'s husband, instead of being placed one step lower than the heir to the throne, and two or three lower than the Sovereign? Prince A. is a noble man and plays his very difficult part most successfully, but he is *hated* by a good many malicious folks—unreasonably, most people consider. He is very handsome, though somewhat too German looking; but why, oh why need he wear striped waistcoats? They are as frightful as Lord Brougham's yellow things. Goodbye.

Your affectionate JANE.

Diary: no date. Last night I went to the House of Commons, and spied through the grating. I heard Dizzy, Lord Palmerston, Gladstone and a number of others speak; but it was just a desultory talkee-talkee, no real speeches. I should like to hear D. and G.[1] upon a speechifying night.

Had an argument with Papa about poetry. I never can understand why people should be allowed to proclaim that they do not like music, whereas if one remarks that poetry, or rather, verse, is uncongenial to one's mind, one is told, that it is impossible! Papa says I *pretend* to dislike it. (There is no *pretence* about his indifference to music, dear man, as he always begins to rake the fire even after he has *asked* for a 'simple air, not fireworks.' Alas! the simplicity of the melody is lost in an accompaniment of tongs, pokers, and shovels!) Certainly there is no pretence about my indifference to verse; I never read poetry if I can get prose—between ourselves, if the most exquisite poetry ever written was contained in the only printed book, that book would rarely be opened by me—*never* if the house contained a piano. Surely there is no reason why a devotee of poetry should be so superior to the music lover? He may care absolutely nothing for any other art, whereas the music man may be devoted also to painting or sculpture. There is admittedly a deficiency of some sort in the mind (or soul?) of a person who cannot appreciate all art, for in a sense, art is art, whether the expression takes the form of music, painting, or poetry. Moreover, I suppose as

[1] Disraeli and Gladstone.—ED.

poetry is a species of melody, it is a curious problem why the melody of words and rhythm should be possessed by people who are absolutely deficient in the power of hearing the melody of notes, and the rhythm of vocal or instrumental music. It is as mysterious as the ear for music and language—the possession of one by no means assures the possession of the other; a person's soul may be full of the melody of musical sounds, and yet be deaf to the melody of musical verse. So again colour and form may be strongly developed in one man as regards the plastic arts, but the harmony and form of a poem he finds quite incomprehensible.

Really the gist of the matter is probably this: what people despise, or at least hold cheap, is knowledge or taste for things beyond their ken. The intellectuals look upon the study of Art and Music as child's play in comparison to that of Classics or Mathematics—simply because they know nothing about the Muses. Nevertheless the Art student and the Musical student look forward to being some day in the position of creators; can the Classical or the Mathematical student ever aspire to these heights?

[Diary. No date; but probably in the early sixties.—ED.]

I was discoursing with the sweetest of musicks

today upon the organ at St. John's, when in walked the Padre: 'How charming that is. Is it Batiste's?' Yes it was. 'But I really came to ask you if you could come round to the Schools as Mr. Arnold[1] is coming today to inspect us, and he asks for some lady on the Committee to judge with him upon the needlework (*with* him! I wonder how much he knows about it!) So of course I went, and after a time, in walked the great man, with his hat duly fixed upon his head, after the manner of a real Englander. We talked of the work. Did I think it good? Yes I did. 'You really do think it is good?' 'Yes, I think it is very good.' 'You are sure you think it well done?' and so on and on—more in the manner of a badgering barrister cross-examining a witness, than a poet. Presently in walks the Padre.

'Oh! Mr. Arnold, how do you do? Let me put your hat down for you.' The Padre has a way of reproving people so delicately and gently that only a few 'see' the reproof. But the outsiders do! Is it not droll, the Englishman's love for his head covering?

I did not lose much time by my excursion round the corner, for the forced entrance through a window of the church of a stinking cod-fish, entirely dissolved any further desire to organise for that day, my enthusiasm having quite departed

[1] Matthew Arnold.

A SPINSTER AUNT

through this energetic proceeding of one of the Padre's anti-church parishioners.

Our parrot distinguished himself today. He is old and has used his time educationally to much advantage. For a bird, he has a superabundance of brains, and he is discriminating in his speech, though frequently giving way to bad language.

We had a visit from an Indian officer, who has been through the Mutiny, and has just returned worn to a skeleton, a mere bag of bones with unkempt hair and beard. We unavoidably kept the Captain waiting some time, and he for a diversion addressed himself to Polly.

'Can you talk, Polly?'

No answer.

'Cannot you speak, Polly?'

Still no answer.

'Are you an obstinate brute or a fool?'

The Captain's voice assuming a more and more aggressive tone, brought forth a torrent of unmannerly expletives: 'You wretch! You ugly wretch! wretch! wretch! Call a cab, you wretch. Go to the Devil, wretch! wretch! ugly wretch!' When I entered the room the worst was being roared out, and of course I had to pacify the criminal and make due apologies for him.

CHAPTER IV

CONCERNING CHURCHES

[THE following letter is not dated, but it seems to possess sufficient internal evidence of having been written between 1856 and 1860 to another cousin, one Ann, who was living, by the direction upon the envelope, in the neighbourhood of Frome, Somerset.—ED.]

DEAR 'SISTER ANN,' here am I coming with an amusing tale, or rather a chapter in the ecclesiastical history of the 19th Century. The *Scene* of my adventure—the Church of St. Martin-in-the-Fields, Westminster; *time*, the Holy Season of Lent; *Day of the Week*, Wednesday, Midday. *Office*, the Litany. Placing myself, one of the necessary two or three in the Free Seats in the middle aisle, so as not to be imprisoned in the high pew of respectability, I caused much trouble to the mind of the white-capped pew opener, who came from her seat in the vestibule by the stove, her headgear somewhat awry, expressly to open the door of a pew, and motion me by the wave of her hand, to enter the same. Parson and clerk

A SPINSTER AUNT

had arrived at our wishful deliverance 'from pride and vain glory,' so I shook my head in negative fashion and remained on my knees. Then whispered she: 'We don't like to see the likes o' you in the free seats.'

Naturally I suddenly became almost as petrified as the marble slabs upon the walls. And this reminds me of another experience. A short time ago I went to the consecration of Colonial Bishops in the Abbey. I dare say you read all about it except a particular part of the Abbey ritual. After the Offertory, there was a great stampede, but as I wished to stay to the end of the office, I remained kneeling. Up came a Verger: 'If you are going up, you can go into the cross benches.' I said nothing. 'If you are not going up, you must go out.' I now became deaf and stupid, and so took no notice, and he slammed the door, but he kept his watchful eye on me. After the Consecration, the man returned. 'You must go up now.' Not a limb did I move. In a most peremptory voice he repeated his order, and one of the clergy in the stalls looked round. This possibly intimidated him, and fearing a scandal he left me alone, though for a moment I wondered whether he was fetching a policeman to remove a brawler. I wonder if brooms and brushes are put under the Altar here as at many churches? You might tell Mr. Bennett of these experiences.

Do you think the extreme Protestants really

desire to return to the manners and customs of former days ? How well I remember the ecclesiastical curiosities of my childhood, and the terrific dullness of church-going to the infant mind! In these days it seems as if one were romancing, in describing the ordinary church service of twenty years ago. There were of course high pews at most churches and a three-decker occupied at the same time by the rector preaching, a curate dozing after the fatigues of reading the service in the middle seat, and the clerk snoring below. But at St. Martin's and some of the other old parish churches, there was a picturesque ceremony preceding the service—a procession of churchwardens and sidesmen preceded by the Beadle in glorious raiment of scarlet coat, knee breeches, white stockings, shoes, and buckles, all surmounted by the cocked or three-cornered hat. This gentleman appears in Dickens' books very often, but otherwise he is becoming an extinct animal, though his like may still be seen rarely on state coaches, and his hat still lives on the heads of Gensd'armes in conservative France. This procession was the only part of church-going that I found interesting. We sang no canticles, only the Glorias of the Psalms, and the existing hymn book was the one with a mitre on the cover. Oh, the droning of the organ and the mob-capped Charity children, singing still more nasally than they do in these days. But one institution of St.

A SPINSTER AUNT

Martin's was amusing. There were two large sash windows one upon each side of the altar upon what might be called the first floor, level with the gallery. The windows belonged to fair sized rooms—they could not be called pews, and private boxes seems inappropriate. I think St. Marylebone has something of the kind with a smaller box above where the Charity children sit in their mob caps and long mittens. Formerly I believe the boxes at St. Martin's were occupied by the King if he ever went to this Royal church, but in my childhood the pews were in the possession of Lord Overstone or the Duke of Northumberland, and it gave me great joy to watch the entrance of the occupiers. First they threw up the sash windows, then they drew a seat to the front and laid their books upon the velvet ledge, for all the world as people do at a theatre, and one expected to see a fan and an opera glass! St. Martin's was a very smart church, for in those days, people as a matter of course, went to the parish conventicle. In the front of the gallery, just opposite our pew (which was on the ground floor against the wall between the windows of the side aisle) sat the Duke and Duchess of Sutherland, the Argyle family and many others of the nobility; but I fear the honour of saying my prayers under the eyes, literally, of peers and peeresses did not impress me as it did my elders and betters. I did enjoy gazing at the Duchess of Sutherland as she was so beautiful, and the Duke of Argyle's golden locks were a feast of colour when the sun blazed upon them—they formed a sort of iridescent nimbus round his pale face; and then the little Marquis of Lorne[1] was exceedingly pretty and picturesque in his Highland attire. Church-going to most children was a Sunday penance, only redeemed by the Beadle and his fellows processing—rather different to present day processions at St. Barnabas and a few kindred churches. But to my small mind St. Martin's was an enormous improvement upon St. Paul, Covent Garden, which church my mother affected because of the preaching of the rector—Bowers by name, afterwards a bishop. And what a grand church St. Martin's is, though of course not equal to Wren's masterpiece St. Stephen, Walbrook. St. Paul, Covent Garden, was a most benighted place of worship. The most dismal of services and no singing but the metrical psalms, Tate and Brady I think, and a hymn at Advent, Christmas, and Easter. To this day, the hundredth psalm, new or old version, and 'Lo He comes,' are the abomination of desolation in my ears. How the congregation roared out the dismal 'deeply wailing' three times, and wished for more! When I think of the ordinary church services of those days, I always wonder that we ever continued our Sunday duties when we arrived at years of independance. Just think for

---

[1] The present Duke of Argyle.—ED.

A SPINSTER AUNT

a moment and contrast it with the modern child's Sundays—and our home ways were what most people then considered very unorthodox. The pews at St. Paul's and nearly all old churches were very high, and I was too small to see anything but the sprawling angels with golden trumpets at the top of the pediment of the reredos, and the nose of the Rev. Dr. Wesley, (resembling the probosis of the Duke[1]), when he was discoursing at the top of the three-decker, over our heads literally, for we sat under him. But a humane medical student, a pupil of my father's, used to lift me up on to the seat from which vantage ground I could survey the bonnets and bald heads of the congregation. I had a book which I could not read, but in which my elders were constantly finding the place, and often that devoted young man used to pass round to the base of the pulpit, to pick up the useless volume dropped or thrown over the top of the pew by naughty me, (remember I was only a wee child in those days). How dismal it all was! and this was the church Clarissa Harlowe attended for early 6 o'clock mattins—rather degenerate in our time!

But there was one joy which Sunday brought round, an after breakfast reading of Robinson Crusoe by the aforesaid medical student, and an after dinner visit to the Zoological Gardens and

---

[1] Wellington, of Waterloo fame, always called 'the Duke.'—ED.

home by the Botanic Society's Pleasaunce in the Regent's Park where we used to see Mr. Rogers the poet of 'Italy.' My father was one of the original members of both Societies. Those were the days when our parks, especially the Regent's, were mere green paddocks for the feeding of sheep; it was many years later that we copied Paris and made them into beauteous gardens. But when it was first done, every one cried out that the people would steal the flowers! and every one was wrong!

I often wonder whether the modern children will give up church *when they get the chance*, for I think they have too much, altho' it is of a lively order; but probably many people, the Anglo-Catholic people, are apt to forget that children are not likely to be as enthusiastic as regards church-going as they themselves are. What think you? But of course the time has not yet come for us to see the *results* of the Catholic revival. Church building and the beauty of holiness are not all that is necessary; and to many of us a great deal of modern enthusiasm seems to be expended upon unimportant but pretty external details. For instance, if a person desires to be thankful for extra church privileges, he wishes to give an offering, and often chooses altar plate, of which the church already possesses all that is necessary. Why should not votive offerings consist in donations to the church's maintenance—such as roof repairing, providing new kneeling hassocks, and so on. But it may be objected that these things are ephemeral, whereas the plate, or lamps, or even a carpet endures for a long time. That is true, but the difficulty might be overcome by the use of a board of recorded gifts and donations, such as one sees in old churches:

> Ann Beard. Two shifts to be given to two old women annually.
> Jemima Jenkins. Caps for the same, at Easter.
> Master Henry Stubbles. A pair of strong socks to seven poor men, duly given at Christmas.
> Mary Ann Bull. Some strong pattens to keep nine old women dry shod in the snow.

This might be imitated thus:

> Mrs. Septimus Higgins. Plumber's bill paid at Michaelmas.
> Lady Thompson. A new roof for the chancel, and annual repairs of roof to the value of Forty seven pounds, as a thankoffering for recovery from influenza.

Such a scheme might be inaugurated in many parishes with great advantage to the inhabitants. At the same time I doubt whether, even in the uttermost depths of the country, a church could be found now which possesses no flagon. Yet not long ago I was present in such a church, and as the Holy Communion was to be administered, the wine was poured into the chalice from a black bottle. And a very short time ago I not only saw this 'use' in a Somersetshire village, but on one occasion the cork not having been withdrawn in the vestry, the parson sent the clerk for a corkscrew! Such a scandal as this it may be hoped, is unique, and surely not even the most ultra Protestants can desire to return to such manners and customs as prevailed in the forties, when religious services were conducted, in many details, indecently and in disorder. The worst of it is that people began at the wrong end. The Catholic Revival was of course partly doctrinal; but one of its enthusiasms was church building—there was to be the church as a central part of the scheme with innumerable services, and schools and missions were to be worked around it; but every one forgot that religion and morality could not be practised by people who lived in the most degraded condition huddled together without any attempt at decency. How could godliness be carried out by the slum-dwellers whose manner of life was completely void of everything like morality and decency? What did such people care for a beautiful church? How could it appeal to their degraded minds? Possibly had the money spent on churches in slums, or half of it, been used in clearing away the shocking dens in which the poor lived, more good would have come of the efforts made by the churchmen and the philanthropists. Zeal is an excellent quality, but it is so often misplaced! We have had an example of that recently in our neighbourhood. A certain bookseller, elected churchwarden of St. Paul's Wilton Place, has been exposing 'Popish practices' which seem to me to consist in the choir wearing surplices, and the Vicar preaching in a surplice. That caused your Mr. Bennett to be so persecuted at St. Barnabas, Pimlico. Mr. Westerton and his set forget that the services are conducted in this manner in Cathedrals which is considered to be quite correct; but in parish churches it is, forsooth, Popish! Can anything be more silly?

Well, dear Ann, as I have to write to Mary, I must wind this long epistle up and post it.

Ever your affectionate cousin JANE.

P.S.—What think you of the presentation of a tract being made to me the other evening in Oxford St. on my way to All Saints, entitled: 'To a drunken Ostler. Where are you going, young man? To the gin palace.' Singularly appropriate, was it not? like another in large print, 'To the aged.' The next I get against Popery and Tractarianism shall go to you!

Diary

Ascension Day.—I went with the children of St. Martin's to beat the bounds, mainly because our parish and St. James' divide the private garden of Buckingham Palace into two halves and I thought I should like to see the grounds. The children all stood before the steps of the Palace and sang the National Anthem and presently the Queen and Prince Albert appeared on the terrace, and of course we all cheered very noisily and the Queen and Prince bowed very pleasingly. The grounds are very pretty with a lake and swans and other birds. It is a quaint custom and we all carried wands, branches of willow I believe.

22nd June 1859.—Selection day of the Festival.[1] It all went off very well, but was decidedly dull. I think Friday will be better, 'Israel in Egypt.' The double choruses sounded well at the rehearsal, and the enormous body of voices was appropriate to crowds of shrieking Hebrews. In the 'Messiah' I thought the noise terrible and utterly wanting in impressiveness. Surely a chorus of thousands and a hundred or so of instrumentalists is an absurd idea. In Paris the vocalists generally double the orchestra—say 150 to 78 or 80—respectively. But Costa's one idea is *noise*. The practices of the London contingent

[1] The first Handel Festival at the Crystal Palace.

A SPINSTER AUNT

were far better balanced as regards singers and players. Sims Reeves of course sang well with his hand on his heart, or holding his music at arm's length, whatever it may be. His sentimentality is the same for ballads and for Handel, and he is so unsentimental in appearance! Clara Novello's voice rang through the building; what a lovely voice it is! but oh! how I detest Saul's 'Dead March.' Would that it were interred decently and for ever! Costa the Supreme, blinked and waved his wand in his white kids. What funny little ways and tricks music people have. Madame Schumann to wit, always comes on to the platform in white kids; why? They have to be drawn off immediately. Then she places them on the piano with her fan. Then out comes her handkerchief, and she dusts up and down the keys and finally places the handkerchief with the other impedimenta. But what a superb artist! and yet she does not draw so very much in London. I am wandering from the Palace. My neighbour is a namesake. Between the choruses she whispers, 'Do you come from Bradford?' 'No, London.' And then she turned her fixed eye upon me. 'Ah! they are all Onions at Bradford; I was before I married; I thought you might be.' This seemed irrelevant as my name is not Onion, and she must have chosen for lunch (provided by the Handel Festival Committee) not wisely but too well. The fare was copious but not very sympathetically chosen for singers. Hundreds of pork pies and strawberries and cream seem strange combinations. The scuffle to find the sandwiches being hopeless, we betook ourselves to a quiet corner and invested upon our own account in foods provided for the audience of a less substantial and doubtful character. After the performance we met many friends, and so home, very weary, about 6.30. Some people think it 'shocking' to sit up on the orchestra singing in public.

. . . . . .

1861. Every one is talking about the new book, 'Essays and Reviews'; one might say every one is fighting over it in word, and many seem to be almost desirous of re-instituting the Holy Inquisition with faggots and matches. What an exhibition of liberty of speech, and conscience, and Christian charity! How will it end? Probably the narrow people will gain the day and the law will pronounce in their favour or shuffle out of the difficulty in some legal way. If people would squabble less, and let others hold their own opinions freely, what a much happier world it might be; but every one wants every one else to conform to his own peculiar dogmas. 'I am right and you are wrong and there's an end of the matter'; in these days the sequel is merely banishment from religious circles of orthodox dimensions—happily. By the way, I heard Dr.

A SPINSTER AUNT

Pusey the other day; what a dull preacher he is! Have you ever heard Mr. Frederick Maurice? He often preaches at our little St. John's. His sermons are so soothing and his views so broad and optimistic in spite of his persecutions. It is a detail that one does not always understand what he means—probably because he does not quite know himself. How then can he explain to others? But his earnestness, his beautiful face and voice, and his true Christian Socialist views fascinate me. I love to listen to him.

RECOLLECTIONS OF

CHAPTER V

SWIMMING

[THE following letter is undated, and I have been unable to discover the year in which the first swimming bath was opened for women, but I think in the early sixties.—ED.]

MY DEAR MARY

I must tell you at once that the Parish folk have decided to let us have the swimming bath in Gt. Smith St. opened once a week for women. There's a concession! Our friends have been agitating the matter for a long while, but there was much opposition, and now we must get as many people as we can to go, and *never shirk* whatever the weather may be! We two, Ada, Louie, and Clara, Mrs. G. and one or two others, so far, are all we have. The opposition held that swimming was 'unnecessary' for women. I wonder why? and when we went to see old Mrs. Taylor the other day she was eloquent and surpassed herself. 'What will you girls do next? Wanting to swim!! Just like men!!!' How shocking! apparently it is as immoral as riding in a hansom cab without a masculine companion. Oh! dear. Shall we never be allowed to be rational? Is Mrs. Grundy always to hedge us round?

However these old ladies, the Grundys, have some of them a few virtues. Are they not truly kind and sympathetic in many ways? And are they not gradually fading away nobody knows where? The younger generation—ourselves—when we are old, shall we be sympathetic to man and beast as these dear old souls are in spite of their narrow ideas? I wot not; but I doubt. Gentle in manner and in word; refined, well educated and kindly to all, from the poor child whose friends want votes to place it in some orphanage, to the rich youngsters who display an inordinate affection for cakes and biscuits—true, kindly, Christian gentlewomen, all of them. Why are we not of the same make? Is it our early training which is at fault? Dear old ladies; simple minded souls who never speak or think evil of any one. I remember meeting one who was sympathetic after the manner of St. Martin. Crossing the Channel one very cold night, she saw a poor silly woman who had not provided herself with a wrap; and she had a baby! One sees not a few such heedless mothers when we cross the evil Channel. 'She did not think it would have been so cold.' What did the dear old lady do? She did not cut her shawl in half; that would have been wicked waste and of little use to either of them; but like a Good Samaritan she gave the woman the entire shawl, pretending that she did not want it until they got into the train, and wrapping mother and babe in it, she retired to her cabin. I know what you will say; you always admire the worldly wisdom of St. Martin in cutting his cloak in half, and his delicacy of feeling in not putting the beggar under an obligation. Besides you will say the cloak was large: but if so the old lady's shawl was not. Well, perhaps both were wise in their generation. But sympathy does not always extend to novel ideas such as learning to swim 'like men'; and as to its being of use, said Mrs. T. 'If you and I tumble into the river, the only difference will be that I shall go down at once gracefully and gently (I hope by express speed,) whereas you will struggle for some minutes, perhaps have a very *mauvais quart d'heure*, and then you will also go to the bottom, slowly but surely.' There is something in that argument, and the philosophy hath truth in it; nevertheless I desire to be able to swim, and I rejoice in this opportunity of learning, and in spite of a probable addition to the other maxims: 'No lady uses slang nor does she ride in hansoms'; I shall swim and swim as much as I can. So be it, but we intend to smash up all young ladyisms.

Ever your affectionate cousin, JANE.

A SPINSTER AUNT

P.S.—You said in your letter the other day that I was unsympathising as regards your decision, and *cold*—no; not cold, I think the expression was tepid like the hot water bottle in the early morning. Am I equally stony? *Ma chère que voulez-vous?* I *do* sympathise with you; in fact I *envy* you from the extreme bottom of the little triangular solid which is called my heart. Think what an advantage it is to have made up your mind upon one really serious subject at 22—and for life! and here am I, 25, and my mind is quite nebulous. And such an important subject too! To resolve at 22 never to marry—that leaves you exactly 48 years to devote to your beloved music allowing that you disappear at the Psalmist's term of three score years and ten. That I consider enviable. For hours, days, weeks, and years nothing need come between you and Bach—nothing need interfere with your devotion to John Sebastian, Handel, Scarlatti, Purcell, and all the band—they are your joy, and you may reckon on 48 years to feast upon them—mentally. I should expire at the end of a week of such sustenance. I suppose I had too much of John S. when I was at school in Leipzig, for I was often taken to the Johannes-Kirche to hear his things. You know (no you don't. How silly it is always to be saying, 'You know') well, *now* you know, he was organist at that church. Forty-eight years of Sebastian's fugues and Herr Handel's sonataṣ. Even Beethoven and old Papa Haydn are too modern for you. Do you ever feel an internal thrilling when you follow a fugue, the sensation which lesser (?) lights cause in my heart, the lesser lights of the 19th Century—Schubert and Chopin and Schumann. Remember I am in good company in my dislike of fugues. Chopin and Berlioz detested them. I suppose the repetition of a movement taken up by one after another, voices or instruments, which rubs me up the wrong way, is to the fugue lover, a joy? It is like lovers' endless twitterings, 'I love you dearest,' in the bass; then the alto, 'I love you dearest,' then Tenor, and finally the soprano, 'How I love you, my own.' How dull! In music I want emotion—murders, deaths, forsaken lovers, excitement caused by any more or less violent passion—all and everything that makes you feel like running headlong into an abyss. This one feels in the music of Berlioz, Schubert, and others of the new school. You of course say the old masters are the models, the examples for us to follow. Is music like architecture then, a completed art? You admit that poetry speaks afresh to us in some of the younger generation—Tennyson and Swinburne and Browning; why should music as a progressive art be dead? We feel that architecture is a completed art; the Greeks and the Mediæval builders perfected their work, and all we can do is to continue in their paths and copy or combine their systems, generally thereby producing hideous monstrosities called 'Victorian' buildings. Painting is also decidedly progressive—we have Turner who is certainly not a mere imitator of Claude, and Constable and Corot who can in no wise be called imitators of any of their elders, such as Poussin or Wilson. Again water-colour painting has developed, may be said to be a new art—Copley Fielding and De Wint broke away from the Girtin and Gastineau schools; and now William Hunt and others have developed into an opaque method called by the French *Gouache*. Whether that is a success remains to be seen; it gives no advantage that one can see over oil colours, and many disadvantages, for oil is really a perfect medium—you can do anything and everything, and if you fail, or your colours fail, it is your own fault; you either have no brains, or you do not use the best makers' colours, or you employ pigments which *must* destroy one another and consequently ruin your work—mummy and asphaltum as used by Reynolds and Wilkie—or you do not let your canvas dry properly. *Gouache*, *i.e.* tempera, *may* be more durable, but it is not nearly so pleasant to handle. The early frescoes are probably as pure in tone as when they were first painted; but are not also the pictures of Van Eyck and Holbein? Surely if we may talk of progress in Painting and poetry, we may be allowed to admire the progressives in music, though we cannot dub them pre-Bachites or pre-Palestrinas. Pre-Raphaelites claim a return to previous methods and theories; in music, the moderns are absolutely original as far as we know at present. Perhaps some day a papyrus or a slab may be turned out of some ancient tomb giving us harmonies or melodies which we have been considering new, and showing us once again that Egypt and Greece were our forerunners in music as in most things.

Well, the summit of all wisdom is to know your own mind, and you know yours now at 22, '*you will never marry.*' That's decided, and you can work in peace. Be thankful that you have settled this momentous question! Be happy! And go on your music way rejoicing—at 22 years of age! I envy you and congratulate you as a new devotee and slave of Art. We are all slaves to some person or some thing. To dogs some of us —I plead guilty; have I not frequently caught a cold in perambulating dear Lill on a chilly night? You will pass a life-long devotion to music, to, especially, Johann Sebastian. *P.S.*—Only don't change your mind at 54, and marry a young gentleman of 31! Remember, please, you are my cousin, and for the honour of the Family, do not make yourself ridiculous. As a 'new composer,' or the 'only feminine operatic composer,' we shall all be eager to claim relationship. 'Are you related to the celebrated Dr. ———' will be said to me one day. 'No, not related to him, but I know him very well.' 'Oh! then I suppose *he* is a brother of the great musician, Miss Mary ———.' 'No, she is *my* cousin.' 'Oh! indeed!' which of course will mean, though unsaid—'both Dr. ——— and Miss ——— having brains, must be relations; *you* being only a poor sort of painter cannot aspire to relationship with such distinguished persons.' I have been to Highgate today painting—oh! the wind! I should like to go to a place where the wind would cease from troubling and painters could be at rest.

[No date. About 1862 probably.—ED.]

MINEHEAD.

MY DEAR MARY,

You asked me in your last letter if I had seen the Alfred Wigans and Miss Herbert at the St. James. Yes, I have in more than one piece. Alfred Wigan's acting in 'The Isle of St. Tropez' was wonderful. I think he and his wife are perfect in their line. Miss Herbert is good and a very beautiful elegant woman; but as an actress nothing in finish and style to Mrs. Alfred Wigan. 'The Isle of St. Tropez' is a thrilling play. When Wigan is seated before the looking-glass, and sees his wife drop the poison into the tumbler his face is a study. I suppose you have never seen

Robson? He is marvellous; one time thrilling the audience with the intensity of a great tragedian, at another lapsing into a comic song.

'Still waters run deep' is a good play and gives scope for Alfred Wigan and his wife's finished style. We know no actors, though I have met one or two at other houses—the Hydes to wit. I used to meet Keeley every morning going to school when I was about 14, and he always smiled at me as if he knew me. I told this to my godfather G. Hyde, who was surgeon to some theatrical fund, and he repeated to Keeley what I said, whereat the great comedian exclaimed: 'Little dear!'

Have you ever seen 'Justicia's' pamphlet, written in 1855: 'The Right of Women to Exercise the Elective Franchise'? The next year a Petition was signed by 8000 women. Of course it will be years before we get the vote; but it must come as a mere act of justice and common sense. It is simply absurd that a woman with responsibilities and possessions should have no vote, and men, with very inferior qualifications, should be on the register. If women are not fit, mentally, to vote, why should they be considered fit to canvass for candidates? they must be acquainted with the political position, or they would not be able to influence the men voters. That I would not do, as I think canvassing nearly as immoral as bribery, and of course they are almost synonymous, for one leads to the other. I would have canvassing made illegal, as it leads to perjury and corruption. I wonder how many men promise their vote to one candidate and then give it to the other? It is very troublesome to find out who are the delinquents, unless you take your man to the poll and see that he gives his vote to the right candidate; and if ever secret voting comes in (the ballot), an unconscientious voter will be able to cheat as much as he likes, and take a bribe from both the rivals.

We have had a delightful time here, the walks are charming and it is a quite paintable country though one is apt to exaggerate the purple. I have a theory about purple or purplish grey. Put in the shadows first in this colour and then wash in the local colour, and in only one painting if possible. If one painting over a thick white impasto be the most brilliant method in oil colours, surely the transparency of water colour work must be lost by using body colour and much stippling. Yet six years ago we all swore by that manner. I remember thinking Edmund W.'s work perfection and Mrs. O. saying, 'if you use opaque colour why not paint in oil?' And she was quite right, though the opacity of oil paint is nothing to that of a chinese white and colour mixture.

    Goodbye; with my love,
          Your affectionate JANETTE.

RECOLLECTIONS OF

P.S.—I met a Mrs. Pink at the Thomsons'. I never heard the name before. I wonder why there are so many colours, I do not mean coloured people, but people with colour names. Greens, Browns, Greys, Whites are common enough and Pink, Blue, and Black rather less so; but I never heard of a Mrs. Red or a Mr. Yellow.

A SPINSTER AUNT

CHAPTER VI

A HARVEST HOME

—— 1862. Salisbury

My dear Mary

I came down here last week; you know I love this country, I mean the valleys, with their countless little rivers trickling through the meadows. The upper country, the chalk downs beloved of Copley Fielding, are not to my taste. My favourite kind of landscape is pastoral, but I prefer the French to the English species. The long lanky trees waving in the wind are far more beautiful than our stodgy elms and oaks; but here in this part of Wilts there are so many abeles that I have named one road not far from here, the French Rd. One side is bounded by a wall and the other by a small river with delightful weeds and wild flowers. Behind the wall is a well timbered park, and between road and river, a row of abeles; then a stretch of meadows with cattle sleepyly grazing, and the spire of Sarum Cathedral peeping out between scattered aspens and white poplars. It is an ideal piece of landscape almost as beautiful as the turf country in Picardie, or the flat land bordering on the Seine, the Marne, the Oise, and the Yonne with their *saules pleureuses*. You don't appreciate flat country, do you? You like mountains and hills; but our English ones are such poor specimens, mere pretence mountains. Heath land also I love, such as you find in the New Forest and all about Poole Harbour, that lagoon district which reminds one a little of the Venetian waters. Thereabouts in Dorset is colour—heather, bracken, gorse, broom; but colour is rare here, and I verily believe English people prefer grey skies to blazing sunlight! There is a charm in greyness no doubt; but it must be a pearly grey, not a leaden grey; and after all it is beauty of a melancholy type. I love the sun and the joyfulness it puts into one's heart. Well, just now we have sunshine for a wonder, day after day, and yesterday, the Harvest Home, it was brilliant. I wish you could have been present, for it was a most interesting function and exceedingly picturesque. It began with a short service at the church. There were three processions; one from the great House, another from the principal farm, and the third from the whitening factory. The principal one was headed by a brass band (somewhat shrill) banners and masses of people in their Sunday-go-to-meeting best. The Countess and all the children walked in front, and met the other

A SPINSTER AUNT

processions at the church doors. Every imaginable fruit and vegetable was to be seen piled up in the chancel; but unlike a similar ceremony which I once saw at Bellagio, there were no offerings during the service, but most of the vegetables and fruit stuck about the churches, all I believe, were sent to the Hospital afterwards. (Oh! this pen, it is *vile*.) At Bellagio there was a great procession of men, women and children bringing offerings in kind which were, after the mass, sold by auction in the courtyard in front of the presbytery and the money given to the poor. These were offered at the altar and blessed by the Padre during the thundering, one may say, by the organ of what sounded very much like the end of an Italian opera! (Church music in Italy, is of the most undignified and frivolous kind). There were loaves of bread, grapes, melons, eggs, all kinds of vegetables, and a young lamb carried on a cushion. Yesterday after the church service, we all adjourned to the principal farmer's house and had a splendid lunch in the garden. Numbers of tables and crowds of people. Then came speeches and thanks, by my Lord and his tenants, the rector of course, and some of the labourers, and after the feast singing began.

I wish I could have written down some of the folk songs in Wiltshire dialect, especially one sung by a quaint old woman, about 'John when he was a'cortin' me,' but the following

RECOLLECTIONS OF

version of 'John Barleycorn' may not be known to you:

> There was three Men come from the East,
> Could sow most Wheat and Rye,
> They made a solemn vow my Boys
> John Barleycorn should die.
> *Chorus.* For my whack fol-de-rol de diddle dolderay,
> For my whack fol-de-rol-de-day!

> John Barleycorn he laid in ground, all for a whole fortnight
> Till some rain from the sky did fall.
> Then John Barleycorn sprung up again
> And quite exprised them all.
> *Chorus.* For my whack, etc.

> John Barleycorn he growed in ground,
> Up to Mid-summer
> And then he had a beard, my Boys
> Longer than any man.
> *Chorus.* For my whack, etc.

> Then came the jolly Mowers
> Which cut him off at lea,
> They throwed him on the back, my Boys,
> And served him cruel-ly.
> *Chorus.* For my whack, etc.

> Then came the jolly puckers,
> Which pricked him to the heart
> And the carter he served him worse than that
> For he tied him to the cart.
> *Chorus.* For my whack, etc.

> They dragged him round and up the hills,
> Till they brought him to the Barn,
> They made a mow of him, my Boys,
> To keep him from all hurt and harm.
> *Chorus.* For my whack, etc.

A SPINSTER AUNT

> Then come the jolly Thrasher,
> That cut him flesh from bones,
> But the Miller, he served him worse than that,
> For he ground him twixt two stones.
> *Chorus.* For my whack, etc.
>
> Put Brandy in the Bottle
> And Cider in the Can
> John Barleycorn in a nut brown Bowl
> Will prove the strongest man.
> *Chorus.* For my whack, etc.

Naturally the words lose much of their effect for want of the tune; but I think if you had heard it sung in the Wiltshire dialect, and at the top of the many vigorous voices, you would agree with me that it was a wonderful performance musically though not quite after the manner of your Johann Sebastian. After dinner the farmer's wife asked the young ploughman who declaimed the solo verses, if he had enjoyed himself: 'Bless you, Mistress, yes, I goes on a eatin and a eatin, and I hardly knows how.' *There* is enjoyment in its highest form!

It was also a pathetic entertainment from one point of view, for it was the first Harvest Home at which the Countess has appeared since she lost her husband, the great Minister. The young Earl is a fine looking, handsome boy, and they say he is clever. He made a little speech, just a few words about doing his duty and so on, and touched upon the loss to him, as well as to them all, of his father.

As I write these notes of the day's doings a little baby Robin is hopping about at my feet while I whistle to him. He cocks his head about, but cannot yet get out a note; and a blackbird is pouring forth his evening serenade to his lady love, who is tucked away comfortably in her nest out of reach, I hope, of our common enemies, the puss cats; and I cannot help wondering, if the birds knew the joy their ditties give to us, the superior mortals, whether they would not manage to sing for a longer period? May not such wee creatures especially if they have humble minds, think that it is throwing pearls before swine to sing to such huge people who count their Grisis and Marios, their Pattis and Luccas among their brethren? And yet, do we not talk of a beautiful voice which is poured out simply and without effort, such as Clara Novello's or Adelina Patti's, as being 'bird-like'? and did not the public name Jenny Lind the 'Swedish Nightingale'? Once, by the way, when I was staying at Sèvres, I had a little too much of Nightingales. I had never heard any except on rare occasions; but that spring there were multitudes of French songsters serenading *Mesdames leurs femmes* in the trees within a stone's throw of my window. At first my sentiments upon the subject were thus expressed: 'How exquisitely beautiful!' and I was content to lie awake until dawn enjoying the concert. That view of the music lasted some

A SPINSTER AUNT

days and was succeeded by less enthusiastic sentiments—an hour or two sufficed. This was followed by a weariness that expressed itself in a mundane desire for sleep; and then there was a feeling when the performance began, approaching *ennui*, boredom: 'What *still* at it!' Finally, on retiring to my rest the window was fastened in spite of the sultryness of the night, my ears were stuffed up with cotton wool, and I echoed the Cardinal's sentiments applied to the little Jackdaw. It is only too true that human nature may have too much of a good thing, but I love to have the birds hopping about all the same. I often think that sentiment somewhat creeps into the Nightingale's reputation. Supposing they sang by day? Surely for beauty of tone, the Blackbird's voice equals or excels that of Nightingales and Thrushes, although for joyousness no singing approaches the beauty of the latter.

But apart from their singing, are not our wild birds the most joyous creatures in Nature, not excepting even our dogs, for they are so essentially semi-human that they are content to sink their own individuality and independence (most of them) and make our joys and sorrows their own. But the birds keep their freedom however much they may love us, and they do love and trust us when they know us intimately. For instance, in winter I have a clan of Titmice fluttering and fussing about the cocoanuts as they sway about in the wind hanging from some trellis near my window. A short time ago there were a pair of the large blue variety, two sweet little coal Tits, and Mr. Thomas Titmouse and Madam his wife. Then one very cold morning came an invasion of the long-tailed clan, beautiful little creatures all grey and pink with just enough black to bring all the coloured plumage into harmony. Whence came these strangers? They fluttered up, apparently having some knowledge of my provision of food during the winter months How did they know they could satisfy their hunger at the cottage of St. Francis? They never appeared before (all the eleven years I have been in the house) nor have I seen them since; they must have come from some unknown purlieus, and they gobbled up the crumbs with what might be called indecent haste, unless they were all but starving. Surely birds must have some means of communicating useful information? Years ago when we were living in the Regents Park with the *loggia* at the top of the house, we cultivated a few plants, and made the balcony a pleasant place to sit and watch the glorious smoky sunsets. Round the *loggia* was the usual Nash ornamental balustrade of the Park houses, and upon this ledge we placed bread crumbs and fat bacon the winter through. The half-starved army consisted of Blackbirds, Thrushes, Starlings, Chaffinches, a Pigeon or two, and the much-abused Sparrows, for whom I have a sneaking affection; for is there not something pathetic in being cared for by Him in spite of their value being so small that 'two are sold for a farthing.' One day I counted forty grimy friends gobbling my festive meal. How hungry they were! In the afternoon they reappeared but I noticed that among them were some country cousins of the Starlings, beautiful, brilliant, clean creatures, iridescent in the sunlight, easily distinguishable from the dull-coated Londoners, whose wonderful plumage was dimmed by grimy coal smoke. Such a squeaking of their shrill voices! and so many were they that the combined clan chivied away all the lesser army. Evidently a philanthropic member of the Town Colony had sent by some unknown telegraphy a message that food abounded in the Regents Park just in the same way that my little Blue Tits communicated with their Pinkish Brethren only the other day. How do the Natives of unexplored countries manage to send messages quicker than our vaunted electricity? There is nothing new under the sun, and possibly were men more sympathetic and less sportive towards their lesser brethren the birds and beasts, some solutions to many mysteries might result. However perhaps it is better that mysteries should not be solved, as we should have nothing to ponder over, if they ceased to be mysteries.

Talking of sentiment, does it not enter into the admiration bestowed upon the olive, for surely the willow is equally beautiful in form and colour? In form perhaps it is superior. There is something fantastic, weird, uncanny in the forms that the stems and branches of olives take; something suggestive of unrestful souls. All other trees have a principle of growth, the stems giving out innumerable branches upon a comprehensible system, but there is no plan for the growth of the olive; its vagaries are maddening and unaccountable; and although its branches are the emblem of peace, it seems in appearance to be the most un-peaceful of trees. May not some pre-historic tribes have made it the symbol, thinking that if peace came through the waving of one of its twisted and fantastic branches, there indeed would be rest from the battle. And then the colour. In spring it wends its way exquisitely among the tender green dresses of other trees, its delicate pinkish grey forms a charming background to the fruit blossoms, and it brings all into harmony (symbolic again of peace); but later on towards summer, or in early winter, it is dull and sad and wanting in the reddening purple tones of the birches and beeches. Had the Garden been a copse of beeches, or willows, or abeles, would the old Classic sentiment which clung to the olive have been transferred to the New Faith? But let me not grumble at some sparks of sentiment

A SPINSTER AUNT

surviving to illuminate our minds in this materialistic age. Adieu dear cousin

Your JANE.

P.S.—I have joined a musical society which is delightful. We sing all sorts of things by Hummel, Mozart, and so on, and we have a fine soprano for the solo parts. It is supposed to be a full orchestra; but that depends upon chance. Sometimes strings are absent—sometimes wood wind. Do you know Hummel's *Alma Virgo*? It is charming, the solo parts soprano and hautboy. Why do we never hear such things at concerts, instead of the eternal Handel? Our conductor is the fine organist of the Irvingite Church in Gordon Square and also of the Roman Catholic Cathedral at Nottingham—Mr. E. H. Turpin; he plays divinely.

CHAPTER VII

POOR THOMAS

—— 18??

MY DEAR MARY

I was writing the other day to Cousin Ann. She asked me if I could find a collection of letters which were kept by Aunt Priscilla as family relics, the old Aunt, *our* great aunt, Priscilla. They were written by several members of the aunt's family upon the death of a certain Thomas, who must have been a delightful creature devoted to his instrument (the violincello), but unfortunately for many years attached to a more or less insane wife. His patience and kindness and self sacrifice were exquisite my mother always said. And he also had a love story, inasmuch as he married the wrong woman through some unknown infatuation. There was an Eleanor who was devoted to him, but somehow the other woman was more attractive, though as I remember Eleanor, as an old lady, she was lovely. Or probably Miss Paxman flattered him by talking music sentiment; any how poor Thomas unfortunately made the

A SPINSTER AUNT

one mistake of his life. He was always called poor Thomas mainly I fancy because he was, according to the rest of the family, unregenerate. You know most of my mother's family were very low church—scarcely church folk at all; only as the 'Establishment,' as they called it, was a part of the British Constitution they held to it as they did to the Queen and the Royal Family. They were the sort of Christians who affirmed that there was only one path to Heaven, and their's was the true one; and so they greeted me when I paid a duty call with: 'Well when are you going over to Rome?' Of course I was a 'Puseyite' (and am still) if not a 'Roman Catholic,' or rather 'a Jesuit in disguise.' Most of the so-called Protestant party even now talk in the same manner; but the curious part of it all is that they themselves always feel so sure, nor have they any compunction or sorrow in putting the rest of us, their really much-beloved friends, in the bad boat. 'Mind, there is only one road, and you are not on it!' So comforting to feel in good health when all those around you are suffering agonies of pain!

I think perhaps you may like to read these letters, before I send them to Cousin Ann; or to save time, will you send them on to her at Frome —the Cottage, Frome, Somerset. Great-aunt Priscilla evidently treasured the missives vastly, for they were always kept in a little box made by herself, painted in patterns, black upon a white ground and varnished to look like the Italian inlaid ivory work; but I will not send the box as it is too heavy. I suppose you remember the old lady? She wore a bombazine gown, whatever bombazine may have been (I have the bill—8 guineas and a half for the stuff only) and a mob cap like the Charity children. Sometimes she dressed in soft grey or mouse coloured noiseless silks and a three-cornered white handkerchief as behoved a Quakeress. I remember going with my mother to tea at Aunt Priscilla's and finding ourselves the only guests who did not 'thee' and 'thou' each other. She was Grandfather Fox's step sister you know. I always felt very much alarmed at the Friends' quiet well-ordered manners. Between ourselves, do Quakers ever explode with excitement, enthusiasm, or anger?

I forget if I told you 'Poor Thomas' was a High churchman, a great and devoted friend of Dr. Newman and Mr. Keble; he was at Oxford with them but I forget at which college.

Letter I. docketted by Aunt P. thus: 'James' views courteously expressed.' (Who was James?) '"Thomas was a queer mixture, I cannot understand a man possessing such liberal views being a member of the Establishment. I do not think he was a Jesuit as many of his family do. Undoubtedly Dr. Pusey and his friend Mr. John Keble are all working for the Pope, just as Dr. Newman does, and they will have their reward.

A SPINSTER AUNT

They said he wore a hair shirt, Thomas, I mean. Of course the others were sure to. What folly! Still I must fain say Thomas was a good man; the way he sacrificed himself for his poor foolish wife was noble. Not a word of reproach for her carelessness about the boy ever escaped his lips, and he devoted himself to making life as happy for her as possible. Often have I known him come home from his work tired and weary (and music teaching is not the most peaceful way of getting a living), and then set to work to read Jane Austen's stories, or Mrs. Radcliffe's high-flown stuff to his poor wife (Mrs. R. suited poor Maria's sentimental temperament); or he would play his violincello if she happened to be inclined for music which did not always happen. Once she smashed his beloved instrument to pieces, poor creature, but he bore it like an angel. But he was terribly wrong-headed upon Religion; if he had given up all that empty formula which early surroundings had bound him to, he would have been probably a better man; but Newman was his curse: it stilted his mind and prevented intellectual growth, and from his youth his intellect was inclined to be warped and narrow. As to his end, Eleanor's comments are all high-flown nonsense; there is a distinct uncomfortableness in dying in church at what they call the altar upon a cold November morning, which I do not like. Solomon says there's a time to laugh and a time to weep, or something of that kind. It is in 'Ecclesiastes' which I often read, being wisdom itself; but surely if there's a proper time for joy and grief, there must be a proper place for being born and dying in, and not an uncomfortable church; its like the children beginning their lives in cabs and such places, though I suppose it is not entirely their fault, poor little animals, but their silly mothers'. Besides, for that matter, I hold all this early church going, and fasting and so on, to be a mere fungus which the Reformers unfortunately left growing upon the Establishment, to sap its very life, a poisonous fungus that ought to have been burned with the images and idols of Rome. Thomas was a good man, though a slave to false gods, and formulas and shams as Mr. Carlyle would say."'

'Sarah's (?) views very decidedly expressed!' That too seems to have been Aunt Priscilla's comment and note of interrogation. '"I always said Thomas would *never* be happy until he had lost his soul. To die like the grass, cut down in a moment, and *unprepared*; and then Eleanor forsooth, thinking it *beautiful and poetic*—just like her, and *she* is just like *him*. All this frivolous nonsense of flowers at a funeral! who ever heard of such a thing except in *Popish countries*. There, say what you will, they are *all* Papists in

A SPINSTER AUNT

disguise. His will proves it. 'A floral *Cross*' (with a capital C) 'upon the coffin and a choral service' (Eleanor calls it a Requiem Mass! what next?) 'Let every one carry a small bunch of flowers which are to be sent (*all* the flowers) to the hospital, *not* buried; and ask every one to *pray* for me. R.I.P.' Good gracious, what next? What *are* we coming to? Pray for his soul, when we know *for certain* that as the tree falls, so it lies. We may *hope* for the best, but to fall *suddenly* with such Papistical thoughts in his heart *is awful to contemplate*. I fear he was always a living lie, false to his supposed creed, and even if he had gone over, he would have been no better, for how can *idolaters* hope to find grace? I always told poor Thomas he should repent while *there was time*. Certainly *I* shall *not* go to his 'requiem' indeed! I heard it once at Exeter Hall but they altered the words, so it did not so much matter; but I like Romish music no more than Romish idols. I was told the other day that there was a doll dressed up in white satin at Antwerp Cathedral which had thousands of pounds worth of jewels on it; and that is what such people as poor Thomas and Eleanor want to bring back to Protestant England! *Idol worship!* Fifty years hence, the *surely saved* will count *very few*. Eleanor talks of the beautiful end and is not at all shocked at the *suddenness* of it, and yet she *prays three times a week* against sudden death in the Litany. Well, there, they are all mad together, or blind if not sinful; for when people, knowing *the true path* forsake it for *false* prophets, we know what the end *must be*. Poor Thomas called upon Christ, but his Christ was anti-Christ. And *he* thought the *church* all in all. There is but *one* path, and certainly neither he nor his friends ever walked by the *only one* which leadeth to salvation. I must ask Mr. Jones when I see him, if he thinks there is *any hope* for poor Thomas; but I fear not, *poor foolish misguided man*."'

'Aminta sympathetically.

"Poor dear Thomas! I'm sure if there is an orchestra of Angels in Heaven like the old masters paint, Thomas will be engaged for the violincello parts. Eleanor always said he had a beautiful mind but whatever his mind was his soul poured itself into his music and I doubt very much whether Saint Cécilia herself upon the very best modern organ would have done better. Poor dear what could she do on that little thing like a harp which she holds on one arm? And it always made me cry I don't mean the harp but poor dear Thomas' music."'

'Aunt Zina writing to her boys.

"I do wish Père Boulanger could have seen

A SPINSTER AUNT

dear Thomas, and I had always hoped he would have been able to come over to Paris. The Reverend Father's influence might have been for his eternal good. He was so near the truth, so near the right path, peeping in at the windows as it were; why could he not have entered by the door of the Church, instead of staying in the misguided Protestant fold.; but I do not fear for a moment that he will be entirely lost, he was so full of good works for Christ and His Church, but it is so sad to remain in heresy when the arms of the true Church are opened to receive you. I shall certainly remember him in my devotions and endeavour to gain for him the benefit of an indulgence. I don't know whether this can be done for one who has died a member of a schismatic sect. I have only been converted so short a time, I must ask our dear Father. But I shall in any case attend the Neuvaine at Sainte Géneviève in January. I wonder if Père Boulanger would arrange a Novena especially for poor Thomas. I will ask him, he knows I always hoped he would follow me and be converted. How any one can reject perfect peace when attainable passes my understanding, but alas! for years I rested upon false doctrine and under the direction of men who called themselves priests, but were not priests."'

The following is endorsed by Aunt Priscilla :—
' I wrote down the following conversation from

Nancy's description in the evening after the funeral.'

'Nancy and Betty at tea after the funeral.

NANCY. "Yes he was a true gentleman, Betty, was your Master; but I do wish he had been more pious."

BETTY. "Pious! why he went to church nearly every day of his life, and often without a bit of breakfast."

N. "Thats where it is, Betty, fastin' won't save souls. And although me and my Missus don't always agree about things like a beefsteak puddin; she thinks the undercrust which gets soddened, and pies too, is unwholesome—and the hard boiled eggs wasteful, yet we agrees quite well about prayer meetins, and I thinks its much more respectful to go to church at the proper times, 11 in the mornin than to steal out before its quite light as if you was ashamed of what you was a doin. It ought to be like doctor's stuff, regler, 11 and 4; only that prayer meetins and church is at 11 and 6 or 7. I holds to half past 6 for evening service. Besides goin at the regler times is a makin no demsteration of yourself, as if you was better nor other folks."'

'Margaret after some weeks had elapsed.

"Pray forgive me, my dear Eleanor, for not having answered your letter of the 2d inst.

A SPINSTER AUNT

before, but I have been ill from my usual complaint, indigestion. The seat of the trouble this time was my right side, where I suffered the most excruciating agony, causing tremblings all over my enfeebled body. And, as if this were not sufficient for poor human nature I have also been suffering from a boil upon my left arm, just above the elbow. This, you may imagine has caused me an infinite amount of pain, and much trouble in the way of poultices, (linseed meal) which my doctor ordered to be kept constantly applied to the tiresome excrescence. On the 9th, no I think it was a day later, the 10th, my servant made me forty-one of these attempts at relief, and I can assure you she had little time for much else, particularly as I was obliged to get her to put cold compresses to relieve the indigestion from time to time. Man has much suffering to go through here below ere he reaches the goal, and some of us seem to be especially tried in this respect. The weather here is exceedingly cold, and was so on the day of the funeral, which was the reason that I dared not accompany you and the rest of the family to the church yard. Your letter was indeed a shock to me, and my husband attributes this last violent attack of my habitual source of suffering, to your sad intelligence. When one is so far from strong as I am, the least shock to one's nerves causes serious consequences. Poor Thomas, we can only trust in the infinite mercy of the Almighty, and hope that he was prepared for his sudden call.

Believe me to remain, my dear Eleanor, with much affectionate sympathy and esteem for you and yours, Eʟɪᴢᴀʙᴇᴛʜ Lᴇᴛɪᴛɪᴀ."'

'From the Rev. Jeremiah Jehoshophat Jones of Salem Chapel, Clapham.

"Sad! sad indeed! To be cut off like the grass so suddenly without the chance of repentance, but let us hope our dear kind friend may not be among the lost. But can we hope with any confidence? Alas! alas! Mr. Thomas refused the true Gospel while there was time; and without Grace, of what value are works? But we can at least, and most profitably, point to our dear friend as an example, a terrible example to our flock, that they may be converted ere they be cut down like the green grass.

Let us prepare for the end, for it cometh like a thief in the night unheralded and unlooked for."'

'The Vicar, preaching at St. Chad's.

"Our dear friend was one of the most holy and humble-minded men whom it has been my good fortune to meet. He had the kindest of hearts, and was ever one of the most sympathetic souls to those in trouble; and he bore his own many trials with the most patient trust as befits not only a professing, but an acting Christian. He made the best of this flitting world; but he looked for perfect happiness and peace elsewhere. He loved his music, but he loved his God yet more. He was most unselfish and self sacrificing, a Christ-like man, and he ever felt 'who am I that I should complain of sorrow? What are my sufferings compared to His?'

Let us thank God that he has taken unto himself our dear Brother, painlessly and peacefully. And who, looking upon that countenance, as he lay in his last sleep, can doubt that his gentle soul has been wafted away into Paradise? Like Stephen, 'he fell asleep.'"'

I wonder what you will think of the letters, and which you will like best. I think I can guess. I will write again soon.

Ever your affectionate cousin JANE.

MINEHEAD, *June* 1862.

DEAREST MARY

We have an unlooked for addition to our family in the shape of twins, a boy and girl. When the telegram arrived and was read aloud.

'God help them!' said the Pater. 'The Twins?' said I? 'No; the parents,' said he.

While I was painting to-day in an ancient quarry, an old woman who was passing stopped: 'That's full of Varmints and Vampires,' said she, and knowing that she meant vipers, I fled ignominiously tho' I doubt the truth of the statement. We go to Lynton tomorrow, drawn by a coach and eight horses. I am looking forward so much to that part of the excursion. Good night.

CASTLE ROCK HOTEL, LYNTON.

We have arrived; but oh! the vanity of human wishes! At the last moment Jehu and his 8 horses were given up. F. had set herself against the coach all along, and at last she persuaded Papa to have a carriage. 'It was safer, for the coach does come to grief some times, and might go over the cliff.' And so we were dragged up Countesbury Hill by two beasties instead of my much dreamed of eight. However it will be all the same a hundred years hence.

This is a charming little inn, a thatched cottage. In front is a lawn with flower beds, over which one looks on to the sea and Countesbury Hill, a lovely view. Staying here is Miss D. the authoress. Why need cleverness in women produce what may be called a Guy? A very short scarlet petticoat, a very small jacket, a tiny pork-pie hat with a brilliant scarlet wing sticking straight up, a looped up blue serge gown, and cropped hair— that is the style of costume affected by working women. Half the students at the schools and galleries, particularly the Turner worshippers, wear their hair short like men. But are men less silly? Tennyson being a man poet, wears his hair very long and curling on his shoulders. Also he swathes himself in a huge cloak and pointed cornered wide-a-wake—for all the world like an Italian brigand; and then forsooth he complained at L—— last year that he was mobbed, and must leave! The 'mob' must have been six or seven boys; but why did he not cut his hair? and mark you, lady poetesses and lady painters cut theirs short. It is a queer world.

Ever your loving cousin.

Feby. 1, 1863.

DEAR MARY

Yesterday I went to the Abbey to see the consecration of Bishops Tozer and Twells. The Bp. of Oxford [1] preached a most eloquent sermon; he is so happy in voice and culture and the choice of words, but personally I prefer H. P. L.[2] as an orator, though possibly he is not so poetic in his similes; but the Bp. is often just a little too suave. Mrs. Maughan and I often argue upon

[1] Samuel Wilberforce.—ED.   [2] Henry Parry Liddon.—ED.

this point. L. is I suppose more of a theologian and his sermons are so well composed, so finished; and then his voice! one could sit patiently and listen to him for an hour or two even if he talked nonsense, so exquisite is the mere *timbre* of his voice. His oratory reminds one of the French 18th Centy. preachers—even of the Dominicans of today, those who are fine orators. I often wonder at the extraordinary influence Dr. Liddon has upon people. One can understand the educated flocking to hear him, the Cabinet Ministers and the Intellectuals; but one is surprised to hear that one's housemaid is desirous of spending part of her Sunday out, in listening to an hour of sermon which must be mostly over her head. If he is ever given a canonry or something of the kind in London, he will do an immense amount of good. As it is, one only gets the chance of hearing him now and then.

I wonder *à propos* of the performance which was unedifying, unimposing, and somewhat slovenly, when we shall see a bishop bearing his crozier and wearing a mitre, and clad in something more ecclesiastical than a black satin gown? At present the use of these symbols of episcopal accessories is confined to the panels of their carriages, and their spoons and forks, possibly also their note paper.

Ever your affectionate JANE.

A SPINSTER AUNT

7 March 1863. *Evening.*

DEAREST MOLLY

We saw the Princess of Denmark today, coming from the Station with her future husband. She is pretty with fair hair. Her mother and two sisters were there also. We saw them all excellently well, for Mr. Wornum allowed us to stand on the paved court in front of the National Gallery. The guardians took out chairs, and as the pavement is raised above the street we saw over the heads of the crowd. Mr. W. was very kind, for he invited us to his rooms if we could not see sufficiently well. I never saw anything more picturesque than the view down Pall Mall with numbers of flags flying across the street, and crowds of gaily uniformed soldiers. We are going to see some of the City decorations, and the illuminations on the wedding day, so I shall not send this off until later on. By the way I heard today from an old lady friend, Mrs. Jonson, that it was very improper to go to a dog show! I wonder why? and I wonder if anything is proper besides paying dull visits to old ladies? I care little what the world thinks of me, yet all these suggestions of improprieties do make one to a certain extent, uncomfortable; one knows not the whys and wherefores—they won't tell us! and so one may put one's foot into a conventional hole so to speak, unawares, and with the most perfect innocence. Perhaps there are no whys and no wherefores!!!

RECOLLECTIONS OF

11th March.—We went all about to see the illuminations with Robert and L. C. The old part of the Strand with its gabled houses all covered with flags looked charming. St. Paul's was fairly well done, but not very effective. We got into a fearful crowd in the Strand, I have never been so squashed since the lying in state of the Duke[1] at Chelsea Hospital. We went single file, as otherwise we could not have got through the crush. L. C., E., R. and myself. They pulled us with all their might, and when we got into Norfolk St. we were all so breathless that we stood panting for at least five minutes. It was all the fault of the police permitting vehicles in the streets; they ought to make regulations as in Paris and allow no carriages within three miles of Charing Cross. They are a danger, and of no use even to the occupants for they only creep along, and some people we know at Wandsworth spent the night within the precincts of the Marble Arch, and having seen nothing, they returned home at dawn. Later on in the evening some people were crushed to death in this very part of the Strand.

Today E. and I took Jack and Tiny to see some of the decorations before they are taken down. London Bridge is very civic, in fact most of the ornamenting business is ugly or vulgar or both. Arches of wood covered with the crudest

[1] Wellington.—ED.

coloured devices and portraits (such things!) of the happy pair. Garish and hideous; and again no regulation of traffic. We were crushed so, near the bridge, that we entered for sanctuary a public house! The children's first appearance in a London pub, and mine too for that matter. Well, it is all over now.

14*th.* I must tell you what a street boy said to Harriett the other day. She wears a *very* mild hoop. So do I, for I hate them. It was in Vigo St. (By the way I forgot to tell you that on the night of the illuminations just outside Scott-Adie's shop, we four met the Pater and Laura. We all went out independently. Was it not curious?) Here is the small boy's observation to the apparently hoopless lady: 'Oh! don't yer look nice and slim; wouldn't yer like a crinoline?' The wearing of hoops leads to comic incidents as *Punch* sometimes demonstrates. I saw myself in Regent St. last week a lady walking calmly along the pavement, having caught up her outside petticoat which left her lower extremities walking in a sort of cage! You know some people wear inflated hoops, india-rubber tubes, joined together by perpendicular tapes; and you also know that Regent St. at 4 in the afternoon is full of footmen standing about by the carriages. Imagine then their stifled laughter. Under these circumstances what ought a Christian woman to do? If one speaks to the victim her distress would probably make matters worse. It is a problem I have never been able to solve. One afternoon at All Saints a worshipper's chignon dropped and hung by one hair. This happened early in the service, and I assure you the whole forty minutes remaining I could think of nothing but, 'what shall I do?' The rest of the women seemed oblivious to the accident—they were more devout than your humble scribe. I am not good, as you know. I waited, and told the poor thing outside the porch. She did not seem grateful. Was she annoyed that I disturbed her equanimity? Or had I not done so soon enough? People are very odd. Sometimes when one moves up from the corner of an omnibus to make room for a lame person who is struggling to appear as if she had the right use of her limbs, the only acknowledgment is a scowl. I admire the action of an American girl I once met at a ball. She had a long curl—*à l'anglaise* as the French call the fashion—it fell off. A man, not her partner, picked it up and placed it on the mantelpiece, and in passing round the room the owner took it up, and replacing it upon her head with a hairpin, remarked: 'I guess that's mine!'

No one would ask Blanche T. whether she would like a crinoline, as she wears the largest I know, a perfect little house as small Tiny called some hanging outside a draper's shop. One day the children being caught in the rain; 'Let's go

A SPINSTER AUNT

under them little houses, Betsy,' said Tiny. The only hoop I ever wore was a very mild one. I believe I was the first to give up the hideous fashion and the last to begin it. When I went to Paris, I took one, as everybody said I should be jeered at if I were what the boy called sleek and slim; but I packed it up again on leaving, and when at Fluellen, I immolated it by throwing it into the Reuss. I saw it float down, knocked about by the torrent and the rocks, and I hoped a sensation story might be invented in the newspapers about a suicide. But I watched fruitlessly for many days, and no thrilling horror appeared. Its end was ignominious silence.

Have you ever been asked at a ball whether you liked oysters? Conversation with a partner at my last rout flagging, somewhat disagreeably, the intelligent youth received a noble inspiration and posed that momentous question! But I met a still more intelligent young man at Dr. J.'s 'slow' last week. It was a true slow, a slower could not have been discovered. I knew not a soul there. I was stranded by an ottoman in the middle of the room after the manner of the woolsack in the House of Lords, only covered with dames instead of ancient dignities; and you know when once you get upon or near an ottoman, it requires superhuman efforts to get away—hence my astonishment when this bold, strong minded, young man came up and asked if I would like some refreshment? Said I joyfully, 'Yes,' and we descended to the dining room and demolished ices, many and sweet. Said he, 'I thought you looked very uncomfortable, and there was no doubt that I felt so, for I knew no one in the rooms but the Dr. and Mrs. J., so I thought the best thing we could do was to come down here.' 'A brilliant thought,' said I, and we chatted on quite pleasantly upon divers topics, and men, and things, for more than an hour and a half, until my respected elders discovered me *en route* for the cab.—Good bye, Your loving JANIE.

A SPINSTER AUNT

CHAPTER VIII

THE DEN

THE DEN,
November 12th 1863.

DEAR MOLLY

My dear little Lily has died and I have lost not only my faithful and loving little friend, but the peaceful consoler of all my minor troubles. The ugly pup lives and resembles a guinea pig, but black and uncomely. I wish I had been at home to comfort poor Lill. When I left her the other day, I had no idea she was so ill, but her beautiful black eyes looked piteously sad, and I was blind and stupid, for they spoke her only language. Why was I not told? They say they did not know, and that she was not suffering. Then why did she die? She certainly did not even moan, or I should have stayed with her. For years she has been my confidant and comforter. She entered into all my woes connected with the marriage; and people say Pomeranians are silly dogs! She was an aristocrat in all her movements. She was born at Apsley House, and being underhung, (a formation of the mouth which, in a dog, is considered to be a blemish, in spite of the fact that many well-born Britons frequently possess this characteristic), poor Lill had consequently to be given away to a more plebeian household. Perhaps she was no loser by the change, for, instead of being one of many dogs, she reigned in absolute supremacy in our home, and she deserved all our devotion, for she was sympathy personified. And she had a heart which, presumably, all aristocrats do not possess as a matter of course. Can any creature be more sympathetic than a speechless dog? What heals a heartsore more completely than to feel a little cold nose thrust into the palm of one's hand? It is like the sympathy of a small child's kiss, but the child's act is an undeveloped instinct—the dog understands with the innate wisdom of a reflective, though silent being. Poor Lill; what hours we have passed together in this old Den. She was not clever, but her lovingness and pure-minded unselfishness would have been a credit to many a human being. People, some people, talk of the affection of cats; but was any puss cat ever known to leave her bed if sleepy, or peradventure sick, to greet her dearest friend? But almost any dog will do so. Where does the little soul of a 'mere animal' go? Can such unselfishness, such abounding love and devotion have no sort of continuance? We cannot tell; but may not the 'beasts that perish' be the noxious beasts only? Reptiles certainly. Why should the expression be taken as including all beasts, *i.e.* all creatures but holy man? There certainly are types of men which should be dubbed the beasts. You remember this old 'Den,' don't you? this home of dear Lill? It is altered now you know; but in the old days before my time, it was part of what was called Bluebeard's chamber. Then, before the greenhouse was made upon the leads, connecting the back and front houses, any one going to the Den had to pass by the yard. The basement of the back house was used as a stable. My father being an oddity in many ways, and keeping a horse and chaise, put the latter at a neighbouring inn; but he liked to keep his horse under his own eyes. Being behind the front house, the only way out was by the yard, which the horse passed through on his way to the street; and in crossing the yard the creature used to poke his nose in at the dining room window to receive contributions of sugar at breakfast time. Then he solemnly walked through the hall—a simple and original arrangement.

The Den gained the name of Bluebeard's chamber, because of its dark corners and general mystery—as for instance being peopled by various curious vases and strange bottles enveloped in straw. One of these, a fine earthenware oil jar of Italian origin, we called the Forty Thieves'-jar. When I was a child it was only a lumber room; but when a stepmother's arrival was discussed, an extra sitting room was obviously necessary.

'Brother-in-law,' said an uncle, 'the girls must have a study, where they can work by themselves'—a most wise and apt remark, for we had already arrived at the same conclusion, and advice is always sweet when it coincides with our own desires. We had secretly held council upon the respective merits of Bluebeard's chamber and a room at the top of the front house; but the former, being connected with the drawing room by the greenhouse, made a most convenient study, and so Bluebeard carried the day, and the 'Den' was evolved from the imaginary scene of that butcher's husbandly discipline, and became the home of Lily and ourselves for many a happy year. How hard we worked to turn that dark chamber into a fairly light one, for the ceiling was only 6 ft. high. But the Oxford Movement having penetrated into our spiritual darknesses, and the Pre-Raphaelite reform having touched our artistic tastes, and Ruskin being then an infallible guide and paver of artistic roads, we were so filled with the correct arguments and opinions which are usual in youth and likewise infallible, (although to older eyes, seemingly rather foolish), that we covered everything in that poor old room with ecclesiastical symbols in divers colours, but with religious enthusiasm, artistic enthusiasm, and all kindred enthusiasms.

First came a skylight round which Mediæval designs enclosed medallions of Saints. This was not only useful for giving light, but was the only part of the room in which a six foot two friend could stand. Then the windows looking on to the greenhouse, were painted with coloured borders, and the corners handsomely decorated and leaded by lines of dark brown paint. The white part was latticed. This had a very pretty effect with the plants of the greenhouse on the other side.

All the woodwork of the room was decorated, and the dark corners were enlightened by little pendant lamps burning before the shrines of our patron Saints standing in niches. Many were the festivals when we lighted up our lamps! certainly far more numerous than those in the Prayer book, red and black put together!

With these surroundings it will be seen that our Lily had all the advantages of an artistic education, coupled with socialism of the best kind, and frequent opportunities of improving her small mind. But her power of acquiring knowledge was not great, and consisted mainly in tapping at the door when she required our society.

There are two ways into the Den, the one already mentioned by the greenhouse, and a trap-door over a back staircase. This was Lill's favourite entrance, as it led straight up from her hut in the yard. It is also very useful for ourselves, for if we see objectionable folks visiting the occupant of the front drawing-room, we have time to slip through the trap-door for a few minutes before our step-mother approaches by the greenhouse, and not a little diversion is produced by the Comedy of the Drawing-room which we witness from our vantage ground behind the plants, when it is safe to return.

'Oh! I am *so* sorry. I thought the girls were in the Den; but no one but the dog is there. They must have gone out.' Luckily dogs speak only a language not understood by all the people.

When danger is at agony point, we do not reappear, but descend the back staircase, cross the yard, mount to our room in the front house, put on our bonnets, and slide out noiselessly by the front door.

In all these comedies, Lily was irreproachable. She never barked, and, when left alone to answer questions as to our whereabouts, gazed stupidly with a blank look in her eyes.

Such is the Den where so many heartburnings have been stifled, and such good resolutions formed —only to be broken. It was in the old days the scene of sorrows, the intensity of which now seems exaggerated, if not foolish. Its walls heard outpourings which, could they have spoken, would have caused many a disaster; and above, and over it all, poor old Lill presided, the Angel of the Den. She, happily, could not repeat what she heard, though I doubt whether she would have given utterance, had she been able. She was ever sympathetic, comforting us with the most loving glances, lavishing devotion upon us without stint. She was never tired nor bored by endless outpourings of griefs and vain repetitions of woes; she would nestle herself close to us and gently lick our hands, the dogs' infallible cure for all sorrows, mental as well as physical. Was it possible that such a creature would have betrayed us by speech, had she possessed the power? Our friend has been with us about 9 years and now she has passed away to the heaven of good dogs, leaving behind that little black woolly puppy as unlike its mother as many a human baby. I shall never forget poor Lill's beseeching glance the last time I saw her cuddling up the pup after I had inspected it. 'I grieve to leave you alone,' she seemed to say, 'but I give you a little legacy to love and comfort.' Tears without number have been shed, hearts are overflowing with sorrow; a dismal void is felt everywhere, but especially in the Den—its Angel had passed away for ever. . . .

26*th*. The pup has been a link with the past; but alas! one day, in its desire to see the world and investigate its mysteries, it clambered up the side of a washtub and fell a victim to its enquiring mind. No one happened to be near at the time, so the poor little pup ended its short career here below, and joined its darling mother.

Three or four portraits of Lily remain in the family picture gallery, ancient attempts in water-colours, but good likenesses in spite of miserably poor *technique*; but to do justice to her beauty, her fluffy white coat, her graceful figure, and her expressive eyes so sympathetic and loving, would require the genius of a Great Master; indeed, the best likeness of her is the Pomeranian in Gainsborough's portrait of 'Perdita,' where the dog—I say it with bated breath—is so much more beautiful (and intelligent!) than the lady. How curious it is that when two great painters depict the same woman, the portraits are quite different; not in colour only, but in character. Who would say the 'Perdita' by Reynolds is the same lady as the 'Perdita' by Gainsborough? But for beauty and for execution, most people would give the palm to Reynolds. Yet there are connoisseurs who consider Gainsborough to be the greater painter.

We composed an epitaph for poor Lill which falls short of all she was to the two occupants of this old Den:

> 'Dear little Lill, best of friends,
> Gone away we know not where;
> How blank is all the world to me,
> Without thy loving sympathy.'

The other day I met the Gospel Truth people; they were furious about the new kind of burial as they termed it—cremation. It was shocking, and seemed to them to affect the future of the soul somehow. I suggested, what happens to the poor souls consumed in a fire, and I might have added the poor drowned folk, the probable prey of great whales and other creatures of the sea; but I did not wish to anger the good people unnecessarily. I did, however, anger them much; for I was led to respond to their explanation that the poor creatures burnt to death in a house, (or a mine, or a theatre), died so 'by the will of God,' by replying that the accident was most probably caused by the careless upsetting of an oil lamp. Oh! you should have seen their faces! But fancy attributing such a desire to the Almighty. Such folk are as ignorant as poor old Jones, who every anniversary of her husband's departure, goes up to Finchley 'to see *him*.' I try to persuade her that *he* is as near her here in Marylebone as up there; but the only comment is, 'No, I must go and see *him*.' And she goes and trudges through the snow on a February morning, very imperfectly shod, catches cold ending in bronchitis, and loses five or six days' charing wages. And people say that Faith is Dead!!!

Much love to you;

Your JANE.

[*Diary.* No date.—ED.]

Tonight, while the state performance was going on in the Opera house, it was picturesque to see the encampment of Life Guardsmen taking the place of cabbage carts in James St. They bivouacked, so to speak. And when the Royalties left, some one had the wit to let off Bengal fire. It was most picturesque; the guards with their helmets and cuirasses glistening in red and green flashes of light.

3rd April, 1864. THE DEN.

DEAREST COUSIN

We have to-day seen the greatest man of the century—I say so advisedly; for the man who has freed his country and takes no reward, is surely greatest among the great—he is a second Washington, and doubtless could have made himself Dictator had he so desired. People feel this, though they dare not say it; and all London poured out to meet Garibaldi; rich and poor, high and low, struggled to do him honour. We stood at the bottom of the Haymarket in Cockspur St. facing Charing Cross, so we had a splendid view. It was a right Royal Progress all the way from Bricklayers Arms Station. Why he was landed there as 'goods,' we have not yet fathomed, but it seems a queer place for an illustrious visitor to make his entrance into the greatest city of the world. He is a magnificent

A SPINSTER AUNT

creature, so handsome, with beautifully chiselled features; and standing up in the carriage in his historic red shirt and grey cloak, bareheaded, he looked every inch a king, which probably he might have been, had he not been Garibaldi, for his unselfishness is only equalled by his patriotism. I am thankful to have seen him, but the crowd was unpleasant—somewhat soiled to put it mildly. The men clambered on to the carriage, and would have liked to have taken the horses out to drag it. The enthusiasm was boundless, and the cheering deafening. It is sad that some persons in high places object to this proof of England's sympathy with Italy's freedom, and with the great Liberator. I do not know if this be true; how can one ever get at the truth of what 'they say'? At all events England and London have paid their tribute through the action of the nobleman who initiated the idea of the visit.

A London crowd always astonishes me, although I am myself a Londoner—it is so wonderfully orderly and good tempered. So are the police. In fact there seems to be a sort of innate understanding, a mutual determination to keep order without any trouble or violence, which is tremendous praise to all parties upon such an occasion as this when most people went temporarily mad. I rejoice that I have seen the hero, as much as I regret that my efforts to meet Mazzini have always proved fruitless. He frequently goes to the Harrison's, and so do I; but whenever he was expected, he never turned up.

Ever your loving JEANNE.

Don't you like the French form better than Jane?

July, 1864. LYME REGIS

MY DEAR MARY

We all of us have witnessed domestic storms in tea cups, but we and our friends have been instrumental in causing, quite innocently, what might be called a hurricane in a sugar basin. It was in this wise. Always ready and desirous of improving our national inactivity as regards novelty, we made the other day, an effort to introduce mixed bathing on to our British shores; with what success you shall hear.

Our lodging has a garden, and that garden ends upon the beach; so we bethought us that if we bathed before breakfast we should save much dressing and undressing, and we could walk down to the sea through the garden. Our party consists—the bathing contingent—of Mrs. D., her two boys under ten, an art student (girl) and we two, ditto, ditto. Nothing could be more seemly than our attire; bathing costumes, really very pretty, blue serge trimmed with red braid like the French suits; and over all, a large waterproof cloak. But we had reckoned without our host: vested interests and British conventionality.

A SPINSTER AUNT

We marched down the garden at 7 A.M., walked across the shore, took off our wraps and joyously entered the sea. It was a lovely morning and we had a glorious swim. After a quarter of an hour or so, we returned the same way very pleased with ourselves. But in the afternoon the Mayor interviewed Mrs. D. He was 'very sorry to cause us annoyance, etc. etc. No doubt we were innocent of any intentional impropriety, but Lyme Regis was not France. It might be prejudice, but Dorset was Dorset, and did not like new-fangled nor Foreign ways.' One of us had a brilliant inspiration: 'But we will pay the machine people the same as if we used the thing' (there is only one machine), 'which would surely be an advantage to them and to their other customers.' An armistice was arranged, conditions of peace were drawn up and Mr. Mayor bid us 'Good morning.' But alas! the host we fought against was stronger than purse power. Ma'am Grundy triumphed, and we had to resign ourselves to the use of the machine, and confess ourselves beaten: as Reformers, we are feebleness personified.

But another incident is even more characteristic of Dorset than the bathing one. Painting under the cliff last Tuesday, I was disturbed by a shower of pebbles and mud upon my white umbrella. Looking up I beheld a crowd of young ruffians chucking missiles at me with the energy of even sleepy Dorset youths. I remonstrated, I threatened; I addressed them in violent language as vagabonds, rascals, brutes and any other expletives which came handy. But it was no use, and I ignominiously packed up my tools and retired, once more defeated by the family of Grundy-Hodge. Probably the instigator was a son of Madam of the bathing machine.

Going home I met my friends returning from their walk. 'What think ye?' I cried, 'I have suffered many things unpleasing for Art's sake, but never before have I been stoned!' and I related my adventure as we walked along. In the evening a policeman wished to see me, and much did I wonder what new offence I had committed in this sleepy Dorset hamlet called a town; but upon interviewing P.C. No. 1 (there are only two officers of the law here), I found that Mr. Mayor had overheard my complaint, and desired to know if I could identify the culprits. I said no, for it was a vast multitude, probably all the school just turned out and in search of excitement. However Mr. Mayor was so shocked at the urchins' behaviour that he instructed the police to shadow me in future wherever I may be at work. So now wherever I go, there lurks Robert with his vigilant eye upon me and my surroundings. I think the persecution arose from a primitive dislike of 'them French folks and their ways':—'hers a Furriner, and us doesnt want no Furriners yere with thems nasty ways.'

A SPINSTER AUNT

For some reason a white umbrella, and the worker underneath, provokes indignation among native populations, or it may be that we painters are considered to be legitimate subjects for sportive mud and stone throwing. In the Béguinage at Bruges, and by the river, the young Flemings were intolerable until a detective took me under his wing and kept off the boys; but the cure was worse than the disease, for the man standing by my side poured forth an endless volley of futile conversation which was most disturbing. One day I chased a dirty little villain across the grass and took him by the scruff of his neck for a good shaking, much to the amusement of all the Béguines, who were gazing out of their windows at this unwonted entertainment. At Venice, too, upon the waste ground beyond the Giardini Publico, my poor *ombrell' vecchio*, as a small vagabond termed it, was a butt for stone and mud, though it was *not* a white one.

Good bye, sweet Coz. Your JANE.

P.S.—Did I ever tell you that I once saw a real Dancing Faun in the flesh? It was on that same waste land at Venice where some recruits were exercising, and boys bathing near by. Presently the latter roused by the too-tooing of the trumpets, and rushed up the bank to see the fun. One of them, a little fellow of ten or eleven divested of his rags placed himself in front of the soldiers, and capering about backwards, gesticulated in the attitudes, for all the world, of a Dancing Faun. It was a Greek marble come to life. The gracefulness of the boy was delightful, and his swarthy skin lent colour to the illusion, even an improvement upon the marble—he might have posed for Praxiteles' 'Dancing Faun' in a previous incarnation—not that I believe in re-incarnation; do you? However delightful it might have been to pass a few years as Jeanne d'Arc, barring the terrible end, I should draw the line at the types of women such as the Princess who disposed of her inconvenient friends by a process of immersion from the Tour de Nesle. Query, did she? History says, Yes; and history says No. What then is the use of reading history?

A SPINSTER AUNT

CHAPTER IX

ART AND ART STUDENTS

[No date.—Ed.]

My dear Cousin

Some one calling to-day was eloquent upon the habitual joyousness of childhood; but surely that depends, like most things, upon circumstances? I wonder if you have still a vivid recollection of our childhood? I do not think yours was particularly happy, but mine was in a way, though it was a very peculiar kind of joyousness for a small child. We certainly were very happy when we got out of the attic window in Millbank, and sat in the gutter admiring the hay barges with their big red sails sailing down the river, and old Lambeth Palace and church as a background; but those were *fête* days, followed for you by many a dull one. Do you remember a hideous man ringing the bell and telling grandmama what we did? and never again could we get out, as she had bars put up. Oh! it was sad. I was happy enough in my playroom at the top of the house, an attic with sloping roof and only height enough in the centre for a grown up person to stand.

But that was of no consequence to me and mine. I held a school there and practised for a commercial career in the drapery line. The school children and the purchasers in the shop were all the same. There were dear old Nipper, the black and tan lady, and innumerable dolls—boy dolls, one Willie, and girl dolls, and baby dolls, and a lovely specimen of that great ship-building success in early times, the ark of the Noah family. How I loved to put the long procession of creatures upon the floor; each after its kind, two and two; birds of the size of sheep, and grasshoppers gigantic, headed by Mr. and Mrs. Noah, the young ladies, and gentlemen of the clan, all standing upon little round wooden plates.

Nip possibly was the only member of the community who ever tired of our play. But she and I felt great joy when a careless maid left the door on to the leads open after carpet shaking, for by crawling up the sloping roof, we could see Hampstead church and the Surrey hills over miles of roof and chimneys; and if, peradventure, no one mounted to the top of the house, the joy of sitting upon the tiles was a joy which lasted many days. Still my child life was what many would call dull. No companions (except yourself) of my own age, no nursery, no nurse—just any one in the house who found it convenient took me for a walk, and at one time across the road to a sort of dame-school down the street where I learnt nothing but to sit still upon a three-legged stool by the side of the old woman, (I daresay she was *not* old), hemming picture pocket handkerchiefs. I have a notion that the one idea at home was to keep me quiet so that the mother should not be worried or disturbed, she being invalidish. I certainly was a very lone child. You see I was No. 5. No. 4 died when he was a year old; the beauty of the family of course! I often wonder if we should have been transformed into beauties, had we, the ugly ones of the family, had the wisdom to disappear early in life! 'Distance lends enchantment,' etc.

One of my passive amusements was to put my mother's work basket to rights, and strange to say that particular work basket had the way of always being disorderly, which was, for me, a convenient quality. And another never-failing amusement was to re-arrange a cabinet of shells, which had become hopelessly disturbed by journeying, imperfectly packed, from the West Indies. The shells formed little patterns with divisions of cardboard, after the manner of Cloisonné enamel; but it was a never ending labour, and the re-arrangement never seemed to advance.

But in the way of outings I had many joys. London was neither so large nor so dirty as in these days. Hampstead was real country; so were Greenwich, Woolwich, Erith, and Blackheath. And then the open air cowsheds in St.

James' Park were delightful; we sat there upon little benches and drank warm milk, I mean just milked milk, and ate curiously stale cakes. That was supposed to be invigorating for London children. Also curds and whey; that was another institution of London park lodges accompanied by similar hard cakes. Biscuits were rare and expensive in those days—monopolies of first class bakers. And remember, evil germs and their cousins, Bacteria and Microbes, had not been discovered and so Park milk was considered to be harmless; and if the creatures existed, they possibly played some rough kind of game, which resulted in a general massacre. Drainage was also in its infancy and therefore afforded a very limited topic of conversation at tea parties; and water from the New River was probably more or less impure; and yet we escaped many ailments which are common enough in these enlightened times. I remember, when my mother visited a friend in the Vauxhall Bridge Road sitting upon a sort of paved balcony where a few plants tried to live; and at the end, fenced off, was what to me looked like a river. Later on I discovered that it was the conduit which flowed from Hyde Park or Marylebone and served the purpose of many a Venetian canal. In these degenerate days I should have received typhoid microbes into my system; but plenty of fresh air kept me pretty healthy in spite of the curious upbringing; and

A SPINSTER AUNT

my many excursions into the country with my father were of more value than the amount of lessons I should have learnt, had I been at school on those happy days.

Certainly the only infantile disorder I ever had was the measles, and during that necessary retirement from the world I was initiated into the cult of the Lower Regions, for the housemaid who looked after me being a Wesleyan, and I being no doubt very cross and naughty, I was threatened continually with a future life in Hell, a country I had never heard of before. Susannah never minced words—spades were spades. But I do not think her information made the slightest impression upon me, nor was my curiosity aroused; besides, I had some sort of misty idea that God being good, was not likely to send me, not having any sense of evil, to an uncomfortable place. My religious up-bringing must have been vague I fancy, for I recollect nothing but that God was Goodness and Truth. But of course, had I been asked to draw Him, I should have represented Him as an old man with long grey hair and beard; just as my idea of the Tower of Babel was obtained from a picture in the old Bible of a sort of Pisa Tower standing erect with little men and ladders all stuck about. How the Old Masters have falsified our religious ideas! Does not that ancient Head haunt us all our days? God being a Spirit, why attempt to portray Him at all? Because we are told He made man in His own image, I suppose; therefore as man cannot be represented as a spirit, which he is not here below, they turned the statement inside out, and made the Almighty in the image of man. Possibly also the 'Ancient of days' expression, may have led to the symbol. I think Mohammed did well to forbid images and representations of Allah; as a Prophet, did he foresee the danger? And a similar blunder was perpetrated by the artist who invented winged Angels. The Bible speaks of them as youths, and they were upon occasion taken for young men, which could not have occurred had they swooped down upon the earth with out-stretched wings. Moreover the Old Master Angel is nearly always painted with the face of a woman. Again, the tongues of fire, surely an allegory—a symbol of light, and energy, and warmth of heart. But what did the Old Masters do? They materialized the poetic idea, and made a flame rising out of the head of each of the twelve Apostles! You may see an early specimen in mosaic upon one of the domes of that glorious church, the church of churches, San Marco, Venice, among many another materialized idea.

Alas! for the corruption of our spiritual ideals by the handmaid of religion—Art.

Talking of art, what a delightful place for a painter is Covent Garden Market with its wealth of colours in fruit and flowers. May we not, some

A SPINSTER AUNT

of us, have acquired our love of colour by living within hail of it? Yet it strikes me as a curious surrounding for our principal theatre, the fashionable Opera house of the greatest city in the world! As the Queen alights from her carriage, I wonder if she enjoys the odour of the decaying cabbage leaves that strew the pavements over which her loyal subjects step on their way to their elevated position on the Amphitheatre knife-boards—backless planks price two shillings and six pence, the value of a reserved velvet seat at the Grand Opera in Paris. But Covent Garden was an artistic neighbourhood, many artists having been born or having lived in its purlieus—Turner in Maiden Lane almost in sight of oranges and lemons which sent whiffs of colour into his soul, and I think De Wint hard by. In Long Acre, now given over to coach builders, fried fish vendors, and pudding shops, lived a couple of hundred years ago one Nicholas Stone (a sculptor of merit, as the French would have called him, the 'statuary' as Horace Walpole named him.[1] Stone in his pocket book, quoted by Walpole, says he made 'a tomb for doctor Donne and sett it up in St. Paul's London, for the which I was payed by doctor Mountford the sum of 120L.' He was a notable man, was Nicholas, who had learnt his craft in Holland where he worked under Peter de Keyser. In 1619 he received his patent as

[1] *Anecdotes of Painting.*

master mason, with a 'wage and fee of twelve pence by the day' from King Charles 'for inspecting our buildings and reparations belonging to our castle of Windsor during the term of his natural life'; and he was also at work 'upon the banquetting-house.' His pocket book reveals a successful business, for he amassed 10,889L. He 'sett up' many tombs, notably that of 'sir Thomas Bodely in Oxford in 1615 for which he was paid 200L good money.' He also built the gate of the Physick Garden and the porch of St. Mary's church, but as he worked for Inigo Jones, he probably only did the masonry. Walpole scoffed at Stone's art, but the tomb of Bodley in Merton College chapel is no worse than the average monumental sculpture of the period, or for that matter, of the present time. The Donne monument is certainly original in design. Was it peradventure designed by the Doctor himself? Stone not only did 'carven work,' but in Scotland he undertook 'wainscott work for the King's chapple' for which he had money 'well payed' and 50L given by the King's command for drink, 'whereof I had 20L.' For work at the 'banquetting-house' he received 'four shillings and tenpence the day.' He also made 'the diall at St. James' and reset the fountains at Theobalds and Nonsuch, and 'other dialls at the Privy-garden at Whitehall and at Chelsey for sir John Daves.' Among the many tombs 'sett up' were one for Dr. Donne's wife at

A SPINSTER AUNT

St. Clement Danes, one of Spencer in the Abbey, and for Sir George Holles, 'also sett up in the chappell where Sir Francis Vere lyeth buried, and for Monsieur Casabon.' This probably led to the assertion that Stone was the sculptor of the beautiful de Vere monument. Nicholas also had commissions for 'pictors of white marbell' for divers persons including 'sir N. Bacon and his lady to be layed upon the tomb that Bernard Janson had made at Redgrave.'

You will wonder why I have written you so much about Stone, but he is interesting to us as being a namesake of our grandparents. Our maternal great-grandfather Stone (possibly Henry as that seems to have been a favourite Christian name in our family) was a fan painter after the manner of Watteau, and you remember our Great aunt Sarah who was a clever painter of birds; so Nicholas may be an ancestor. He died in 1699 and our great-grandfather must have been born early in the 18th Century, so the gap is not very wide. But although Stone had three sons, there is no record, as far as I know, of their having children, which is awkward! Henry, who painted and is called Old Stone, and Nicholas, the son, travelled in France and Italy. John was educated at Oxford and took part in the Civil Wars. He died the same year as his father, 1699, and was buried in the family grave near the pulpit of St. Martin's-in-the-Fields, where Charles Stoakes, a kinsman, erected a monument inscribed with the customary eulogy in the flowery verse of our ancestors. It is a long rigmarole about 'miserable fate' and naming Henry 'the Sun':

> 'The sun setting all too soon' . . .
> 'Thou shouldst have lived such statues to have shown
> As Michael Angelo might have wished his own':
>
> 'Four rare Stones have gone, the Father and three Sons.'

You see there seems no conclusion to be drawn of any children having survived, for surely they would not have left the erection of the monument to a distant kinsman. However, whether or not our ancestors, the 'four rare Stones' seem to have been fair craftsmen, considering the low water into which sculpture had fallen in the later Jacobean period. Fancy having an ancestor equal to Michel Angelo! Oh ye Gods and little Fishes!!!

Your loving Cousin.   J.

LONDON,
October 186?

Mary dear, here's to your health, and many happy returns of tomorrow. We have started an institution, not charitable, or only indirectly so, but social—an After-work Tea in this dear Den. After painting at the Studio, or the Galleries, we return here and bring our friends to partake of a dish of tea. It is a delightful idea and is carried out with much enthusiasm. We are not beholden to the domestic authorities, as we make our own tea in our own pot, boiling our own kettle upon our own hearth, and we toast our own muffins at our own fire in our 'umble Den. And above all, We Talk Shop—and there is no one to grumble thereat! Another delightful feature. What can be more improving than a discussion upon Art after the day's labour? Labour! What a dignified name to apply to what some of the 'circle' (as the Germans say) find a day of pleasing chatter. How we talk and rave and dispute (in the French sense of the word). I wish you could step in one afternoon and hear us damage the reputation of many a Master, new and old. The other day poor Murillo had a bad time of it. Well, is he not truly mawkish and woolly? But he was absolutely crushed, by reason of some of the band who are enthusiastic followers of the Oxford movement, being unable to trace any religious feeling in any but the early Florentine and Flemish painters and their imitators, Millais, and that set of pre-Raphaelites. As to landscapes, 'is not Poussin a poor creature' says L. O. 'and Claude certainly is *not* Turner.' Well I agree with Marian H. in that, don't you? To me, Turner's most 'absurd' and fantastic pictures are a feast of colour, and I fancy the future folk will agree that he was justified in desiring that his 'Sun rising in a Mist' should be placed between the two Claudes. Yesterday some one (not a painter) jeered at me for my devotion to Constable. He, the Jeerer, remembered the painter, and one day had been sitting upon his knee while he was palette-knifing. Suddenly he exclaimed to the child: 'Some day people will see that my dabs of white, "snow flakes" as my enemies call them, are right.' Whereat I replied to the Jeerer 'I believe the future will corroborate Constable's opinion as to palette knife work and light.' However the Jeerer mentally cried: 'Stupid Idiot!' Though of course he was too polite to utter such expletives even to poor little me! Very few artists are really appreciated until they have been some years out of this world's turmoil. 'Who cares for De Wint now?'

'De Wint! Black and no finish,' cried C. H., 'You don't call that Nature?'

'Finish, what do you want finish for? If a picture represents the phase of Nature the artist meant to convey to the spectator's mind, what matters it whether it was executed in a dozen strokes of the brush or a thousand? Is not De Wint as true as Millais? I adore much of Millais' work; but Ophelia's pond and brambles are to me not quite so true to Nature as a river of De Wint's. I mean his sketches; those washed out and stippled up things he did in his Studio I hate. It is just the difference of vision. The modern people paint the entire picture, looking at and imitating each square foot of the landscape in succession. De Wint probably stared at the whole landscape, and then with one deft and skilful sweep of a brushful of watery colour rendered the general effect of the scene.'

'Yes,' said I, 'but is not the modern way the best for beginners? By imitating each tree, and painting each leaf you see, do you not acquire, by mere length of observation, a vast amount of knowledge as to the anatomy of Nature's work? And then when you have learnt all her mysteries, you can throw off detail and generalize. The mere fact of sitting days and days before a particular object must teach you a great deal which a few casual glances would not.'

'Ah! but why not stare only? You cannot *imitate* Nature—it is impossible.'

'Of course not: but I am only advocating the execution of the Pre-Rs as a means to an end.'

'That is what people say; but surely Velasquez arrived at the end by a different kind of training, and also the divine Corot, and all that French set. There is no niggling up individual leaves in their work, and yet few pictures convey with greater truth the idea of a certain kind of landscape, the soft grey of the Seine and its willows, which he has made his own happy hunting ground.'

'Yes, his work is beautiful in a way; but I am like a certain distinguished Frenchman who is said to have remarked that he liked Corot's work, but, as to the truth of his landscapes he could give no opinion, never having been out of doors early enough in the morning.'[1]

And so we go on discussing and almost quarrelling over some reputations; for instance the other day some one mentioned Egg and Danby and Noel Paton and the rest of what we call the Vernon Gallery tribe. Down came the opposite party like a sledge hammer.

'You had better read your Ruskin.'

'I do read Ruskin, but I don't hold him to be an infallible guide, and I can see some virtue in Ward and Frith' (chorus of Oh's!). 'Well, there is good composition in some of Ward's work, and Frith's engrave well. He is no colourist; but possibly a hundred years hence people will be glad to note the details of the "Derby Day" in the same way that we are now interested in Hogarth's pictures of the manners and customs of the 18th Century. A painter who sends down to posterity the fashions, follies, and customs of his day is not doing bad work, whatever his mannerisms and *technique* may be. Of course, artistically, he is not a Hogarth.'

'Even if his colour is black and his models mere lay figures? I do not mean Frith, who, I am told, hunts about to find people to sit for his various characters. But all this school paints out-door pictures in their Studios, so that

[1] An *on-dit* of the Emperor Louis-Napoléon.—ED.

whatever they do as regards taking notes out of doors and on the spot, the pictures *must be* more or less false. I once asked an old model if one of the Vernon Gallery School used a lay figure. "Lor, bless you, my dear, he's got dozens of them!" If you look at the faces and clothes in such works as the "South Sea Bubble," you see at once that the effect is that of the Studio, not of a street; but for all that there is plenty of character and go in the picture. And who but a landscape painter ever works entirely out of doors? and even he, in former times, I question, only made sketches and painted the picture in his study. Do you suppose Salvator Rosa did? or Ruysdael? Do you think Rubens ran about with huge canvases? Possibly some of the Dutchmen may have worked in the fields; but was not Turner probably the first who saw that light could only be obtained by working in it? Does not the light somehow get on to your canvas and into your paint?'

What inconsequent but delightful discussions we have as we toast our muffins, and sip our tea in the dear old Den. Of course we say and do many foolish things, but none that equal a joyful outburst of enthusiasm related to me by an old Prix de Rome student. The excitement of their success was so great, that having supped well but not too wisely, they lacked still another outburst, when it was suggested that the piano should have some champagne; and thereupon, one of the young idiots poured the contents of a bottle into the unfortunate instrument's interior. I wonder what the owner thought of the matter!

We are a happy circle—but already one gentle soul brimming over with love of art has left us. Shall we any of us be able to prove to the world that women have brains, and given equal opportunities, can do as good work as men? How many of us will go under, as numbers of our brother brushes do? How many of us will realize our hopes and ambitions—fears we have not! Our theories are excellent. Given some brains, and an unlimited supply of love and enthusiasm, and an untiring energy and power of work, shall we not be able to move mountains, *i.e.* force open the doors of the R.A. for women students and women Academicians? Surely Art Schools opening for women ought to develop some painters superior to Angelica Kaufmann and Madam Moser? Poor dears! we shall at least know our craft better than they; but whether we shall overcome the mountains of prejudice, rivalry, and jealousy which have to be scaled, is another matter. There are women in France who equal their brethren; why should there not be here? At present women students suffer disabilities as regards drawing from the Life; but if women painters were elected as associates of the R.A., *they* could superintend that class, and one more barrier would be removed from the feminine path

A SPINSTER AUNT

to knowledge and distinction. At the same time, there are disabilities from the mere fact of being women. The *camaraderie* of the club; when will that be supplied? Shall we ever have clubs after the manner of the man's club? Will women ever be admitted to our Universities upon the same level as men? Certainly a Rosa Bonheur would *not* be *decorée* here; and if, peradventure a woman should make some wondrous discovery in science, would she receive the highest honour in this country, a Royal Society medal? The prejudice in these Islands is overwhelming, and so far, the enemy is somewhat justified in his narrow mindedness. Perhaps we have no woman painter who is equal to the best of the R.As.; but I take it Sir Joshua Reynolds did not think the sentimental Angelica *his equal*? Nor I imagine did he, in his inmost soul, think his R.A. *confrères* his equals! We have a woman astronomer;[1] she is not and never will be a Fellow of the Royal Society. Why not?

Probably the main disability of womankind is a lack of vulgar push. Men will always push harder and more successfully because they agree to push each other. 'If I push you, you must push me, and we will all push together; in this way some, if not all of us must arrive.' Have you ever read Scribe's 'Camaraderie'? If not, do.

Girls now certainly have more facilities as

[1] Mrs. Somerville.

regards Art Schools than formerly. In my young days there were only Leigh's in Newman St. and Sass' in some purlieu of Bloomsbury. I went to L.'s remarkable classes. He was said to be the original of Thackeray's Gandish in the 'Newcomes' but if so, the novelist exaggerates somewhat. Still, there really were (and are now I suppose) the wondrous 'High Art' pictures all over the house—in the rooms and on the staircases; and what a wonderful house it was! Not too clean and woefully hugger-mugger. But had Leigh not been bitten by the High Art fever of his youth, he might have become perhaps a painter of distinction; his sketches were excellent, some of them, and he directed fairly well; but he was wrecked upon those terrible rocks which have ruined so many artistic lives, Michel-Angelesque imitations—staginess, muscularities, and conventionalities, such as used, I suppose, to be admired at the Academy, in the huge works of poor Haydon, the President Benjamin West, and divers others, now, not only wrecked, but drowned probably for all time. The world rolls round, and art, like everything else, is partly a matter of fashion; but surely this our British School of yore, like their masters the Italian Eclectics, must really remain defunct? Will the blown-out muscular Saints of the Caracci ever again be glorified, and the 'sweet' Virgins of Carlo Dolci and Sassoferrato ever be loved again—except

A SPINSTER AUNT

perhaps by mathematicians and other distinguished scholars and savants who know nothing of art. As to instruction, we did very much what we liked with little correction and much talk and theory—it was just the sort of school that is so pleasing to the young; as *they* say, 'they keep their independence!'

I think a good deal of teaching in the fifties was decidedly limp. At Queen's College, those girls who were desirous of acquiring knowledge, got it; but we, who disliked work or were indifferent, and who held all teachers and pastors and masters to be our natural enemies, learnt little or nothing; nevertheless our reports were 'good' or 'satisfactory.' Surely one function of teaching is to put information into the minds of the stupid and the lazy; the clever, and those thirsting for knowledge are sure, some how or other, to acquire it, with or without help. But the lazy and stupid do not. For instance, at Queen's I learnt music for one term. I disliked the master cordially, and he probably found me offensively idle. My previous music master at another school was also a natural enemy. I loved music, but I hated practising scales and exercises, and still more I detested 'arrangements' from trumpery Italian operas with variations racing all over the piano. At Queen's I had hoped for better things, but did not find them; my work there was to mangle Beethoven. When examination time came I had to appear before Professor Sterndale Bennett. He sat at a table writing, and we girls were ushered into the room, one by one. It was very alarming, especially to a shy girl who could never play the simplest thing when any one was in the room. When my turn came I felt like a martyr being thrown to the lions. I trudged into the room and sat down with my Beethoven sonata before my eyes, but saw nothing; and by the time I arrived at the eighth bar my confusion was complete. Then came a kindly sympathetic word from the Professor: 'I think you are very nervous? that will do, thank you.' How I blessed him, but I expect he was horrified at the frightful massacre to which I was subjecting poor Beethoven. All the same, as the report was 'Satisfactory' or 'Fair' (I forget which), it was a terrible farce.

And the French and German classes were no better as far as my instruction went. We learnt parts of 'Athalie' one term, which I never knew; but the greater part of the hour was occupied by talk between the Professors and the Lady Visitors whose duty it was to prevent flirtations between the Professors and us. In those languages my reports were also 'Good' or 'Satisfactory' although I never worked. Of course I was a non-compounder—I only attended a few classes; and I dare say the compounders learnt more as they were coached up by tutoresses. Certainly the only

A SPINSTER AUNT

classes at which I really gained any information were the English Literature ones under Dr. E. H. Plumptre,[1] and the drawing class conducted by Mr. Armitage; and why? Not because the system was better, nor I suppose because they taught better; but because I was interested in the subjects, and was therefore willing to work. Now when I think over my school days at Leipzig, the picture is quite different. Although I was only there about a year, I was always happy doing my lessons and I can safely say that all I acquired when young of general knowledge, I learnt there. The Masters interested us in our studies (four hours in the morning and little or no home work); and of course my knowledge of German being very imperfect, I had up-hill work: but the Masters had the faculty of making dry facts agreeable to the young, and they were many of them enthusiasts in their subjects. For instance Fräulein Weber (a niece of Carl Maria) who gave me private music lessons. With her I was not shy, she brought me out instead of heavily stamping upon me, mentally, as Mr. Goss did at my Brompton school. He walked up and down the room in his spectacles, saying nothing, but rubbing his hands in a provoking manner; and remember, I was with him two years after Fräulein taught me, so I must have been more reasonable. She was delightful, she gave me the

[1] Afterwards Dean of Wells.

sort of music I liked, Mozart's, and made me sing and encouraged me, but did not blink facts. Had I continued with her for four or five years I might possibly have played decently, and sung too. It was just the difference between the application of sympathy, and of wet blankets.

By the way, did I ever tell you about a wonderful ball I went to in Leipzig in those early days? It took place at the works of a great printer and upon a Sunday evening—tell it not in Gath! In my childishness I certainly felt many qualms in my conscience, the legacy of my Puritan ancestry; but cowardice and a desire to do as others did, made me accept the invitation. My feelings now upon this Sunday question are that things wrong on Sunday, must be wrong on week days; though they may not be expedient on the first day of the week. In this Leipzig case, the work people were free on that day and no other. Six days of twelve hours work was the rule for labouring men at that time, and certainly from all points of view it was delightful to see so many men and women innocently amusing themselves. Church going in Germany was mostly over by nine or ten o'clock in the morning, so there was no more interference with Sunday duties than where people have entertainments on Saturday evenings which stretch into the small hours of Sunday. All the same I passed many an uncomfortable *quart-d'heure*. But it was worth seeing all the same. The works were situated in large and picturesque grounds, and the opening polonaise was a perambulation all over them. In and out of the paths, up and down the avenues, we all walked two and two. It was a lovely warm moonlight night, and in addition the garden was illuminated with coloured lamps; also the stringed band was superb.

Good bye; this letter is all too long. Ever your loving,   JEANNE.

CHAPTER X

THE DEN

[No date.—ED.]

THE DEN,

DEAR COUSIN

Can you, and will you come up to see the Exhibition of Horrors, equal to the Baker Street's upper chamber.[1] It is as good as a screaming farce played by Buckstone and Keeley, or 'Norma' by Paul Bedford and Wright. (*En parenthèse* did you ever see that 'Norma' adorned with a wreath of carrots?) Well, our farce is the show of copies at the British Institution in Pall Mall. You know the owners of the pictures of Old Masters exhibited every year, leave a few for students to copy with a view to study, and at the end of the time these so-called copies are placed on each side of the original, the best next to the master, and the worst at the extreme ends of the two lines. It is exceedingly funny to see this regiment of pictorial horrors, mere caricatures, many of them, painted by the colour blind; the only use, apparently, of the exhibition being to

[1] Madame Tussaud's Chamber of Horrors.

A SPINSTER AUNT

show the difference of eye sight in people, and the semi-blindness of so many who, presumably have been taught to draw. Squints, grins, smirks, frowns, all invented by the copyists. Reynolds' beautiful dames turned into vulgar fish women; Romney's innumerable Lady Hamiltons gazing so Heavenward that the eyes are lost somewhere in the upper lids, or are rolling about at the back of their skulls; Gainsborough's poor ' Blue Boy,' a really intense Prussian blue or French ultramarine young man with scarlet cheeks all ablaze. And the landscapes! Cuyp with chrome sunsets; Poussin and Wilson alarmingly green; Canaletto's gondolas of most peculiar construction; Van de Velde' ships with such extraordinary sails that the tenth part of a gale of wind would make them founder with all hands. The only use in the Exhibition is to show what to avoid, and as to the results of the study, they are hard to find. Some few copies are really good, Mr. Paul's terribly good! The rest, completely worthless from every point of view, except as affording an excuse for flirtations—that study is carried on very well, but of course it always receives more attentive enthusiasm, and more practice, than pure painting which is merely a means to an end. But what we do enjoy, we who believe in pleasant *cameraderie* is the luncheon time with its talk. Of course in the gallery with Mr. Nicol in his little box, talking is only carried on in a seemly whisper; but below, in the basement, where the caretaker provides us with baked potatoes, we have many a joyful half hour. Some of the Students revel in more serious lunches, but the true Bohemian meal of the place, is the baked potato. Curious this cult of the baked potato. At Charing Cross opposite Drummond's bank, there stands a man in a white linen suit with a bright metal vessel resting upon a short pole. The thing is in the form of a basket with lids and a handle over the top, made of tin with brass bands, and in it are baked potatoes to warm wayfarers when waiting for omnibuses after the close of the theatres. I believe he sells sandwiches also, or sausages, or both; but originally the contents were only potatoes. It is not a bad thing on a cold night. The vendor has a deft way of putting the butter (which is best Dorset) into the potatoes so that it spreads about but does not leak out—hence the vegetable warms your hands before eating, and like an orange or hot chestnuts, is clean food, if demolished in the proper way. I fear our old lady friends would think this as bad or worse than swimming, for not only is it like men, but not a distinguished thing to do even in the dark; but a little mild Bohemianism does no one any harm, does it? Besides, if it is distinguished to sit in a carriage in Berkeley Sq. and eat Mr. Gunter's exquisite ices, why should you not stand at Charing Cross, and eat a very superior potato,

A SPINSTER AUNT

provided by a gentleman in white? It is all conventionality. The potato man always reminds me of the Paris *Marchands de Coco*—equally well turned out, and so clean and polished—I mean their machines. The Charing Cross man also serves as a finger post indicating a back way to Hungerford Market.[1] How quaint the old wharves were with their straw barges; now only seen at Milbank. That market was the scene of the theft, by me, of the sucking pig's tail, but I believe the story is a mere tradition,[2] got up by L. and F. in order to tease me. 'Who stole the pig's tail?' was a very familiar cry for years, and about as true as the miracle of San Januarius.

Speaking of flirtations under the name of study at the Galleries, I had a sort of adventure a short time ago at the Brompton Boilers.[3] A girl I have known for years, but who rarely appears now at the National Gallery, came up to me and said mysteriously: 'Hush! don't look round!' Naturally, instinct made me half turn my head, and I saw a man I remembered vaguely at Trafalgar Square. He was at work copying some picture. 'Come into the next room,' said Miss R. When we had found a quiet corner, she began in a trembling, excited voice. 'He'll kill me if he sees me talking to you. I married him,

[1] Where Charing Cross Station now stands.—ED.
[2] Related by Aunt Jane on page 7.—ED.
[3] Slang term for the original buildings of the South Kensington Museum, now Victoria and Albert Museum.—ED.

and he beats me. What should you do? I hate him.'

Hatred and fear seemed natural forces likely to result from violent chastisement; but under the circumstances advice seemed difficult to offer. I tried to comfort the poor frightened creature, but I felt my comforting to be very weakly, for it is not easy to put oneself into the position of a beaten wife, particularly when one has no personal experience as to the proper behaviour of wives in general—and this case was, I suppose, not one of usual occurrence. I hope not, but 'one never knows, my dear,' as old Mrs. Martin says. Besides, there are so many things to be considered. For instance, one of our big Justices holds the opinion that it is doubtful whether beating a wife may not be legally a 'just and fair chastisement' for erring partners. He holds that a husband 'can lawfully use disciplinary punishment,' but whether with or without a weapon, Mr. Justice D. does not explain. Now how was I to discriminate between a just and an unjust discipline? How could I tell all of a sudden, whether the wife had improperly irritated her legal master? How did I know whether his discipline was reasonable or excessive? How at a moment's notice could I give advice on so serious a matter, and also only having heard one side. I explained my difficulty to my unfortunate friend, and I tried to pour gentle streams of sympathy into her soul; but my comfort crumbs were stale and hard. However, after a long talk on her side, and an equally long listenment (if I may coin a word) upon my side, we parted; she, 'happier'—she said; I most miserable. Her last words were, 'You have done me good.'

Miserable does not adequately describe my feelings for I felt acutely my foolishness and weakness; and dreaded lest the result of pouring the balm of patience and long suffering upon the poor creature, might lead to a terrible domestic tragedy. Upon reflection I feel I ought to have said, 'the man is a coward; if he attacks you, go for him with some handy instrument, umbrella or tongs; give him a black eye for a black eye, and destroy a tooth for a tooth. Being a very handsome man, he will probably object to facial disfigurement, even for a time.'

Poor Grizzle, I have never seen her again, and I have no idea whether her end was peace or a bruised body.

Did I tell you before that we have started a French maid? unfortunately she understands no English, so some of our visitors get confused. A young fellow who has been staying here was obliged modestly to ventilate his French; and I must say his diffidence was justified.

'*Rosalie! s'il vous plait, mes chasseurs.*'

'*Vos chaussures, Monsieur?*'

'*Oh! oui, merci. Et un tire-bouchon.*'

RECOLLECTIONS OF

'*Vous voulez dire le tire-bottes, n'est-ce pas, Monsieur?*'

'*Oui, c'est ça.*'

But Rosalie according to Cook is not always so intelligent. Said Cook this morning, 'I can't make her understand at all. Shout as much as I can, she won't hear me.'

This reminds me of a drive I took once in Switzerland with L. He tried to make use of his German, but the driver did not understand him at all. 'These fellows pretend not to understand,' said L.; 'they could if they liked.' And one day in a Paris omnibus I heard this diverting conversation between two young people who looked like brother and sister. She asked, 'What is Octroi?' 'I think it must mean Post Office!'

You say I am hard upon the world, that it is a 'delightful place.' Yes, to the successful—but to the poor? Take a case like this. A professional man spends his entire life struggling to make both ends meet; there was a constant necessity to sell out funds for small deficiencies. Says a friend, 'Why not reduce expenses?' which sort of advice is on a par, with 'going into the country and living in a cottage.' For if your daily bread has to be paid for by work which can only be done in the town, how can you live in a village hut? My case is that of a professional man of parts, wanting 'customers' as an old lady called a dentist's patients—not inaptly. 'Reducing

A SPINSTER AUNT

expenditure' pre-supposes spending more than is necessary; and retiring to a cottage means a fixed income of sorts. To return to my example. Financial worries for years, age, and diminished powers to fight the battle of life brought on by diminished coffers, led finally to brain trouble. When the end came, it was found that the last £50 of a little funded property and savings had been sold out some weeks before the final collapse, and that £50 was all he had been able to leave his wife. This was sold out to pay the last, *his* last rent. Is not that a pathetic tale? No doubt there are hundreds of such catastrophes. People who go to the wall through no fault of their own—simply adverse circumstances, or through some deficiency in their temperament, or because they dropped upon the wrong road. There is no lack of brains, or energy, or will; but somehow they fail where inferior brains and lesser consciences, perhaps, succeed. I often think that one great quality for success in life's work, is never to see the other side. The man who can argue for his adversary, who sees from his enemy's point of view, who considers conscientiously that his rival is the better man, is lost. One great item in the recipe for this world's success is pigheadedness; only it must be tempered by commonsense, that rarest and least common of senses.

Some one, I think George Sand, said somewhere, '*Il ne faut jamais faire agir un homme dans un sens différent de son caractère*'; and the words came into my head today when E. announced that she thought going on studying art was a useless waste of time and would lead to nothing. She wants to make a living, she must earn money, and she wants to be of use also, to her kind. That she considers to be a duty, and as doing our duty generally means doing what we dislike, she may be right in forsaking the much adored art; certainly choosing the hated path often decides the question: 'Shall I go to Kamschatka or the Red Sea?' Here is E. M. never tired of work, her aim, the honest accomplishment, not of poor old Leigh's High Art, but of the simple rendering of the various moods of Nature under ordinary phases of every passing day, and she suddenly thinks she will give it all up and take to hospital nursing as a higher vocation! No doubt it is, and for a woman possibly the highest, and most useful work she can pursue. But is it a life that will suit a somewhat dreamy mind impregnated with artistic ideals? She is not disillusioned—no true artist ever is, because the true artist is ever hopeful. Each time he fails to carry out his ideal he thinks, 'Next time I shall succeed.' He fails again and again, and hopefulness carries him on perhaps through a long life, without ever obtaining success from his own point of view, even when the public is more or less of the opposite opinion. If he really became disillusioned the game would be up. He is, in spite of every thing, 'a man of happy yesterdays and confident to-morrows.' He may never make more per annum than a dock-labourer, and yet he goes on hopefully, ever seeing an imaginary and goodly turn in the road, and a future recognition by the world at large. Days of depression come, many and sad, enervating for a time his whole soul; but the rubber was not left out in the recipe for his mind, and he bounds up with all the elasticity of a ball, and starts afresh, more hopeful than ever. Surely this quality of hopefulness, measured by those who do not look upon money as the end and aim of all things here below, this ever striving for a noble ideal makes art the most exquisite of callings in this dull neutral-tinted world? What think you? Mind you I include in art, music and poetry; but we are neither of us led away from our own particular art by that!

> 'Whereunto is money good?
> Who has it not wants hardihood,
> Who has it has much trouble and care,
> Who once has had it has despair.'[1]

Those lines I endorse with all my heart; but all the same, filthy lucre is necessary, even for such mild pleasures as Den teas accompanied by muffins, to say nought of rent, rates, taxes, butchers, bakers, and candlestick makers—though

[1] Friedrich von Logau, 17th Century, translated by Longfellow.

RECOLLECTIONS OF

I spend little on *him*. Know you that my collection of old brass and copper candle sticks increases rapidly—4 pennies to 6 pennies a-piece Don't you agree with me that the greatest curse of this world is gold? It is a curse to him who has too much, and the need of its possession is a curse to him who has too little. The mere fact of one's mind dwelling upon money, or the want of it in ever so small a degree, is degrading. A competency obtained by our own exertions with both ends meeting nicely, is my ideal. Was it not Dora Greenwell who said the meeting of both ends was a somewhat sad ideal at which to aim; she would like the ends to tie in a nice bow. So should I. A small fixed income, increased by the proceeds of work, with a margin for getting out of this hideous country every winter, and a nice bow for innocent worldlinesses social and personal, is what I desire—and never shall obtain!

Adieu, fair cousin. J.

Christmas Day, 1865. THE DEN

MY DEAR MAUD

Can you believe another year is all but gone. Today we receive cousins, great aunts, and uncles, and simple aunts. Also innumerable grandchildren and great nieces and nephews, and of course the whole morning is taken up by preparations. *Is* Christmas joyous? I always wonder, and personally, I dislike the festive side. Of course it is a joy to the children, but for the grown-ups, well . . .

Le jour du Boxe,
as the French call this day, 1865.

I was called off yesterday, as the table seemed only capable of holding 23 persons, large and small, and 26 were coming. However we squashed in somehow. The dinner went off very well; only a few verbal catastrophies by the children, who, with a natural desire to improve their small minds, are apt to make unpleasant remarks upon all sorts of things and subjects.

I always wonder at the fulness of the bird and butcher shops at this season, for, given a certain number of birds sold, the supply of meat does not seem to diminish. If you eat bird, you don't want beef. If you eat beef, how can you eat turkey? And yet, shops at this season reek with poultry, and the butchers are running over with meat. This is another hidden mystery, for human powers, even allowing for gifts to the non-eaters of flesh meats, must of necessity be limited.

Says an old book: 'It is as bad to overeat yourself as to wallow in the mire of drink.' 'A waste of money upon unnecessary viands leads to a waste of health'; wise maxims both. There are of course many modern remedies for overdoing Christmas fare; but some of the old ones might be worth trying. Our ancestors had remedies for the unpleasing results of overeating, and also for the prevention of the same—and we all know prevention is better than cure. For instance, *Christes roote* and *Christes herbe*. These 'lyke virtues hath to be taken in potages, or to be sodden with boyled meate. The broth of meate in which this seede hath been sod, dronke, is good for the cholike. Dronke as a decoction, it openeth the stoppinges of the liver.' And it may be added, though irrelevant to the subject of 'beef and puddings noble,' *Christes herbe* 'is useful in all venemous and naughtie humours; and powdered, it kills myce and kattes and suche lyke beastes; and to drive them away.'

In the sermon of a worthy pastor recorded in an old magazine of 80 years ago, we find great stress laid upon the Christianity of good cheer: 'I wish to speak of whatever has taken place in the order of Providence,' said he. 'I wish to think the best of the very evils . . . that a good has been got out of them.' Thus the good remedies above quoted cure the evil results of 'the beef and pudding noble; the mince pies— peculiar; the nuts, half playthings, and half eatables; the oranges as cold and acid as they ought to be, furnishing us with a superfluity which we can afford to laugh at; the cakes indestructible; the wassail bowls generous, old English huge, demanding ladles, threatening overflow as they come in, solid as roasted apples when

A SPINSTER AUNT

sat down.' Why should mince pies be dubbed 'peculiar'? Were they like the cakes 'indistructible'?

Then the 'heaped up fire, the *over* heaped up fire' seems to suggest extravagance; but no; 'it is the inciter to mirth, the universal relish':

> 'Who can hold a fire in his hand
> With thinking on the frostiest twelfth cake.'

Alas! where are our Twelfth cakes, and the 'characters' we drew as children, and the joy of sitting at the supper table as king and queen? Gone, like the maundering pastor.

And what says the ancient 'musician'—save the name! who hears an organ in the street: 'Thou old spirit of harmony, wandering about in that ark of time, touching the public ear with sweetness and an abstraction!'

Let us think over this 'abstraction' and bear with its doubtful 'sweetness' as we enjoy our 'cold and acid oranges, our indistructible cakes, and our mince pies—peculiar'—thankful that Christmas comes but once a year in the 'order of Providence.' But alas! to us it comes three times a year in the form of three dinners at 5 or 6 o'clock, three Turkeys, (sometimes four, one being boiled) three rounds of beef, three times three courses of smaller eatables—'peculiar'; for do we not find at one house a sucking pig! and sometimes underdone. Ugh!

Have you ever had a Christmas present of a pheasant? and did you ever send it on to a friend as a suitable Christmas gift? I have done so, and I devoutly hope not with the result which I read in some French book, that after passing through the railway parcels' offices many times, it returned to the original owner. Happily the intermediate donors did not know this.

Diary. July 1866. At last the Atlantic cable is laid and the big ship is proved to be of use. What an age she was trying to be launched. She stuck fast; and month after month passed and still she stood fast. You will see the account in the paper.

The Engaged Ones have been staying here, and as a natural result, we have been unable to call the very smallest room our own. Drawing room, dining room, work room, my dear Den, when I went out, all occupied at their sweet pleasure—'even the pantry,' said a friend in like misfortune. I think Parochial Homes might be provided for the Engaged, as for the quite insane—*Maisons de Santé*—and I would attach to them, in a wing, practising rooms for young musicians. The lovers are always so pleased with themselves, that they would not hear the discordant sounds of the pianos and the families would be delivered from two incubusses (or incubi?), not to say in some cases two nuisances. Of course care must be taken that the young musicians do not meet the Engaged in the corridors and gardens, lest their unseemly manners be propagated.

Last evening we went to see 'As you like it.' Said my father's neighbour, 'Do you know this play, Sir?' 'Oh! yes, I have often seen it.' 'Then it is not a new play, Sir?' 'No, it is by Shakespeare.' 'So I saw on the bills. Then he is not a new writer?' 'Not quite new,' quoth my father.

Diary. 1868. Much wrangling over the Disestablishment of the Irish church. It is supposed to be a sop to the Irish R.C. party; but they will probably never cease to grumble and never be at rest. What if the Roman Catholic church took the place of the disestablished Anglican? Why should not Cardinals sit in the House of Lords? Also of course Scotch Moderators; they are the heads of the Established Church of Scotland, I believe? I cannot see why the three kingdoms should not be on the same plane. If all English peers sit by hereditary right why should not all Scotch and Irish? Though it would be better to make a selection from all three peerages. As to the Roman Catholic church in Ireland, I believe it would save no end of trouble if it were the State Church. The R.Cs. might not agree, but I doubt them refusing loaves and fishes even with loss of some independence. From an artistic point of view the cardinals would look well sitting up in scarlet as they do in 'Henry VIII.' Some people are prognosticating that this will be a step towards Disestablishment in England. But there is a great difference, as the majority here belongs to the church: in Ireland only the minority. However that too (English Disestablishment) would save much disputing and may come some day. The Nonconformists would like that change (Reform they call it with a big R.) but the 'Establishment of Popery' even in Ireland would, I suppose, be adverse to their principles.

I was asked today a question; it might be called—in derision, (though the questioner was quite serious), a problem of pure mathematics. Here is the problem. 'Had your mother and your father married a different man and woman, you would have been two instead of one person. Now, reflect for a minute,' said Ethel, 'you inherit the superb curve of your nose, it is quite Roman, from your dear father, your eyes and the colour of your hair from your mother. And so on with all your physical and mental traits of person and character. Also, possibly some qualities from grandparents and aunts and uncles; for instance, I have a cyst at the back of my head under my hair, and a nephew has one just a little higher up on his head, which is beginning to show as he is getting bald. But these inheritances from others

A SPINSTER AUNT

than parents do not upset my theory, as qualities in a grandparent may skip a generation, or be dormant; and so a bad temper, or a cyst may be in one of your parents but unknown to him or her for want of circumstances to develop it. Well,' continued Ethel, 'if your parents had married otherwise, what you inherit from your father (your Roman nose, say) would be attached to other eyes, for the sake of argument, squirmy eyes; and the large grey eyes you inherit from your mother would be attached to, possibly, that peculiar kind of nose that may only be seen in this country, a true pug—I don't mean a *nez retroussé*, that is universal and pretty, but a true British pug. Now whether this would have made two people as good looking as the one, is a question beyond the power of argument, and matters little. To put the matter plainly. A. and B. have a child C. Had A. married D. there would have been a boy or girl E. partaking of the qualities of A. and D. instead of those of A. and B. Then supposing B. had married F. their child would have been partly B. and partly F. otherwise G. So that instead of being only C. that is you, yourself, you would be at once E. and G.'

'Oh please, Ethel,' said Sophie, 'my head is swimming,' and all the rest laughed immoderately. 'Poor girl,' said my father, 'she will soon want my certificate to lodge her at Hanwell with your poor illused lover.'

RECOLLECTIONS OF

January 1868

MY DEAR MARY

Did you get the scrap I copied from my Diary the other day about the mathematical problem? If so, I dare say you wondered what my father meant by my 'ill-used lover.' So I am going to send you the story. *I have had an offer of marriage!* It took me by surprise, so my theory that a girl always feels that it is coming, and can prevent it, and so save the man trouble, is not proven. You know, I think that it is a disgrace for a woman to boast of the number of offers she has received, for it usually means vanity, or heartlessness, or both; but evidently it is not to be foreseen always, and therefore not preventable.

Accidents will occur to the best regulated minds. Only think! I have been following a man about on Constitution Hill who I have never seen! So said my Pater at dinner a few months ago. 'No,' said I, 'it is of course my attractive sister.' 'Not at all,' said he, 'the accusation is brought against my youngest daughter.'

Much fun was poked at me; I had been seen 'flirting behind a conservatory door at a ball'; that might be allowable in these modern days; but to follow a man about the town—Oh! fie for shame, Janey! However it was a nine days wonder, and we thought no more about it. But some ten days ago, I received the following letter from a man living near us.

A SPINSTER AUNT

Dear Miss

I have noticed with pain, that you have followed me about the streets for some time past and although I give you no encouragement, you seem desirous of knowing me. In fact I can see by your conduct that you love me and wish me to return your love. This, I am sorry to say I cannot do; but I will endeavour to make you all the reparation I can for being the cause of your unfortunate passion. I am shortly going to New Zealand, and I am willing to make you my wife, and endeavour to be a kind, if not an affectionate husband. I cannot promise to love you. Love is a spiritual gift which we cannot command. It is an accident. It comes or does not come. It is sent by the gods. It comes from Higher Regions. You did not probably intend to love me intentionally; I provoked the feeling, and the result is sorrow to us both. To me for having innocently been the cause of your infatuation; to you for finding your sentiments unreciprocated. But if you like to accompany me to New Zealand, or Canada if you prefer it, all shall be well. But do not expect the love which is Heaven born, for within my heart, as yet, I feel no chance of it coming on.

Your unfortunate ALBERT ERNEST PERKINS.

P.S.—When you answer this, do not send it by post, as my sister will open it. Leave the letter at the Ham and Beef shop at the bottom of the next street, Charles by name!

Naturally I took no notice of this effusion; I did not even know the man by sight. But I wondered whether he was the creature we used to call our guardian angel when we went to school. He followed us all the way at a respectful distance; and one day when it began to rain, he came up and said to the servant, 'the little girls will get wet; take my umbrella and leave it at the Ham and Beef shop in Charles Street.' But this was pure speculation as we girls never saw him—I mean the latter man.

A few weeks later, I received another missive.

DEAR MISS

I am sorry to find no letter at the Ham and Beef shop, but perhaps I shall tomorrow. I sail in three weeks, so there is not much time for you to get your Trousoe; and as I hear you intended leaving London for Paris, I am writing to repeat my offer. Since I first wrote to you I have been sent to Hanwell. My sister and brother pretend I am mad, because they want to keep the business to themselves; and your father aids and abets them by signing papers. I do not bear him any grudge or malice; he knows no better; but I am no madder than he is, for I notice he always carries his umbrella the wrong way up. However I forgive him for helping my poor sister. Will you write and let me know whether you will be ready by the 12th and whether I shall call for you, or whether you will pick me up. As you may not like leaving the letter at the H. and B. shop in Charles Street; the apple stall woman at the corner of North Street opposite the baker's, will receive it and give it me, she says, if you give her a penny, or buy some nuts.

I remain
Dear Miss
Your sincerely unfortunate Friend,
ALBERT ERNEST PERKINS.

There, Mary, I don't think you ever had such an offer as that, and mark you, he is so very anxious to impress upon me that he wishes to make *reparation* for the misfortune of being so fascinating as to awake in my heart an enduring, though unrequited love! Poor fellow, he has again returned to Hanwell. But for a short time I lived the life of my terror-stricken friend who was in fear of bodily hurt, for who can tell whether the unfortunate victim, *my* victim may not resent getting no reply to his letters, and send a shot into my head some day as he passes? I am totally ignorant of his appearance, so that I have no means of avoiding him, and I might run against him at any moment. However just now he is safer at Hanwell than had he gone to New Zealand, with or without me, so I can walk about in peace until I get out of London.

Wednesday. I had a model today who told me an extraordinary chapter in the story of her youth, a most mysterious affair. I have put it into story form, but I can find no end that is suitable. I have no more idea of inventing a plot than of inventing a musical instrument which would play itself like Mr. Home's violins that fly about the ceilings playing sonatas and romances without bows or hands to move them. I have tried many endings, but all are foolish. Why cannot a mysterious story end in a hidden mystery? Why do readers want cut and dried endings, happy, or otherwise? Perhaps when you have read it, you may be able to find a winding up.

The poor old lady had found life too much for her; 'she did not understand it. She and her husband had always been hard working, sober, honest, she hoped, and yet they had gone under, and now her only means of earning a living was sitting as a model.' Her husband had evidently been above her in station (an undistinguished actor I believe) but had sat to a few artists when they wanted a gentlemanly type of man. 'Ah!

A SPINSTER AUNT

Miss, we most of us get one chance in life; a few get more, but very few, and the wise man is he who seizes that first, and most likely, only chance. The weak wait for the second, either through indecision, or the love of putting off. As for the fools who let chances go by without seizing them, they don't count; possibly they cannot help being foolish; or they are vain, and think themselves so indispensable that the world is sure to want them later on; but it very seldom does.' Poor old thing; reading between the lines I fancy her husband had let his one chance go by. Here is 'The Mystery of a London Street,' much as the poor old soul told it me, for I wrote it bit by bit during her rests.

RECOLLECTIONS OF

CHAPTER XI

THE MYSTERY OF A LONDON STREET

It was Christmas Eve, about 3 of the clock. I am not likely to forget the day by reason of a fierce toothache to which I had been doomed for some weeks, coming to a crisis. The wind which had been blowing all the East End smoke our way, had now dropped and left a deposit of coal dust to mix with the indigenous fog; and to our amazement the sound of St. Paul's big bell striking three cut through the yellow curtain. It was not often that we heard the booming of the Cathedral bell even in the stillness of the night or chilly morn; so that when it startled us that afternoon it seemed to betoken something unusual. Was it the Christmas message sent a few hours too soon? Or was it a reminder to me not to tarry on my journey dentistwards?

I ought to say by way of explanation, that I am a reduced widow. My husband was a sort of artist—he painted pictures which rarely sold. Some folks said that was because you could not see what they were meant for, or which was the top. Others said they were too blue, or too purple; but John always persisted that he followed Nature, and that the sketches were no purpler than the celebrated Papillon's *Sonatas* which always found an admiring public; and besides, Mr. Ruskin always said, so my husband told me for I never read his books, that Nature *was* purple. I know nothing about it, but it always looks green to me; but of course my husband and Mr. Ruskin must be right. Whether my poor husband called his work 'Studies in Grey' or 'Harmonies in Blue and Silver' or plain 'Sunsets' or 'Moonlights' it made no difference. They went the round of the exhibitions, taken generally by me, formerly in cabs; but as that ran away with too much money, I latterly wrapped them in brown paper and took them by omnibus. Little did my fellow travellers suspect the hopes and fears which were tied up in that shabby paper, and generally strangled by that much knotted string.

Sometimes the Committees snubbed them and snuffed them out at once, always politely of course, as far as words go: 'They regret that want of space prevents,' etc. etc.; but they never added, as the Editors of Magazines do, that 'inability to accept,' or 'rejection' does not imply an opinion unfavourable to the quality of the MS.—that formula not only takes the palm as regards politeness, but is kindly and sympathetic; but the result is much the same.

RECOLLECTIONS OF

My husband used to say he thought they ought to print at the end of the Catalogue the names of the artists whose pictures were really unhung for want of space. If you say they were accepted but not hung, nobody believes you; but printing the names would show people that you were not absolutely rejected. And *I* used to wish they would not put so many crosses in red and white chalk on the backs. You don't know the trouble it is to wash them off, and of course you must get them off before a picture goes another voyage.

Sometimes the pictures were accepted—by a miracle or a mistake—for my husband never begged to be hung, he was too proud; but even then they rarely sold. He used often to say that if he could bring an action against a critic, or write a pathetic letter about the Hanging Committees only hanging themselves and their friends, and then shoot himself like poor Chatterton his pictures would sell. Poor man, that would have done him no good, the dealers would have got the money, not even me; and I am very glad he did not. He was the kindest gentlest member of the S.P.C.A. that ever lived, and his only fault was wasting money in homeing stray dogs and cats and burying them in the garden when they died. We sometimes had three or four, and there were lots of little crosses in the garden over their graves. That was when we lived at Hampstead.

When the end came (that was in London) it

A SPINSTER AUNT

was very peaceful; a sort of fading away for want of encouragement. Poor John! I found a letter addressed to the Coroner to the effect that his death was due to the Hanging Committees 'not to the kindly rope,' which showed that he had thought seriously of destroying himself at some time or other. There was no date on the letter, and of course I burnt it. He also left me a large collection of canvases, a few easels, 6 portfolios full of sketches in oils and water colours, some two or three dozen of empty tubes and enough elderly furniture for two or three rooms. So as the house contained eight rooms, I determined to let the ground floor and kitchens, and live as best I could, upon the pension allowed me by the Artists' Benevolent Fund and any odds and ends I could pick up.

For some years we had living with us to do the work an elderly couple who had seen better days, and who were glad of house room and a very small wage in exchange for doing some of the house work. Properly speaking, I ought to say that the woman did the work, for the man, poor fellow, being terribly asthmatic only smoked some nasty smelling stuff, and dusted the studio in a limp and inefficient fashion. I think he was lazy too. We always gave them coals and gas, and so they were fairly comfortable; and it came about that, when John died, and I told them I could not afford to give them even the small wages any longer, nor coals, that they declared that they would stay with me all the same. Good, kindly souls! Mrs. Morgan 'would go out charing if I would allow her, or perhaps the new lodger might want her.'

The next thing to do was to put a bill in the window: 'Flat to let.' We thought that as flats were becoming the fashion, it would be more taking than 'Ground Floor'; and it really was a Flat—'self-contained' as the agents say; two large rooms and a small third one leading into the garden—a delightful set of rooms looking into the Park.

Day after day passed and no one came of any use, though many people looked over it for a 'friend in the country.' What heartless work it is looking out for some means of money-making which do not turn up; whether it comes from art, or lets, or writing, or teaching, or what not. Poor John used to write for the Magazines sometimes, and now and then was paid; but generally, he only got flattering letters which were thought to be sufficient remuneration for hours and hours of hard work; and often the Magazine died before the money arrived.

It is droll too, if it were not so serious, that the public looks upon money in connection with art as degrading; artists being ideal creatures who should be above such vulgar trafficking as money making; 'art is not commerce' they say; but all the same it is only another sort of commerce to groceries, and unless all artists are to have an income provided by the State, I don't see how they are to live without selling their pictures. That would enable them to dream, and think, and produce works of art possibly; but more probably it would make the mass of them mere idlers. My poor husband would always have worked because he loved work, but that is rather unusual. If exchange and barter were to be revived it would be very delightful (my dear husband always said we should be quite rich then as we had so many pictures we could have exchanged with the butcher and baker and the grocers), but as we are obliged to give money for all we want, the confusion in the public mind about art, and artists being properly paid for their work like other people, is deplorable. We once had an example of practising exchange and barter. By some extraordinary accident, one of my husband's pictures was hung at the Academy and in a very good place; and one day he had a letter from a man in the country asking if he had any small sketch or copy of this picture. He liked it so much, but he was only a tradesman and could not afford the 15 guineas it was marked in the catalogue. Would John accept, for a small sketch if he had one, a very beautiful Dresden china pipe? John wrote back that artists, like tradesmen and other people, could not keep body and soul together upon pipes and tobacco;

and he added rather in joke than otherwise, that if the writer had goods which might be useful to him, and not perishable, and would send 4 guineas' worth to London, John would send him the original sketch by return of post. The man replied that he was a grocer and would willingly send tea and other things to the value of four pounds if John would let him have the small Impression. That made us laugh, as it was the new term for a sketch and we wondered how the country grocer knew it. However, John agreed, but begged him not to send tea as he, (I mean John) never drank promiscuous tea—many of John's friends who spent four times as much on beer and spirits, sneered at his 'extravagance and waste of money on his tea.' That's like people; it's always extravagance in others to spend on things they themselves don't care for. John also said further that the country grocer must pay the carriage. After a few days the parcel arrived, for the dear good man thought John was serious, and a very fine set of contents it had. We had groceries enough to last us for months. For my part I think such exchanges substituted for coin of the realm would be an excellent arrangement, for most of us possess more properties, as the actors say, than gold and bank notes. The only difficulty would be what to do with so many pictures? It is true they could go to the local museums in the Provinces where they would be more interesting than dusty, moth eaten stuffed birds with the straw coming out of their insides.

But to return to our flat letting. I think it must have been at least eight weeks, that, day after day, we went on hoping against hope. People came to see the rooms in shoals to get out of the rain, or snow, or biting wind. Some found them too large, others too small; some too low, others too dark—but all too dear. I had many mean offers which I refused; and many more parties wished to take them, but I saw they were undesirables. What is the use of letting to people who would run away without paying the rent? Thus time went on and Christmas Eve arrived. I had dressed myself to go to the dentist when up came Morgan.

'A gentleman to look at the rooms, Ma'am, and I think he will take them.'

This was by no means the first time Morgan had thought that some one was going to take the place; but I, for my part, had very little faith left as to the probability of finding a tenant; it all seemed to get more and more hopeless, each sun that tried to rise over the dismal fog. However I went down stairs to interview this last arrival, somewhat put out at being detained, and I determined to get rid of him as soon as possible. A stout, pleasant looking man confronted me, and we discoursed.

'Your rooms will just suit me, Mrs. Burton, and also the terms.'

'Indeed, Sir!' (I *was* astonished!) 'Is it for a business place, Sir?'

'Oh, no; only for a shakedown where I could stay when the weather is bad.'

'You live in the country, then?'

'Yes; Great Western.'

'Far down, Sir?'

'No, an hour or so.'

Evidently my efforts at discovery were quite fruitless.

'Well, Mrs. Burton, can I come in this afternoon?'

'That is rather soon, Sir; we generally want references on both sides.'

'Now my good lady, let us be practical. You want to let your rooms, and I want to take them. Of course you also want to be sure of your rent. Is not that so? Well, if I pay you the three months in advance, isn't it as good or better than references?'

This proposition seemed to me so straightforward, and under the circumstances, so exceedingly handy, that I naturally favoured it; but it was also so very unusual, that I bethought me that I should like to consult my friend Miss Tomkinson who happened to be upstairs, waiting to accompany me to the dentist. So I begged my new tenant to sit down while I ran up to tell my dear Amelia the extraordinary news. She, as usual, thought me quite mad. To let my flat to a perfect stranger; to have no references as to respectability; 'to have a man coming and going who might be anything'—these were her objections, and all, of course, very plausible. But I put it before her that it seemed a godsend after waiting so long, and that I might wait still longer and fare worse. However it was no use trying to make Amelia hear reason. Poor dear Amelia does not know what it is to want money to pay the quarter's rent and to go without all but absolute necessaries. I was as usual 'Quixotic'; I was 'Visionary, Hopelessly Hopeful, Imprudent, Wanting in due Caution!' and every other virtue (or vice?) of that kind—all enunciated with the vehemence of a worldly-wise person. I knew, alas! by Amelia's opposition what I should have to encounter from my relatives; and then, if anything went wrong, there would be the usual chorus of cousins: 'I told you so!' But what could go wrong? Was not my instinct invariably a just guide? Was I ever led away by following my first impulse? Was the man likely to burn the house down? And why? And then, I was so worried and bored by people who would 'call again,' or 'write'; it was always 'for a friend in the country,' and so on; it is always the same story when any one is trying to let. So I made up my mind to run the risk, for I liked the look of the man. He was so frank and honest looking, gazing straight at you with far-seeing eyes. And then there was an amused expression about his mouth that I took to at once, a sort of undeveloped smile not quite properly born. He was dressed in a thick grey suit, and a great coat with a velvet collar. He was not good-looking, but had a friendly twinkle in his eyes. 'But what in the world can a sea-captain want with your rooms?' was dear Amelia's remark when I described him to her. I went down stairs.

'You have decided, Mrs. Burton?'

'Yes, Sir. What name shall I make the receipt out to?'

'Well'... a long pause. 'Ralph Lewis, if you please.' So, thought I, that is *not* your name; and I wonder if I have been extra foolish. However, I said nothing, but wrote my name across the Queen's head on the paper I had brought down with me; and Mr. Lewis handed me three new five pound notes out of a pocket book which contained a bundle of them. I had not seen such a lot of bank notes for many a long day.

'There, Mrs. Burton, now we are quits, and I'll send my things in tonight. Your man will keep the rooms dusted, I daresay, if I give him five shillings a week.'

When I told Amelia going along to the omnibus—'Just like you! I've said so before, and

A SPINSTER AUNT

I'll say so again' (alas! how true), 'you are always erratic, impulsive, wild; you are no better than an Irishwoman or a baby—and you a real born Londoner; that ought to make you wiser and thankful. But you never will change; you are just the same as when you bought that cheap remnant of brown alpaca, knowing all the time that Uncle White was at death's door. Silly sentiment not looking facts in the face, and then having to borrow 14/9 of me to pay for a bit of black.'

It is needless to relate the torture of awaiting your turn in a dentist's consulting room, and then the curious half-conscious night-mare condition which gas throws you into. Various sea-captains, bank notes, rooms to let, yellow fogs and falling snow flakes all dancing about together in a jumble, making one imagine the end of the world, or of oneself, had absolutely arrived. When we returned, we found one of Maple's furniture vans at the door, and Morgan taking in divers boxes and bundles from Mr. Lewis who was issuing from a four-wheeled cab holding a legal looking black leather bag. He left about eight o'clock, and being Christmas Eve we did not expect to see him for a few days; but it was a fortnight before he re-appeared with a huge black box on the top of a cab. I see you smile, Miss Jane, of course Mr. Lewis was inside the cab. That day he stayed some hours, and there was a great deal of noise in the big room as if he was shunting about the box he had brought.

Naturally every one, ourselves included, felt very curious as to Mr. Lewis' reasons for taking the rooms. No letters ever came for him, and he posted all he wrote, himself. When, once or twice, he left in a hansom, the only address Morgan ever heard him give the cabman was, Paddington, Main Line—that betrayed nothing. Sometimes he came often; at others he did not appear for three or four weeks. My friends were eloquent about my 'mysterious lodger.' One called him 'the Burglar,' and wanted to strew flour on the floor, thinking of the story of Bel and the Dragon; the 'inner chamber with its exit into the park was just the place for such a person.' Another called him 'the man with the frank countenance,' which was a hit at me, of course.

One day Morgan was most excited. Mr. Lewis had come in a handsome landau and pair, with two grooms on the box, all beautifully turned out, and a lady inside. 'Had I not seen it? what a pity!' Mr. Lewis got out with the usual black bag in one hand, and a railway rug in the other, for all the world as if he had come off a journey. Was he a diamond merchant, depositing his stones in the inner chamber for safe keeping? Or was he a detective? This theory was the most popular view of the case.

One day I met Mr. Lewis in the passage.

A SPINSTER AUNT

'You are an artist, I am told, Mrs. Burton?'

'Oh, dear no, Sir; it was my poor husband that painted.'

'May I see his pictures?' So I asked him to walk up, and he said some of them were very good, and perhaps he might be useful some day in selling some for me. When I told Amelia this, with some joy, she replied: 'There you are again; you always believe everybody who tries to be a bit civil.' Amelia, though I love her very much, is sometimes a little too outspoken to be pleasant, and she hates art and artists—a 'nasty idle lot, wasting their time in painting things nobody wants, and wasting their money in paints and frames and canvases.' She never would listen to me when I said that was good for trade.

As Lady Day drew near, we became very anxious as I had let the rooms over his head to a charming barrister and his wife (I mean she was charming; I had not seen him). They took the rooms on faith as I could only show the front one and describe the excellences of the large one by showing my own back room which was the same as the ground floor, being over it. They came on the 26th as they expected to find them vacant, and I had to ask them to wait until the 29th to come in. On the 28th we had seen nothing of Mr. Lewis. His time was up on the 25th, and I could not write to him having no address, so I determined to look about in the front room.

I found a blotting book and some paper and envelopes, but no address. I thought I might find the key of the large room door, for of course I had a right to enter the rooms now his time was up, but no key could we discover. Then I tried all my own keys, but none fitted the lock. All the time Mr. Lewis had had the flat I had never entered the rooms, but I rather suspected Morgan had peeped through the keyhole of the inner room door. In the small room there was an inkstand besides the blotter, a few volumes of paper-covered books, and some pipes and tobacco in a Japanese bowl. The books were those that travellers are told not to bring to England. Then I thought I might find some name in the blotting book on the paper, but there was none. But just then Morgan picked up a scrap of cream-laid paper which was half burnt. It had on it stamped *Halle Court*. I flew upstairs to search in the old book of somebody's 'Roads,' and although Gloucestershire is the land of Courts I found none named Halle. Baffled again, there was nothing to do but to break open the door of the inner room, but I did not like doing it; it seemed like an invasion. It savoured also of prying which I hate; and it appeared mean and unduly inquisitive. Besides which I was just a little fearsome of what we might find. All the loose talk of burglars and dead bodies and other mysteries was of course nonsense; but still the fact remained that the man had taken two rooms he rarely used, and paid a high rent to no purpose as far as we could see. And then a queer noise and a curious smell came up from the garden sometimes. Strong-minded persons may laugh, but I never pretended to be the possessor of a large stock of physical courage; and if I say I trembled all over when I put an old key into the lock which seemed to fit, I should be understating the fact. I never felt so terrified in my life since the days when as a child I shuddered at a black slug, and screamed at the sight of black wadding. Even singing 'Love Not' at parties did not make my legs shake more; and yet I did not even know for certain that the key would open the door. So I was doubly foolish, but for a few minutes skeleton keys, corpses, stolen jewels, dynamite bombs, Anarchists and goodness knows what were all mixed up together in my agonized mind.

'Courage, Ma'am, courage,' said Morgan from behind the ambush of his wife's and my skirts. Morgan is not a brave man; and you know, Miss Jane, I am a very nervous person. I turned the key gently. Yes it did turn; but just then, smoke, strong smelling sulphurous smoke, issued from the crack in the door and blew out the candle. We relighted it, but I instinctively put my apron over my head for protection ere I turned the key further round, and I felt so terrified I could not look. Morgan went on talking of courage, but when the puff of air blew out the candle he too trembled like an aspen leaf, and the ever-present pipe dropped out of his mouth. As to his wife, she was the colour of a pale boiled turnip.

'Morgan,' I gasped from under my apron as I opened the door, 'look in and tell me what you see.' He peeped in, but another strong smelling blast banged the door to so violently that it almost caught his nose, which I have forgotten to say was long and pointed.

'It's a ghost,' quoth Morgan, 'or a murder, or both; but I can only see the room enveloped in smoke;—it's a fire!'

Again we closed the door, and looked through the keyhole, but saw nothing.

'Bless me,' cried Morgan, pushing the door open again, 'it's empty!'

Quietly I took my apron from my head, and looked. Yes, the room was all but empty. There was the famous shakedown Mr. Lewis had spoken about, with a railway rug thrown over it—no sheets nor blankets. A common deal box was open, and contained a quite new tin kettle tied up in whitey-brown paper, an empty soda water bottle, an old hearth broom, and a small pair of scales. In another box, a smaller one, some yellow powder, and a very large bottle of salad oil. On the mantelpiece was a spirit lamp, a large biscuit tin with a few scraps of Alberts, an empty Sherry bottle, a comb, a pair of rusty

A SPINSTER AUNT

scissors, two spoons, a very black saucepan, a tumbler, a broken knife, the remains of a cigar and a cake of toilet Windsor soap. That was all in the great room. Stay; what was that just inside the doorway leading into the little entry? Something covered up in green baize—no doubt a handsome piece of furniture, or books thus protected from damp. We approached it, Morgan declaring it must contain a corpse, but the box, the large black one he had brought on the cab, was not long enough. We proceeded to investigate, and warily and gently lifted the green baize covering, to find another box within this one. This still further added to the criminal sensation of prying into the good gentleman's secrets. But it was his own fault. Why had he not returned and moved his things at the end of his three months? Gently and cautiously I raised the lid and saw, or tried to see, a red earthenware pipkin full of burnt sulphur—hence the smell we noticed on opening the door.

'But stay, there's a letter at the bottom, Morgan.'

'No, ma'am, only a post card with some rigmarole written on it.'

THGIE THGINOT
NORAB
! TSIHW !
P.R.U.

What on earth did it mean? . . .

* * * * *

Next day to our extreme satisfaction Mr. Lewis arrived with a man and horse and cart. I told him I had let the rooms, and had intended stowing away his goods in the basement if he had not turned up, as the new tenants wanted to come in.

'True; I owe you another week's rent, Mrs. Burton.'

'No, Sir,' I said, 'I really could not accept it, knowing how little you have been here.'

'Now, my good lady, which think you, is the poorer, you or me?'

'Well, Mr. Lewis, very few persons can be much poorer than I am just now, I am sorry to say.'

'Then oblige me by taking the rent for the extra week, for I am sure it has put you out, my not coming back to time, but I was away, so could not come earlier. And now, Good bye — *Au revoir—auf wiedersehen.*'

He shook my hand in the most friendly way, and before I could say a word he had turned on his heel, jumped into a hansom, and was gone.

'And to think,' cried Morgan from the area steps, 'he hadn't even the decency to tell the driver where to go to.'

* * * * *

One day, some weeks later, it suddenly dawned upon me that Morgan's 'rigmarole' on the post card might become intelligible if it were read from the bottom upwards. I took it out of my desk, and then I saw the P.R.U. which I had not noticed before. I read the card backwards, and spelling it, found the following vague result: 'Whist, Baron, tonight eight.' What on earth it meant I have no idea. Was Mr. Lewis really a detective? If so, why should he have taken my rooms?

. . . . . .

Travelling up Regent St. in an omnibus one morning some time after Mr. Lewis' departure, I saw his burly figure sauntering along the pavement near Hanover Chapel. I pulled the cord vigorously, but before I could get out, he had disappeared, and from that day to this I have never seen him, nor have I ever solved the mystery.

RECOLLECTIONS OF

CHAPTER XII

RHEINLAND

The Den, *July* 1868

My dear Mary

It is all settled. We, *i.e.* M—— of the same name but no relation and I are going for a couple of months on a sketching tour to Germany. Our funds are limited. We are borrowing—perhaps I ought to say, I am borrowing from Peter to pay Paul; in other words, I have screwed the sum of £15 out of clothes and paints monies, to apply the same fifteen golden sovereigns to a German trip, with a view to getting some of it back by pen or brush.

My letters will be unconnected in substance. They will be written at odd times, mostly in bed after the day's work, so the writing will be worse than usual and the expense of sending them horrible: 5d for very little. We are going by boat from London Bridge to Rotterdam, and then per steamer up to Mainz or Mannheim *en route* for Heidelberg, and back the same way, as that is the least costly manner of progression, and moreover will enable us to stop at small places along the river, and so escape tourists in a great measure. So good bye for the present.

Ever your affect^{te} cousin JANE.

On the steamer 'Marianne,' voyaging up the Rhine. *July* 10*th* 1868.

DEAR MARY,

We left London by the 'Leo.' It was smooth all the way, so absolutely no one could manage to be ill. The worst part of the journey was getting to the ship in a small wherry. The boatmen and the porters fleece you right and left; it would be better if the ships of the Steam Navigation Co? would go alongside the wharf.

We left at 11 A.M. and arrived at Rotterdam at 5 A.M. next day and had to find our way to the Rhine boat, so we saw a little of the watery city. I am now ensconced under the awning scribbling this for your edification. Our fellow travellers are all but *nil*—only one young Englishman; though of course natives, mostly market women, step on board at small places—*we* three being of course, first class passengers, have the aft part of the boat all to ourselves. One's first impression of Holland is of a land of windmills, water, steam boats, willows, and bulrushes. It is, to my mind, much prettier than our country; but then you must remember that my passion is for the aforesaid windmills, water, willows, etc. and not for gigantic elms, oaks, and such like Brobdignagian cabbages. I love the north of France which many people call flat and ugly; it certainly is flat, but how can the willows waving in the wind be ugly? Or the sand dunes with their little tufts of grass sticking up at intervals after the manner of the Camargue country around the Bouches du Rhone. Holland is very prim, for the windmills seem to be built in rows. All this part reminds me of the country about Bruges, which is first cousin to Dutchland.

Time goes slowly; we creep along under a passive blue sky, and for some reason, the church clocks always seem to tell the same time, though they may be 6 miles apart. We pass heaps of cows, but the milk in our coffee seems limp; owing to the watery land possibly.

12 P.M. We are nearly at dinner time—that will be an epoch in our lives. I was sketching our young man just now, and looking up at him I discovered that he was sketching me. We both laughed—so glad at having something to laugh at. We compared our sketches and laughed the more —I with my face half shut off by my hat, he with his 5th pipe in his mouth. So we were introduced by art and we became rapidly friendly, so friendly that we agreed that the works we had perpetrated were poor things, but we mutually claimed the worst work as our own. You see we English are

sometimes polite, in spite of the assertions of Foreigners, born mainly of the Briton's dislike to raising his head covering, even when his head is sufficiently covered by Nature.

Emmerich is the Prussian frontier, and we have to be inspected. They fuss very much and open everything and find nothing, so the officers depart to the fore part of the boat and rummage about among the peasants' baskets and parcels.

I note that our waiter appears in a variety of costumes, changing hourly *pour passer le temps*; he speaks 'the Inglische' fairly well.

8 P.M. We have had three meals and a half to-day so we are going to retire for the night. There is only one cabin, where we should sit were it wet. No sleeping arrangements proper; but the captain, a charming man, gives up his cabin to 'the ladies.' It consists of two seats covered with shiny leather and 8 or 4 camp stools. These we arrange long ways so as to lengthen the seats, they being but a yard or so in length. Here we shall pass the night, which is warm—happily there is a port hole which we keep open. . . .

Morning, 5.30 A.M. The night passed fairly well, but we had no means of washing except by hanging our sponges out of the port hole. We asked for a basin—none. For a pail—occupied. However we found even a wet sponge pleasant and luckily had soap and towels. The worst part of the night was the slipping off the seats, and thereby disturbing the camp stools. Our young man occupied the Saloon.

KÖLN. Joy! we have the prospect of a bath! ... I once heard of a French woman who said: 'The English must be very dirty people, for they always wanted a bath.' Köln is delightful. After our bath we wandered up to the Dom and arrived for the end of High mass. Also we saw the Dombild by Meister Stephen with its wonderful stagbeetle, but not the 3 Kings' reliquary containing the skulls—Gaspard, Melchior, and Balthazar; it cost too much for us—two thalers each; and so we leave them for another visit when funds have increased. Then we toiled about, and at 12.30 fed in the 'Restauration' at the railway station and very well upon *côtelettes de mouton* and beautiful *kartoffeln*. We walked over the bridge of boats to the 'Belle Vue' Gasthof at Deutz, which I remembered going to years ago on the way to Leipzig. We partook of coffee during the concert (a stringed band); but as an N.B., never cross that bridge in the sun. The river is quite spoilt by the new iron railway bridge. After a good rest we returned and explored some of the beautiful Romanesque churches. Santa Maria im Capitole is a splendid specimen; indeed all the churches are very fine. When we left at 9.45 P.M. the city looked so pretty with the lights reflected in the water, and the cathedral spire standing up against the greenish sky. The last time I saw it, in 1851, the roof was not all connected; I mean the nave had a break in the centre. It has still to be finished, the towers especially. We had to change boats in the night but we slept 4 hours well in spite of the sofas being convex, and woke to find our 'Marianne' express boat gone from Coblenz with our luggage, through the fog having detained us somewhere *en route*. . . .

Wednesday. I think the Rhine much overrated, and consider the Rhone far finer, but no one screams over that, probably because most people travel up and down it by night. . . .

MAINZ. Alack! alack! our luggage has gone to Mannheim. . . . We had to divide. M. went to Heidelberg with the young man where they arrived 11.80 P.M. and with no luggage, and I came on here (Mannheim) with a nice German girl. We are obliged to stay the night for, although the luggage is here, we cannot get it. It was directed Mannheim, but the numbers did not correspond with our tickets, and the clerk had gone, so no one would believe us. So much for the charms of registration of baggage. In England you see it labelled, and when you arrive you poke it with your umbrella, and hail a cab and off you go;—and how often has any one lost his goods? Certainly not oftener than abroad where it is frequently left behind at junctions. We stormed and raged, the girl in German; I in

Polyglot, but to no effect. Who can melt a German official? I even gave him my key and told him to open the box and he would find so and so. No, *he* could not; I must see the most important functionary. Nearly all the morning has been taken up by luggage troubles, and we arrived here (Heidelberg) late in the afternoon.

Such a droll set at the Pension in the Anlage, many British and more Americans, whole families with children more or less offensive. A happy father desiring his small son to hold his tongue, the child replies, 'Hold *your* jaw,' and then catching hold of his tongue, says, 'I *am* holding it.' We have a German Jewess with much stuck out hair and such a crinoline! She is short, and thick and smiling and has a little girl with similar characteristics. She wears much jewellery. Mamma Yankee is a distinguished looking woman, and pleasant. Papa: well, he says they live at Chicago. The grown-up daughter has yellow hair—undyed. The three boys are rude little ruffians. 'You mind your own business,' to 'Puppa' when he interferes. I am learning the American language; why should we mind the inhabitants of the States having one of their own? 'My drawing is very cunning'; that may be the proper meaning of cunning, as conceit is used by them in the old uncorrupted sense. But it is a little startling to be told that one 'looks very ugly to-day, my dear.' Then these terms seem popular: 'Oh my Goodness, my good woman, isn't it an elegant day?'

A little legend (?) the following story of an Englishman here, who being a captain, is called by us and our particular friends in the house, Capt. Jinks of the Horse Marines. He, the Captain, went to the Baden Post Office and asked for stamps. Receiving them, he said he wanted English stamps. The clerk explained, in German of course, but the bold Captain only raved and stormed. Said a neighbouring Briton, 'Do you know where you are?' The Captain glared, caught up the stamps and fled, leaving his change. . . .

We accomplished the Koenigsstuhl yesterday, with the Parkers in a temperature of 98° in the shade. Almost tropical; too much so for climbing. . . . A Miss Thicksome is here. She is 'of a certain age,' more correctly an uncertain age, and cocks her headpiece at every man—the two or three who are here. She sings three songs—only; and is frequently encored. She is amusing in a way, as she believes all the American stories, and when we go into convulsions of laughter she mildly asks why we laugh. The other night when we went up to bed, M. and I mewed cat-like out of our respective windows, which are some distance apart. In the morning poor Miss T. complained that she could not get to sleep for '*so* long, because of two cats that were quarrelling.

Of course you heard them too?' 'No, we heard no cats.' And she never tired of grumbling at the number of cats in the garden.... Some one asked one of the children if she loved strawberries? 'No, I don't love them, but I like them.' 'Why don't you love them?' 'Because I can't hug them.'... Miss Thicksome asked me to-day if I thought she would see Vienna from Schwetzingen. She wanted to go there, and as 'both places were on the Danube, she thought perhaps Vienna might be visible.'

At the Grünewald, Caub. You see we have moved back. This Green forest is not a bad inn, and very cheap; not quite 8/- a day and very quiet. At Heidelberg the night trains are a great nuisance as the railway is close to the house. Also the crowing and cackling of cocks and hens; this morning I felt I could wring their necks; but it is a curious fact that the eggs producing this happy screaming ought to have been laid long ago, so ancient are they at breakfast.

There was a great discussion to-day at dinner upon the subject of annexation to Prussia, followed by a great squabbling; but all unite in detestation of the French, and take it for granted that they, or the Austrians would have taken Baden, had not Prussia done so.

The church communities here are so united that they use the same building divided down the centre, and it seems specially arranged that when one congregation is praying the other is singing and *vice versa.* No sermon, but after their respective offices, the Roman Catholic priest and the Protestant minister adjourn to the *café* and play dominoes. The people sing hymns in the vernacular all through the mass. What they do the other side I do not know.

July 30th. There was great excitement in the night. A tremendous scuffling of feet and crying and screaming and ringing of bells. I got up and looked out of window to behold the castle lighted up by red fire, but going out on the balcony I saw it was a real fire. We dressed as quickly as possible and went out. Such a noise; clanging of church bells, howling of people all shuffling along the road; and although anything but a quiet place, these noises were unusual in Caub.

The excitement was tremendous, the engines small; for a time there seemed no reason why the whole village should not be burnt. The little engines spurted out a few jets of water at intervals, but the only means of getting water was by forming chains down to the river. And millions of gallons flowing past us unattainable! Luckily there was no wind; but the poor folk could only save their furniture and clothes by throwing them out of the windows, and it was delightful to see how everybody helped. When we returned to bed, it was impossible to sleep, for the noise and clatter kept up all night.

Note. You know the fondness of the true Deutsche Männer for smoking. They smoke everywhere, at their work, at their meals, even at concerts, and you catch a glimpse only now and then of the performers' heads or feet, from the occasional dispersing of a puff of smoke. Be it known that during the excitement of the fire they all had their long porcelain pipes in their mouths, and all the night, after the worst was over, and all the next day, those pipes remained in their usual positions. I suppose smoke is consoling, but one would have thought the fire produced enough for that purpose.

Next day to Oberwesel. In the church there is a curious picture of St. Catherine on the wheel; the latter split, and the scalp of the executioner flying upwards in a shower of blood. That is a part of the legend unknown to me. There is another curious early picture in 12 compartments. In one of these people are being blown down by the wind, while in another St. Jerome is calmly reading a book. Hills are falling upon a number of people starting out of their graves—half skeleton, half skin; others with clothes on—the recently departed? Certainly these Primitives were very realistic in their representations of the future! In another panel fishes great and small are poking up their heads from the sea or river. On the banks each side stand some people. A woman with a sugar loaf head dress, a man in a cocked hat and high boots, and a priest. Is it symbolic of the rejection of the truth by the world, but the acceptance thereof by the fishes of the sea?

Friday. We have had a drama. There is a certain lady here, and at Bacharach lives a doctor, young and handsome; the lady is neither. The Bacharach M.D. visits the lady very frequently and they walk together in the neighbouring woods. The lady we will call Frau Sonnel. She said she was engaged to Dr. Schwarz. To-day she went over to Bacharach to see the treasure, and found him flown; so back she tears, packs up, and returns to Bacharach to stay with a friend, who, scandal on this side says, is also engaged to the villainous Don Juan. She, the Traitress, told the young man's Papa, and he fetched away his son out of danger. Result: Frau Sonnel weeps, and the Traitress affects sympathy. Will she be revenged and leave the other lady in the Rhine? It is not an unusual story, but here it has made a tremendous sensation, especially as Herr Sonnel is on his way to meet his wife, and Frau S. has lent the M.D. a good deal of money! That seems to complicate matters—we did not know she had a live husband.

This Rhine is terribly foggy and I am minded to try some ancient remedies. Did you ever hear of one Lockyer a Medicine man who cured fogs and their results. It was during the reign of

Charles the 2nd of blessed memory, that the mischief of fogs was cured by a valuable medicine, at what price, history doth not relate; but obviously, the loss of this recipe hath been grievous in its consequences, for is not our beloved isle as well as this great river still girt with mists, and our huge city bathed in unwholesome fog? The inventor of this particular bolus was a 'Licensed Physician and Chemist,' who, sitting astride a piebald horse, sold his wares upon Tower Hill; and if you desire to know his name you will find it carved upon his tomb in the north transept of S. Mary Overy, newly called S. Saviour's, together with some beauteous verses:

> 'Here Lockyer lies interr'd: his name
>
> A name so great, so gen'ral, it may scorn
> Inscriptions which do vulgar tombs adorn.
>
> His virtues and his pills are so well known
> That envy can't confine them under stone.
> But they'll survive his dust and not expire
> Till all things else at th' universal fire.'

Lockyer's secret was his method of 'extracting from the sun's rays' certain essences wherewith to pound his pills—*Pilulae Radiis Solis Extractae*. Naturally such heavenly physick would have wondrous curative power over a 'Regiment of Diseases,' known and unknown. 'Two or three in number, taken early in the morning, preserves against contagious airs,' and if a man would remain in health, 'let him take them once a week.' Not only did they prevent the 'mischief of fogs,' but they 'increased Beauty' in the young, and made 'Old Age comely.' Now here's a chance for us all; we can cure the fogs or make them of no ill effect, and also make our future 'comely.' I commend the pills to you, dear cousin. It is a pouring day, hence my above digression.

Monday. I cannot put dates; it is as much as I can do to remember the days of the week for there is nothing to mark them. Last night we had a lovely show; the Drachenfels lighted up with red fire and the edge of the river outlined with little lamps. It really was very pretty, though somewhat cockneyfied. The day before we went over to Köln again. It was Sunday and we heard the celebrated Dom choir in the Cathedral; only men's voices. It was very severe music, possibly Palestrina; unaccompanied, but beautifully sung. May I say I should have preferred a mass by Mozart with boys' voices added. The organ seemed very fine, but there was very little of it. The church is disgraced by many Munich painted windows; and there is little old glass. Certainly the Germans are very reverent and a great many men go to church. We ran about a good deal and purchased divers pots, pans, and glasses; and then to the Station to find we had not enough money for 2d Class, but as there was no room in the 3d we were obliged to get into a second class carriage. Presently the guard appeared and asked for the supplement. '*Wir haben nicht genug.*' '*Wieviel haben Sie Fräulein?*' We showed the contents of our purse, which were only enough for the extra fare to Bonn; however the guard was civil and told us to get out there, which we did, and he put us into an empty 3d class. In going round one of the churches the man showing it pointed to a fresco, 'The Ladies of the Bible—Judith, Deborah, Jael,—that.' It reminded me of a Salon catalogue, 'A naked lady,' as a translation of, 'Etude du nu.'

Wednesday. We have come to the conclusion we will make a *détour* to see Hildesheim, an old Mediæval town upon the way to Hannover, as we find the Rhine very monotonous. We wanted to stop at a charming hotel at Bonn; but as it was two *thalers* a day, we bowed ourselves out, mine host politely ejaculating, '*Auf wiedersehen, meine Damen.*'

MEHLEM, *Friday.* We arrived here yesterday; it is the quaintest old-world place with two Romanesque churches, unfortunately spoilt by Rococo additions, but happily the bronze doors, the silver-gilt reliquaries, the font and the crypt are untouched by restoration. The bronze doors were made for Bishop Bernward in 1015. They are panelled like those by Ghiberti, but much ruder in design and execution. The subjects are the usual Biblical incidents from the creation of Adam onwards. God presenting Eve to Adam

A SPINSTER AUNT

is quaint; but quainter is the Fall. Adam accused by God, points to Eve, and seems to say 'she did it'; and Eve not to be behind her spouse in excusing herself, switches a finger over her shoulder to the father of lies clinging round the apple tree. Mean creature, Adam. But the charm of the town is its domestic architecture. Most of the houses are of the 15th Century (restored of course) and have legends or texts painted along the beams.

> *He who builds upon the open street*
> *Must not be disturbed by useless chatter;*

and we coming from Rhineland desire to add ' clatter.'

> *Weigh just and equal, says a grocer*
> *So will you be happy and rich.*

. . . . .

We turn a corner of the street and read :

> *I rejoice at thy Resurrection*
> *Which surely vexes Satan.*

. . . . .

An inn invites guests with :

> *Here on earth we only have a resting place;*
> *In Heaven we shall dwell for ever.*

. . . . .

An elaborately carved frontage has this motto :

> *My beginning and my end,*
> *All rests in God's hand.*
> *Ill will of others cannot do much harm,*
> *For what God wills that must be.*

. . . . .

RECOLLECTIONS OF

But there were Pessimists in those days:

Ah, God! why is it
That those hate me to whom I do no evil?
Those who spare me nought, those who give me nought,
Must yet endure that I should live.
If they think that I am lost
Let them also look to themselves.

Then the Pharisee adds:

But I trust in God,
For believe me, good luck comes every day.

. . . . .

Over an apothecary's shop:

Will you have medicine or sweet wine?
So come in here, where both are to be found.

Which motto is a curious example of the conservatism of German customs; for to this day, the best old wine is kept at the Druggist's, presumably for sick folk.

MEHLEM. At the sign of the 'Goldenes Schiffe.' We are back you see at our old quarters and we go on tomorrow. There is an awful 19th Century child here: '*Bitte, Mutter*, pull down the blind I don't want the Angels to see me in my bath.' Sorry I cannot put it all in its native tongue. Between ourselves I think I have seen that before; and it's not so good as an authentic answer a French child made to its English teacher when asked what God told Abraham to do with Isaac. 'Cook him.'

A SPINSTER AUNT

A charming procession passed through a village near by while we were sipping our coffee. They were blessing the grapes with much ceremony, but with no priests, merely the lay and poor folk. There is an odious arrival in the shape of an Englishwoman, who finds our little humble *gasthof* 'too vulgar.' Her 'precious ones' must not consort with the child here (the bath child). 'Since she lost her darling boy, she cannot bear to hear her Bessie sing or play'; which seems a pity after letting her learn of Madame Schumann. All the roads here are lined with fruit trees. Either the German peasantry, especially the boys, must be very honest, or the laws about taking your neighbour's apples must be very stringent.

Tuesday. Our parting was touching from Germans and Dutch. We all hope to meet again after the manner of travellers, knowing that such a thing is never likely to happen. Crossing over to Koenigswinter we found fruit enough for 21 groschen to make us and two other people quite ill. It is a provision for the voyage. I had a shock after I left. I always keep my sketch book in a certain pocket and it was only seeing a girl 'sketching a little in water colours' upon the boat, which reminded me of my book. I felt, and lo! *my pocket was empty!* Hence I had left it at Mehlem, and it contained portraits of the delightful but not too beautiful Dutch ladies. We had left our address, and happily the German girl we chummed with returned it to me . . . *I wondered if she had looked inside.*

At Düsseldorf we changed boats, and lo! once more we had our 'Marianne' conductor. '*Ach, Fräulein, noch einmal Sie fahren mit.*' and we almost embraced. Arrived at Rotterdam another shock. Where was our luggage? We had been delayed by fog again, and custom house officers at the frontier, and we had little time to hunt for the goods. We saw them at the office, but the General Steam Navigation's men could only speak Dutch, and they would not give up our things. What to do? I saw an old gentleman passing who looked pleasant and benevolent, so I rushed out of the office: '*Sprechen Sie Deutsch?*' 'Anything you like, German, English, or French.' Blessed man; I could have hugged him, but I only asked him to help us. We pointed out our luggage, and said we wanted to be off in fifteen minutes by the boat for Antwerp. The Dutchman was delightful; explained about the luggage, showed us the way to the boat, said 'Good Bye, my ladies,' and off we went.

The journey through the canals was charming and makes one wish to tour in Holland. Dortrecht is most picturesque, and all the landscape is that delightful grey green of the Dutch painters' work. Part of the way we went by train, and we duly arrived at Antwerp on Saturday evening.

ANTWERPEN, *Sunday evening.* We have seen

Rubens, I only wish one could see him in a well-lighted gallery instead of a dark church. His 'Crucifixion' is of course magnificent—there is no painter like him for richness of colour; but his reading of such subjects is quite out of place in a church. Luckily it was Sunday, and so we had a long view of the pictures free, instead of a few minutes and a fee of a franc. We trotted in several times, also to the High Mass which was lovely—Mozart; and it is so delightful to worship where you like. You pay a *sou* for your chair and walk about with it until you find a quiet corner where you are in peace undisturbed by your neighbour's little fidgetty ways as in our churches where you are all obliged to rise together and sit, or kneel down together. I see the Cathedral spire from my room and hear the bells all day and all night, chiming merrily.

Monday. We climbed the Cathedral tower this morning and found on the top a little lame man who had mounted all alone. Round the platform of the tower there are steps a foot high which he could not mount, so he asked us if we would help him to move a small ladder that he could climb along to see the view. This we did of course, and then we talked a good deal. He seemed to have been everywhere alone, and was quite happy, although terribly crippled; but his condition did not prevent travel fever. The view is charming; one sees for miles and miles over the flat country with inter-winding rivers and quaint villages of white houses with red roofs.

When we were going down I asked if we could be of any use to him, but he said 'No'; and when we had descended, in asking the guardian if she knew he was so badly crippled, she told us she tried to prevent him mounting. It really was dangerous, for the steps are dreadfully worn up the tower. Here endeth my last letter from the 'Continong.'

A SPINSTER AUNT

CHAPTER XIII

PARIS

PARIS, *April* 1869.

MY DEAR MARY

I have at last settled down in a Pension, rue de Provence. It is entirely French even to my bedroom, which is a semi sitting room all blue—a sofa, easy chair and bedstead with a round bar at the top from which hang the curtains, also blue. It is a pretty room and sunny, and on the ground floor; I have only to step out to be in a garden. It is one charm of Paris that you find gardens in all sorts of impossible places. You pass down an ugly street of dismal houses, you go up stairs to see a friend, and you find her sitting at an open window looking on to trees. Delightful. In London you mostly find a back yard, possibly used by a workman who has a stove which ejects much smoke into your room. There are several French people here and no Foreigners; so I ought to pick up a little French; but inasmuch as I am tired when I come home from the Studio, I often retire after dinner and relinquish my chance of improvement in *la belle langue française*.

Chaplin's is more a play studio, amateurish, than a working one. I wish now I had gone to Jullien's but every one said all manner of things about it, and praised up M. C. so much as a teacher, that I chose his *Atelier*. He is not bad; prides himself at being of English extraction—considers himself quite English, even to his whiskers. Of the students Mademoiselle Nicolay is considered the swell. She has 'exposed,' which is thought much of. She is not beautiful, but charming in her manner. There is another girl also charming, but being always posing for charm, is wearying to a degree. Another is also mightily tiring with her perpetual chatter. Then comes a Russian lady whose husband belongs to the Danish Embassy; she really *is* charming and speaks every language well, so we often have a chat; she knew the Princess when she was young and told me many things about her simple life; she also knows a number of people of note here in Paris. Then we have an American, of course; poor lady, middle aged, and not too clever. She is always blundering, and keeps her brushes dirty; so dirty that Monsieur, the other day threw one after the other over his shoulder: 'Do you think I can paint with these?' and up he started. Not over polite!

A Madame de T. is great fun. A beflounced gown and pork pie hat. It is quite a cosmopolitan place for we also have a Spaniard, another Russian

A SPINSTER AUNT

and a very nice English girl, Miss C. B. The master is tall and gaunt, and drags half a dozen hairs over his bald head; fussy, short of speech (except to Madame de T. and the Russian-Dane) and generally disagreeable. I shall change quarters soon I think, for I learn nothing either from C. nor of French *chez* Madame Boulanger.

Much love to you, I must go to work.

Yours very affectionately JANE.

P.S.—There seems to be some disturbance going on in the workmen's quarter, Belleville I think. The Prefect of Police recommends us all to keep at home. Some people seized an omnibus and made a barricade. The Emperor and Empress drove in an open carriage through the disturbed part, which was plucky of them, and the barricaders were soon arrested.

May 12 1869.
RUE BLANCHE, PARIS.

DEAREST MARY

Here I am installed. I have a bedroom on one side of the street and a studio across the road on the ground floor, looking into a garden. The house and studio belong to an old artist, Tissier by name, '*un homme de talent*,' as French people say when they do not know what to say. I descend to a Restaurant for my *déjeuner* and dinner, and I brew tea in the Studio when I want it. I was abused like a pickpocket by the Concierge on my arrival, about the *denier de Dieu*, (an institution I know nothing about), and which she said I had not given her; but as I had no idea what God's pence in relation to concierges meant, I was hopelessly feeble in my explanations. The brutes—the only name for concierges male or female, scowl at me every time I pass their room. I have a model tomorrow, so I shall ask for information.

— My model, half English, says it is the custom to give the concierge a fee on taking a studio or rooms; so I have asked her to do it and explain that I intended tipping her when I left. Such are the differences between England and France, and as a general rule if you always do exactly the opposite to what you would do at home, you cannot go far astray. It is curious, and just as if the two nations, when enemies, (which happened pretty often in former times), had determined upon this antagonism of social duties and customs.

I am working in the garden, it is pretty; but I hope Madame does not object to my forced observation of her little domestic arrangements. She has girls living with her—students. One over my head sings gloriously; is going on the stage they say. The *déjeuner* must be a restless meal. The bell rings and then a clatter of voices. Another tinkle, tinkle; Madame evidently wrathfully addresses the maid who runs out with a small pot, and returns after a minute or two with what I suspect to be mustard. Another day it is salt, showing the economy of the middle class French *ménage* in never taking in stores of eatables and drinkables.

— *May.* I have given up the 'Restaurant du Progrès' and am compelled to descend, and what is worse, to remount the street. You know it, Notre Dame de Lorette, where the extra horses stand to drag the ponderous omnibusses up the hill, silent models of duty, for the beasts always march to their places in front of the others, entirely of their own accord. Duval is more expensive than Progrès but it is not poisonous, I think and hope. I came to the conclusion that the 1 franc 25 '*menu* at Progrès was really and literally too progressive. *Mouton Rôti* becomes *Ragoût de Mouton*, and possibly, afterwards, *saucisson*—but that I never tried; then *Bœuf Nature* or *Bifstek* evolves into stew or *Bœuf au gratin.*' And so on, day by day, *ad infinitum*, a style of *menu* which is only suitable to extreme youth.

I still go to Chaplin's two or three times a week, but shall give it up at the end of the month as I learn little or nothing there. His own work is good, though conventional; his ladies' portraits elegant and *à la mode*; but his colour is too flimsy and pastel-like. There is a want of manliness about his work; a sort of echo of the *élégance* and charm of the 18th Century men, without their strength. Hence I find his water colour work better than his oil paintings, which are too 'pretty' for that medium. Indeed I find no end of good water colour painting here. It has always been so endlessly dinned into our ears that the English is the finest of all schools of Aquarellistes, that I never dreamt or expected to see such fine things by the French Society. To my mind they are far ahead of us, and their work is a revelation. I saw the other day a very slight sketch by Jacquemart—delightful and pure Water Colour. They also work in body colour, *gouache*—tempera, but they do not mix the two —both are distinct methods. The combination of transparent skies and opaque landscapes is not attempted as far as I know. Then the Barbizon painters; Millet for instance turns out exquisite work in water colour; so does Mauve, who is I believe a Belgian.

I am going about a good deal; to the Salon of course and also to the private clubs, the Mirlitons and the Volney. So put away all your ideas of 'Our incomparable school of water colour painters,' with your Birket Fosters and all their tribe. If you must stick up for the Englishmen go back to David Cox and De Wint and all the pure wash people; they possibly taught the French to paint

A SPINSTER AUNT

au premier coup, but we have left all that behind and niggle up with Chinese white and a tiny brush. Well, you want a tiny brush or a steel pen to put little spots on a child's pinafore if they are to be so done that you can count the respective numbers upon body, skirt, and sleeves! I suppose reaction will come and bold washes will take the place of stippling.

I have made another discovery in relation to the French Aquarellistes; they are mostly, if not all good painters in oil. We in England are taught to begin in what is called the 'easier' art! Easy to wash in a sky! Of course if you resort to Chinese white, you can plaster over mistakes (not on a sky) but you lose your surface and your transparency. Look at the flowers of Fantin-Latour and Madeleine Lemaire. Is it easy to work in that way and not re-touch? I believe the right way is to begin in oil; you can work on a larger scale and you can correct better. I don't mean by loading on one dirty colour over another; but by scraping the paint down to the foundation and repainting the offending part.

20th June. One charm of Paris is that you can get into the country quite easily; as easily as we used to go to Hampstead and Greenwich in our childhood. Paris is a village compared to smoke begrimed London, and so clean. Here I slip down in the afternoon to the river, get into a little *Mouche* and go to Sèvres where I wander about in the woods until six o'clock when I return to town the same way or by the omnibus. It goes all the way to Versailles on rails. In the woods at Sèvres and Meudon one finds wild flowers, and one can still walk about for hours without meeting a soul. And then the lovely sky effects upon the river coming back! Neuilly, by the river, is also charming; there is a little classic temple which I think I have seen in one of Corot's pictures. I believe he painted a good deal at Neuilly. Another delightful walk is from Suresnes home through the Bois to Passy. Also more difficult to get at, are Charenton and St. Mandé and Vincennes. I love Paris; it is the place for artists, for every corner gives you subjects for work. Not only in quaint scraps of buildings, but in the people. Compare the French labourer with ours. The one in blue blouse and trousers—the Auvergnats in blue or brown corderoy trousers *à la* Lord Dundreary, and then the Englishman in soil-coloured clothes or the worn out ones of a better class. And the women. White caps and coloured handkerchiefs, short skirts and neat though clumsy foot gear, and the English woman's dirty black bonnet and jacket and long gown all be-draggled and muddy—all set off by shoes with high heels worn down and toes bursting out at the sides. Compare the appropriate costume of the *femme de ménage* with the worn out lady's dress of a charwoman!

A SPINSTER AUNT

I find so many painters here work upon a white ground; they put on an impasto of white paint (zinc white is the purest, but it has less body than lead), and let it dry thoroughly, and then scrape it down to an even surface, and paint upon it *au premier coup*. Monsieur Delaunay works in this way and I believe also Paul Baudry. Hence the brilliancy of their colour. The only objection to this system is that one must keep a number of canvases ready, as one never knows the sizes one may want. It takes weeks to dry properly—the white foundation, I mean, so you have to look a long way ahead. The Impressionists of course paint thinly, but one would not go to them for colour! I wonder if they use grey canvas? It stands to reason that what is underneath must work through in time. There is nothing nicer to work on than an old failure with white scumbled over it. But impatient people would not wait long enough for the canvas to dry and then a nicely cracked picture would be the result. I wonder if the Impressionists will go on painting as they do now, or if it be simply a craze? Is not the great fault of the Impressionists the eccentricity of making their subject on too large a scale for their canvas; and so having the frame almost touching head, hands, and feet.

I had a shock on Sunday. You know how devoted I am to Batiste's organ voluntaries and still more to his manner of playing—it is a lesson for me, and when I return home I always try and make my free and gratis lessons profitable on the St. John's organ by buying some of his works. He has a manner of accompanying a reed melody upon the tremolo and vox humana or vox celeste stops, the effect of which is like far off voices, one might say Angels voices if Fra Angelico's Angels really sang; it is exquisite; and since I came back to Paris, I naturally migrate on Sundays to St. Eustache. The other day I conceived a burning desire to see this divine soul-ful organist, so I waylaid him at the foot of the organ staircase. The door opened and he came forth from the darkness. What did I see? A little fat Frenchman filling up the turret stairs with a bald head and common place, pasty countenance—Alas! it is a mistake to desire to see the envelope of a great mind, or of a poetic soul. He is the finest organist I ever heard, not even excepting Saint Saëns—Batiste has so much soul and taste, which does not mean that S. S. is soul-less; but Batiste to me, is more sympathetic.

I wish you could have heard an old Colonel at the Pension I was at in the rue de Provence talk of art. He discoursed volubly: 'Art! Art is Dead! there has been no art anywhere since the 15th Century. Look at pictures, statues, carvings, all Dead, Dead.' I can only express his emphatic manner by putting capitals to the words.

A SPINSTER AUNT

'But,' said I in a humble and meek manner as if I were talking of army administration of which naturally I know nought, 'but do you not allow that Millais and Leighton, and Bonnat have done a decent thing or two?'

'Bonnar, who's Bonnar, I never heard of him.' I saw a grin passing round the table.

'Well, he's a painter they think a good deal of here.'

'Ah? I cannot admit that I think much of French art, it's worse than English, for our painters—of course I don't mean Mr. Leighton—our painters mostly have some sense of decency. But here the Salon is crammed full of indecencies—naked men and naked women; the whole place is quite unfit for a modest woman to walk through.'

'Also the garden?'

'Oh! sculpture is different, there's no colour; but even there, it's not nice to be obliged to sit and sip one's coffee between two or three nudities. No, I say again there is no art now; neither painting, nor poetry, nor music, especially in France.'

'Poor us. Poor Hugo, poor Tennyson, poor Gounod.'

'Gounod? is that the man who wrote the "Grande Duchesse" which my son dragged me to see the other night; a disgusting opera. Luckily my daughters were not there, or I should have been obliged to leave.'

'Which of course you would have preferred?'

No answer. In the evening the old man took me aside, saying he wanted to speak seriously to me. 'Have you a mother?'

'No, only a step.'

'I suppose she has no influence upon you. Have you no father?'

'Yes, the most upright and kindly of men.'

'And yet he allows you to come to Paris alone, to study degraded art. What an extraordinary man. Is he old and foolish, or a dreamer, or what?'

'He's a doctor, and he wished me to come.'

'Good Heavens! A Doctor who ought to know life, and especially life in Paris, and in a Paris studio! And he, a doctor, lets his daughter come here for the purpose of mixing with the most degraded of people—artists and models. He ought to know better.'

'So ought you,' I wanted to say; but what is the use of arguing with an ignorant bigot?

I am glad I left the Pension; I hate them, though one does sometimes meet pleasant folk. Even this old idiot's daughter was charming and we chummed together. But what a life those girls must lead! Thank goodness, doctors are not so worldly wise as ancient Indian Colonels.

I wish you could see Manet's 'Toreador tué,' it is such a fine thing, although it finds plenty of detractors. Of course it is suggestive of Velasquez'

A SPINSTER AUNT

'Warrior'; but is really more suggestive of Goya in style. Still I do not see why a Modern should not try and emulate the masterpiece of an Old Master when it is a *tour de force* as both these fore-shortened figures are. But Manet is at times crude and hideous, as in the 'Olympia' and her black woman and the 'Déjeuner sur l'Herbe,' vulgar and ridiculous. One wonders how the same man could have produced the 'Fifre' and the 'Guitarero' as these others. Good bye dear cousin.

Your affectionate JEANNE.

P.S.—I am adding this because I do not want you to think I object to the nude. There is nothing objectionable in painting Nymphs and people of that kind who are in the habit of living out of doors without clothes; and presumably, if they had meals at all, would have taken their food in a wild state, uncooked, and without knives and forks. Can anything be more refined than Henner's pictures? But for Manet to place his model, (I suppose she is not a lady friend?) even as Eve before her natural gluttony got the better of her; to place this woman on the grass, as nature made her, with himself and a friend partaking of luncheon as the god Pan and his family might have done, is just a little—well I was going to say indecent, but let us say indelicate—certainly it is not an example of refinement in a painter who has done better things. Probably it was only painted to shock people (pictures are frequently painted here for that purpose), and so to draw attention to his work. One felt inclined to adapt a story of Aunt Priscilla's to the poor chilly model. A quakeress seeing a lady in a low dress, remarked: 'Take my shawl, Friend; I fear thou wilt take thy death of cold.'

May 29th 1869.   RUE BLANCHE.

DEAREST COUSIN

I have been pursuing processions, *Fête Dieu* ones. At Montrouge it was very quaint, but at Sèvres it was quainter. The old church is rather tumble down, but the streets dressed with sheets on each side and festoons of roses were very picturesque—it might have been a hundred miles from Paris. We processioned from the church through the town and then through a part of the park, headed by the Suisse in gorgeous attire. It was very pretty, and the children in white strewing rose leaves, not the least pretty part. In a way, the French are very conservative; they hold to old costume and manners, and so are never commonplace, and not often vulgar; I mean the labouring classes—there's plenty of vulgarity elsewhere. The other day there was a review; the Emperor we missed, but the Empress passed us in a carriage and four, and then the small Prince with an escort of 30 or 40 soldiers. He is a delicate looking little fellow, with a pleasant face like his mother. I wonder what will be his future. You will wonder when I work, for I seem to be seeing Paris a good deal and prowling round. Did I tell you in my last that on Easter Sunday I went to the Russian church and saw the babies make their first Communion? During the mass they ran about upon the carpeted floor, which is not very diverting; and then they were taken up to the priest who gave them the Holy Eucharist in a spoon. To the Western mind it looks just a little irreverent. Archbishop Darboy giving the blessing at Notre-Dame was far more impressive. I like the Russian singing, but it is very monotonous. At first one feels it to be charming; then you get a little tired; and you end by never wishing to hear it again. The other night, Madame F. and I went to the Lyrique to hear 'La Flûte Enchantée.' What exquisite music it is. Cavalho sang charmingly, and Nilsson, as the Queen of Night. Cavalho was Tamina. People are not obliged to dress at most of the Paris theatres. At the Opera they generally do; but dress not being compulsory you see our compatriots in travelling checked suits, which of course no Frenchman would wear in the stalls even if he did not feel himself obliged to be *en habit noir*. The only theatre where dress is rampant is the Italian Opera, where nearly every woman is covered with diamonds. The theatres are all abominally hot, but one can get air between the acts in the *foyer* and on the balcony. After the performance was over, Monsieur G., who went with us, suggested ices, so we went to Tortoni, and I thought now the desire of my heart will be fulfilled; viz. to sit out on the Boulevard at night. Arrived at the Café, what did we do but mount the stairs and enter a *cabinet privé*. Alas! for human wishes; there we sat, we three, and had nothing to look at but four walls papered with false trellis and false roses. My heart sank into the depths of despair. There was an exciting ten minutes on Wednesday during 'Don Giovanni.' Just at the end of the down below part, which here consists of strange shades flitting about in red fire, there was some allusion to Liberty in the chorus, when up started a man in the gallery, clapped his hands and shouted '*Vive la Liberté!*' Poor fellow, he was requested to depart peacefully, but silently.

I saw what would make a pathetic picture the other day going to Versailles, where I am copying a portrait. It was a pouring wet day, and in front of a miserably poor looking cottage was the coffin of a baby child resting upon two old rush chairs, and covered with a ragged sheet. There was all the conventional paraphernalia of the *chapelle ardente*, but oh! so poor and squalid; the candles guttering in the wind, the broken jug for Holy Water, the one-legged Crucifix and a small wreath of *immortelles*. And by the side was a half-starved dog tearing up the poor little babe's headless doll. No one was near—only a donkey grazing upon the shabby grass along the side of the road. Was the child the only one, that the puppy was allowed to destroy its doll?

I was reflecting as I wandered through the Louvre on Wednesday whether museums are really attractive to the multitude; for much as we may value them in the abstract, in practice we leave them very much to enjoy an unbroken solitude. What can be more delightful than to improve our minds? What can be more attractive than to study pictures, or coins, or sculpture, and gems? Even stuffed birds and dried plants have their admirers; and yet, when we enter the gates of these dwellings of miscellaneous objects of interest, especially if it be a provincial assemblage, a kind of torpor enters into our souls, with the lamentable result—a prematurely languid body. And yet how delightful some museums are to the cultured and to the enquirer! a kind of materialized 'Harry and Lucy' or 'Sandford and Merton,' without the tiresome French governess, the superior 'moral-drawing' mama, and the ineffably boring Mr. Barlow. A museum is essentially a mart of knowledge-made-easy, which ought to be as entertaining as a ballet or a quick-change actor. But is it? One often sees the 'Masses' at South Kensington, and occasionally at the National Gallery; but they mostly wander about in a vague, aimless manner. And as to the 'Classes,' they, being supposed to have some knowledge of art, feel themselves justified in visiting the National collections of pictures occasionally, but never even give a thought to the marvels in Bloomsbury, unless a millionaire has bequeathed his valuables to the nation; and then the fashionable world crowds to see those wonderful vases and knockers and jewels, which are priced at £200,000. That is the attraction; 'Only think,' you may hear over and over again, 'the 265 objects in this small room are worth, on the average, some £751 or thereabouts a-piece.' 'Dear me!'

But if the fascination of a museum in London does not outweigh the terrible depression caused by the stuffy atmosphere, what are we to say of those emporiums of dusty, moth-eaten, stuffed birds, and astonishingly bad local pictures which we find in small provincial towns? It is true, South Kensington sends various exhibits on loan; but it usually happens that if the industry of the place be pottery, the headquarters' staff consider jewellery a fitting loan; and if, on the other hand, textile fabrics or carpets are made in the town, carved wood or ceramics are placed in the museum for the education of the factory hands. Now could not our Provincial Museums be made of more use by a system of classification? For instance, if pottery be the local industry, why should not the main exhibits at the museum be specimens of ceramic art of good design? If it be carpet manufacture, let textile fabrics abound; if fishing, all that the fishermen may study for edification,—stuffed fish, boats, tackle, and so on.

And again, why should not the museum be a centre of technical study, and a lecture hall, where discourses upon the local industry could be given by experts?

Salisbury, besides the celebrated Blackmore collection, possesses a miscellaneous collection of objects, and at Wilton there is the well-known carpet factory. Is it impossible to work the two together, and so improve the carpet industry by setting forth first rate examples of Persian, Indian, and other Textiles? And then as to lectures. The mere placing of specimens, valuable in themselves, higgledy-piggledy in glass cases, cannot teach the ignorant—explanations are necessary. In fact the museum ought to be a part of the local technical school, and should teach designing and other matters connected with the local industry, besides affording pleasure to those who visit it, by exhibiting objects which appeal to the workers' knowledge of their particular industry. Surely the museum of a district of potteries might show specimens of Foreign pottery and encaustic tiles. Is it too wild a dream to hope that if specimens of Persian and Rhodian tiles were exhibited in the local museum of some pottery districts, an improvement in taste might result? At present we all suffer agonies from every sort of inappropriate design bounding our fire-grates—vases of flowers, bunches of roses shaded to give them the appearance of being in high relief, and coloured in the most hideous tones; and yet the persons who design these horrors, wherever they may be made, are probably students of some local art school, the master of which cannot have instructed them in the simplest and most elementary principles of design. Why then should not the museum be made an educator, and why should not South Kensington send, on loan, objects which would be of educational value to the local craftsmen? There is no reason why glass workers and carpet hands should not have iron work and wood-carving to look at; but the bulk of the exhibits ought to be such as will interest the men in their own line of work, otherwise they will not visit the museum at all. The man who forges iron gates would gain by seeing designs or models of fine wrought iron work, but jewellery, however exquisite its workmanship, or lace of the most excellent design, would probably be quite uninteresting to him. On the other hand, specimens of fine lace would be of great interest to workers at Honiton and Beer.

In France, most of the provincial towns possess admirable museums both as regards their contents, and architecturally. At Rouen the staircase is decorated with one of the finest works of Puvis de Chavannes, a labour of love; the great gallery contains some very fine Corots, and other examples of the French School of painting; but the principal attraction is a first-rate collection of Rouen ware. Of course the practice of the State purchasing pictures at the Salon, and presenting them to the painters' native towns, not only encourages art, but fosters local patriotism and emulation. I was painting at the Louvre one day, and these ideas were flitting across my brain as I walked back to my seat and went on with my work, when up came an American lady. 'Can you tell me where the French pictures are? I don't mean the old things, I am sick to death of Madonnas and Children. Wherever one goes in Italy, there is nothing but "Madonna and Child," "Madonna and Child," and they are all alike' (accent strong of New York). I offered to take the lady round and we walked through the rooms of the early French painters—Clouet, and the illuminators of divers manuscripts. 'What queer things these are,' saith she.

Arrived at the Greuse mediocrities, she warmed up slightly; the 'Cruche Cassée' was nice; but 'Madame Récamier' *was* queer; she looked 'very uncomfortable on that hard sofa.' 'And her curls —Just like Ma's.'

At last we arrived at Robert's 'Vintage' pictures.

'Ah! I do like them. Could you copy one for me? How much?'

'That depends on size.'

'Well, say half.' Price stated.

'Oh! all that. Well, I guess I'll wait till I get back to Italy; they are much cheaper there.'

'But you won't find Robert's "Vintage" there.'

'No? Well, I'll find something.'

The Louvre sets an excellent example for teaching the public in its lectures by the Curators, called the Ecole du Louvre. But these are not much affected by the upper classes. Will they ever care for art? One hears at the Salon on a Sunday such criticisms from men in blouses as you would never, or very rarely hear at the Royal Academy, where most well-dressed people begin at No. 1 and go respectably round to No. 750.

'What is No. 70, Dear?'

'Oh! is not the child a love?'

'Yes; but I want to know the subject.'

'Mother's darling.'

'Well, she is that. And what's 91?'

'The Meet.'

'Well, that is pretty; and how the dogs' tails all stand up. One can fancy they really are wagging.'

'No. 105 seems to be a wedding; so many flowers and fine dresses.'

'No; it is a Spanish Child's funeral.'

'Oh! Mary, do look at the carrots and onions in that No. 205.'

'It's called "Still Life." I never heard carrots called that before, did you?'

Not one remark about the work, the colour, or the drawing. Certainly we do not love Art with a capital A. for Art's sake.

Dear Mary, this is all too long a letter, so I bid you farewell. Ever your loving   JANE.

[No date.—ED.]

PARIS.

Have you ever, dear Mary, seen any translations from 'the Book of the Dead'? I was amusing myself yesterday at the Louvre. The Egyptian sentiments are very much akin to ours, and the following is as true of a 19th Century mother as of an early Dynasty lady: 'Bitterness finds no entrance into the heart of a mother.' And here again is Solomon: 'Do not act according to the counsels of a fool.' Has it ever occurred to you that if a saying is not Shakespeare's it must be Solomon's?

The next is a morality which might be written up in letters of gold upon our public buildings, with advantage, perhaps, to some members of the modern world: 'That thou mayest not ill-treat thy wife whose strength is weaker than thine own; but that she may find in thee her protector.'

And the religious sentiments are really beautiful and quite Christian in feeling:

RECOLLECTIONS OF

'... Great God living in thy dwelling-place; thy name is a mystery to all the gods; thy form is hidden ... living ... Thou givest breath to every one.' And here is a prayer of great beauty: 'O Saviour! who art in the great temple, (turn) thy face towards me, give unto me my lips and my speech; give me back my heart ... that I may not be rejected by heaven nor by the earth ... turn thy face towards me ... open my mouth that I may speak; give me my legs that I may walk, and my arms that I may overturn mine enemies eternally.' ... 'O! I possess thee, turn not away from me ... that my heart may not be carried off by the (torturers?) ... the light is placed in mine eyes that I may walk by night and by day, that I may contemplate his rays eternally. His desire is that I should travel over the world unto the horizon of heaven; and he will not let me die in the place of burial ... I see with mine eyes! I hear with mine ears; I am the possessor of the second life for ever.'

All the world's akin.

Returning from Egypt, I passed through the galleries where some illuminated manuscripts are displayed, and overheard a most interesting conversation symbolic of British culture and showing the advantages of travel.

A lady and her son.

'Look at this one, Cecil. Italian, 16th Century. Is it not singularly like a mosaic?'

A SPINSTER AUNT

' Yes, mother, you are right.'

' It reminds me of those we saw in the church of Monreale, you know.'

' Monreale ? '

' Yes, the church, you remember, covered with mosaics. In Sicily; surely you have not forgotten Monreale ? where the Guide snuffled so.'

It is time I left off, so goodbye.

Oh! I forgot to tell you a friend took me the other day to see the new Sardou play with Desclée as poor Frou-Frou. She is wonderful: in the great scene there was not a dry eye in the theatre, masculine or feminine.

[No date.—ED.]

DEAR MARY

I am offered a post, looking after the girls at a Studio, Monsieur Bertin's, three days a week, and I have accepted it as I shall profit thereby all ways. Monsieur dislikes the mercantile part of such work. Who likes it? but doing it for another person is not so disagreeable as for oneself. The wind is roaring so I can hardly keep my thoughts straight. I begin tomorrow. . . .

I wrote the above three weeks ago. It is not bad working rue Blanche at M. Bertin's. There are some nice girls there, a daughter of Edmond About, and two Italians, daughters of a sculptor. Also my old fellow worker of whom I told you,

Madame the Russian. A funny old French lady who paints miniatures, a South American and some more French girls, complete the party.

The other day a new girl arrived with her Papa, I should think from the Faubourg St. Antoine; evidently a *commerçant*. 'I wish, Monsieur, my daughter to study seriously, very seriously for a couple of years, as I want her to become a professional artist. When do you think she will be able to send to the Salon?'

'Has Mademoiselle worked before?'

'Not since she was at the Pension.'

'Have you brought any of her drawings to show me?'

'*Oui, Monsieur, les voilà.*'

Thereat the drawings were displayed. Terrible things; groups in chalk of plaster fruits and leaves. Monsieur looked at them quite seriously, and replied equally so: '*Eh bien, Monsieur, nous verrons plus tard; mais pas cette année, je pense; elle a le temps.*' Whereat Papa departed to tell Mama, that '*sans doute*' Monsieur Bertin will let our daughter '*expose*' next year or the year after; 'and from his manner he thinks her extremely clever.' The girl told us this at the next lesson. Poor innocents. . . .

I take up this letter and add to it from time to time. Le Patron has gone away to examine schools in the south, so we are now under the care of Messieurs Baudry, Toulmouche, Hébert, and

A SPINSTER AUNT

Delaunay, his friends. An amusing thing happened on Tuesday. I had not got beyond drawing the head in brown umber when in walks Monsieur Toulmouche. He found fault with my work, and corrected it according to his views. After he had departed we all talked of his corrections, and did not think much of them. In walks Monsieur Delaunay—he had mistaken the day. When he came round to me he said: 'How in the world' (something to that effect) 'how in the world can you have seen the girl like that?' Of course I had not seen her 'like that,' but how could I have said who did it? Every one looked at me, but I held my peace. Monsieur took my palette and brushes and thereupon painted the head in entirely fresh. When he had gone every one screamed out, 'Why did you not tell him?' 'I would not have let him think I had done it,' and so on, and so on. However I was rewarded, for I kept the canvas as it was as a Delaunay, and began another.

We have had a model who poses for Christs, a villainous looking fellow; and you should have seen his face when I said he would do better for a Judas. I did not think of his understanding English. I hope he won't murder me.

.   .   .   .   .   .

I went today to see De Jonghe and tell him I could not have more than one lesson a week at my own studio, and I came in for a treat. Litolff was there, and after much persuading he sat down at the piano, and thundered away a selection, improvised as he went on, from the 'Huguenots.' It was splendid! and he not only works with his hands, but with his whole body and his hair. He must have posed for that German print of the *Virtuoso*, where, in the last picture, arms and legs and head are all mixed up together. The perspiration fell from Litolff's face as in the print, and in time no doubt the pond would have been seen!

Hébert's corrections were nearly as imaginative as Toulmouche's, only of course he is a far greater artist; but he always makes long necks whatever the person's own may be like; just as all Rossetti's women have goitres. Is it beautiful? I always thought the likening of a woman's neck to the swan's was its whiteness?

Goodbye dear Cousin. I am going home in two weeks and I do not think I shall write again before I find myself in the old Den. . . .

I said I would not write again, but I must relate a dog story to you. I saw some performing dogs the other evening who acted a Tournament, and after fighting, one was supposed to be killed. A bier was brought in and the dead animal placed upon it. Then four beasties came in walking on their hind legs, and the bier was put upon their shoulders. Thereupon every one clapped, and the dead beastie unable to restrain his emotion wagged his tail, whereat there was more applause and roars of laughter.

A SPINSTER AUNT

CHAPTER XIV

THE FRANCO-GERMAN WAR

THE DEN. *May* 1 1870

MY DEAR MARY

I am off to Paris tomorrow, and this year I intend keeping a diary which I will send over from time to time. It will be really a letter or letters, in the form of a diary as I mean to try and write every evening, and jot down anything in the day's work which may be interesting; so Goodbye. I daresay you will have the first instalment soon.

Ever your affectionate   JANE.

AVENUE FROCHOT,
PARIS. *May 3rd* 1870.

MY DEAR MARY.

I came over by the night boat and third class train. It is not exactly comfortable, but walking up the jetty and through the old gate—Hogarth's 'Calais Gate'—by moonlight is pleasant enough. It was a lovely night and not cold, and I always feel elated, however I may travel, when I first hear the pattering of *sabots* and the clattering of voices, shrill though they may be. There is a sensation of something running down one's back bone which one never feels in England; it is, I think, grey depression taking flight. It is the same feeling which makes my little dog shake the sheep skin mats when overjoyed at my return.

I found the woman and her keys at the station, and as is my wont, I asked her to unlock the Ladies waiting room, and there, upon two velvet chairs I slept from 3 to 5.30 while the 'bloated aristocrats' were hurrying on to Paris by the express train. At 5.30, or before, I made some tea and enjoyed my breakfast. I then went out and wandered round the old walls and ramparts and hearing the clanging of Notre Dame her bell, I went into the church for the first mass. Only a few white capped women were there. It was soothing after the disturbance of the boat, mental if not physical. At Amiens I stayed a few hours to see the Cathedral with its lofty nave and tiny *flèche*, the top of which is the height of Sarum spire. Think of the relative heights of the naves. The porches as in all French churches are very fine. Why did English builders always make such mean entrances? The North Transept porch of the Abbey[1] is deep and imposing, but the church was probably built by a Frenchman. The town

[1] Westminster.—ED.

A SPINSTER AUNT

of Amiens is picturesque, a good deal of sketching might be done there in the way of old houses, and in the country about—watery things; it is not far from the peat country with its long lanky trees. You know I am enamoured of French meadow and pasture land. There is an elegance about it ours does not possess, except in Wiltshire beyond Salisbury along the little river Wylie, where abeles flourish, and wave their grey, silver-lined leaves in the wind. All, or almost all flat land in France has tall lanky trees of some sort— of course fashioned to grow so for fuel; but wood is getting scarce and coal is taking its place— worse luck as far as cleanliness of living and skies are concerned.

I arrived here eventually by the omnibus train. All things come to an end, even a 3d class journey in France. A friend took this place for me from an artist named Boutibonne; I believe he helped Winterhalter in his awful Royalties, and he was somehow mixed up with the Crawshays and painted a picture of a smelting works with fires blazing up at a white heat. It is not a bad little house standing against a larger one, but very isolated. Surely, had I known it was so isolated, I should not have taken it. It is near the end of the Avenue which is an *impasse* giving on to the Boulevard de Clichy, so it is very quiet, as one only hears a distant rumble of vehicles on the Boulevard. Mrs. Greata came in and I made some tea, and we had a nice little chat; but she was rather more flabbergasted than I was at the idea of my sleeping here alone. The gates of the Avenue are locked at night, and only artists inhabit the houses, so burgling is not a very probable danger. The entrance to this delectable spot is in the rue Laval. The Studio is a large and ghostly room, the whole height of the building; a little entry leads to it and beyond this is a tiny kitchen. Above is a bedroom with two windows; one looking into the garden, the other into the Studio; so you see it is very compact, and just the thing, but I should have preferred a studio with apartments in one of the larger houses. But I am too great a coward to admit my want of courage, so I must make the best of it. Days are getting longer and nights less dark. The old servant interviewed me and said she came every morning and would get my coffee and do the *ménage*, and would come again in the evening if I liked; but as I am sure to go about a good deal I said no. So you see I am truly what one of the nephews calls me, a bachelor aunt.

In the Studio which is deliciously large and light, there are a number of huge canvases, some on easels, and some with their faces turned to the wall. Notably a large copy of Madame Venus by Rubens, and a good copy it is as regards colour. Looking into the Studio from the little bedroom, she seems ghostly—in fact the whole place is, and the sensation that one might be robbed and murdered and no one any the wiser until old Adolphine arrived in the morning is not a lively one; and it is a drawback *de plus* that I have no means of communication with the world, but hammering at the wall, a feeble idea, as the wall may be that of a studio which is sure to be empty at night, and possibly also by day. However, one could shout and one *might* be heard —consoling, that! I daresay I shall soon get used to it, and when one has plenty to do, one soon becomes superior to imaginary terrors. The Concierge comes up the road and puts my letters upon the doorstep, and I peep out of the window, and we give each other a pleasant '*Bon Jour*'; and I fancy I see in his long thin face a contented expression as if he were glad I am yet alive. That of course is foolishness born of untoward circumstances.

6th. I began to work this morning. I have the same model that I had last year; she is an agreeable woman, knows heaps of artists and is useful in many ways and pleasant to talk to. We had some tea in the garden, and I have made a few little sketches which may be useful some day and are good for study as regards light and shade.

9th. Madame Caron has found me a child of about four. Her grandmother brought her today and I shall do something with her. The Master uses her and says she sits well. I had a letter to-day from Mr. Johns asking me if I could find out where in the rue des Martyrs a certain Baron lived who is said to be a hundred and nine years of age; and if I can find the address, will I interview him. 'He is probably an old humbug,' saith Mr. J., 'but I want to be sure of that.'

10*th*. I find I am getting tired of trotting down the street and up again twice a day, so am dropping into my ways of last year—one journey midday, or rather 11 o'clock for I begin work at 8 and am ready for a substantial meal by 11.80; and then in the evening I consume eggs—or *galantine*, or other portable food. But I am also getting weary of egg cooking and shall soon, I expect depend upon *Madame la Charcutière* almost entirely. Figure to yourself the limited ways of disposing of eggs: *à la coque, sur le plat,* poached, *omeletted*, scrambled; that seems to be the end; then one begins again—boiled, poached, fried, scrambled; what should we do without the Lady Hen. I reckoned I must have consumed last year in my three months some 120 eggs, and all the winter I felt I must leave them alone; but now you see I am starting fresh, and Paris eggs are not as London ones, 'fresh,' 'superior,' 'newly laid,' 'good cooking,' and so on, but really, newly laid; *i.e.* within a day or two.

18*th*. The child sits very well. This afternoon

A SPINSTER AUNT

I discovered the antique gentleman in a little apartment high up in the street of Martyrs; he evidently thinks himself a true and veritable centenarian. He has relics of the battle of Austerlitz. He is tall and thin and talked much; but he only convinced me that his claim to be the *twenty-first* centenarian in his family was very pure fiction.

20*th*. I have not written for some time as my daily life trudges on with nothing very interesting to record. Work, the river, walks in the woods, museums, and so on. The Salon has taken up a good deal of my spare time; there is a wealth of good things, especially landscapes; I wish English people would study the wonderful pictures of the Paysagistes of this country, and cease to talk of good landscapes and water colour painting being peculiarly the outcome of British talent. Some of the American men are coming on. Of course the States have no school, but they do the wise thing in coming here to study. Their work is certainly French in character, but some day they will break off from servile imitation and start an American school founded upon the best in the world. The Scandinavians are doing likewise. But the *clou* of the Salon is Regnault's 'Salomé'—Paris has gone mad over 'Salomé,' and we may expect next year's Salon to be a Salomé year, for it is curious how '*les beaux esprits se rencontrent.*' One year it is pigs—pigs in styes, pigs grubbing for truffles, pigs being slain. Another year it is Hospitals—operations with doctors in white aprons holding instruments, nurses attending to patients, poor little dying babies watched by disconsolate fathers or mothers. There seems always to be an inspiration running through the brains of a dozen men at the same time. But this year 'Salomé' disputes the first place with no one. Every where you go: 'What think you of "Salomé"?' She is 'superb,' 'crude,' 'vulgar,' 'marvellous,' 'unique,' 'the finest thing ever painted,' 'the most deplorable example of colour gone mad.' It is 'grand art,' and '*grand art manqué.*' All the papers talk of 'Salomé'; she has a crowd round her all day long. M. Edmond About calls it an '*incontestable chef-d'œuvre*'; Théophile Gautier finds it the East itself: '*Prim, c'est toute l'Espagne; Salomé, c'est tout l'Orient.*' Another critic calls it a '*Souillon de harem que la fantaisie du peintre a lavé et paré.*' (This I think was the *Figaro*; Louis Veuillot probably; but I had such a collection of newspapers to read my brain may be confused.) You don't know what it is to have a 'Salomé' on the brain! Then other wise men call Regnault a mere 'imitator'; of whom I should like to know? And a few will wait to give judgment upon the talent of the painter until he produces more original work. '*Nous attendrons pour nous prononcer qu'il nous ait permis de dégager les éléments de son originalité.*' Paris is once again in the throes of civil war; and the two camps are the admirers and the defamers of 'Salomé' the murderess. Perhaps the best criticism is: 'How could such an animal, for she is merely the embodiment of a female biped, fascinate even an Oriental potentate?' But that is a matter upon which the rest of us can form no opinion.

Have you seen any photographs or prints of 'Salomé'? though they can give no adequate idea of the picture. I daresay not; so I will just jot down the list of colours and tones worked into this marvellous picture, which seems to knock you down when you approach it, with its extraordinary richness of colour and harmony. Of course one sees in it the fascination of the East—Regnault like every other painter who goes to the lands of Islam, is Orient-mad. Then also, there is an echo of Fortuny, that marvellous colourist. Regnault, living at Tangiers in a Moorish house where the absence of a chair is said to be a fact, is of course influenced by his surroundings. And is that astonishing? Who that has ever crossed the Mediterranean is not fascinated by the gaily dressed North Africans, in Alger, or Tunis? The higher classes of men seem to belong to a spectacular representation of 'Othello,' and the poorer folk appear to be Abraham's descendants straight out of Bible land. And the *Fantasias* which take place—the richly apparelled steeds of the Kaids, the beautiful Arabs themselves, more beautiful than any European horses, and the wondrous costumes of the riders. They say that Regnault did no end of work in the Alhambra before he went to Tangiers, in water-colour or rather *gouache*, but I have not seen any of his sketches. But to return to Mademoiselle 'Salomé'; she has quite taken the shine out of poor General Prim who dominated last year's Salon. The main feature of the picture is light—it is a study of light, glistening, sparkling light. In the centre you get the contrast of the woman's thick wavy hair, a mass of black upon a pale lemon coloured background. 'Salomé' is a hideous creature, a grinning monster framed by a mass of tangled black hair. She is sitting upon a stool incrusted in mother of pearl; upon her knees is the charger, a large embossed brass dish. Her left hand holds the sword or scimitar, her right rests upon her hip, which gives the necessary trait of vulgarity to the woman. Her body is swathed in yellow drapery, her waist in a mauve scarf, her feet are partially resting in gorgeous violet slippers lined with scarlet—not the usual yellow of the Moslem world, and the knees are covered with folds of sparkling gold and green transparent gauze drapery. Add to all this a little touch of rose red on one shoulder and a dove-coloured scarf embroidered in gold hanging over one arm. What think you of that *mélange* of colour? And yet it is exquisitely harmonious in tone, possibly brought into harmony by a border of ebony round the canvas. Here you may frame your pictures as you like; the appropriateness of the frame to the picture, is considered—whereas in England pictures are looked upon as wall decoration only, like the paper or paint; so they must all be in gold whether that suits their complexions or not. And I cannot see that the rooms here look worse than the R. A. ones—indeed I prefer them.

It is curious that when first the Salon was opened 'Salomé' was passed mostly unnoticed. It was not well hung. Regnault is lefthanded, and so the picture being lighted from the left, did not look well; and it was only after some days when it was placed with the light to the right, that people recognised its brilliancy. Every one expects 'Salomé' to get the *médaille d'honneur*. I wonder if she will. Her merits certainly are great, but it is a small picture and the *méd. d'honneur* generally goes to some huge thing, historic or religious—subject being of more importance with the Academy than *technique*. On the other hand Regnault was a *Prix de Rome*, and they generally stand a good chance of the honour.

Is not the main point in a frame that it should be becoming to the picture, a point rarely missed by a Frenchwoman in her dress, but only now and then obtained by our countrywomen. And so with pictures. Although one sees here all manner of frames, the aspect of the rooms is better than in London because each picture is becomingly attired, its frame being designed to enhance the picture's beauty. Such is 'Salomé,' and I may add that she is worth crossing the Channel to feast your eyes upon if you love gorgeous and harmonious colour; and even if the wind bloweth where it listeth and more powerfully than is pleasing to your vile body.

16*th June.* War seems to be in the air. The papers most of them speak of the Prussians not daring to invade the sacred soil of France; and the mob talks glibly of a '*promenade à Berlin*'; while the Government panders to the people. The only sensible folk seem to be the Liberals who are speaking out as they never have before—men like Grévy advocating calm and prudence. Supposing it comes to war, are the French the equals of the Prussians? Again the French have great faith in the hatred of the population of the Rhine provinces towards Prussia; but when we, Margaret and I, were pottering about the great river two years ago, we heard of no love towards France. The Rhenish folk hate Prussia, but they hate France still more. Some people say the Emperor is against war, and now the Hohenzollern man has retired from the candidature of Spain's throne, there seems no reason for quarrelling, though it is possible that Bismark desires war, being ready, whether France be or not.

A SPINSTER AUNT

17*th*. We are getting more warlike, and they say the Empress is egging on her weaker (?) half. The poor man is also said to be ill. We foreigners of course know how things are through our papers; the French ones have suppressed all news. I devoutly hope it will be warded off as I do not want to leave Paris, and if it came to a siege, of course I could not stay; it would worry the father; but all the same I should like the experience and I could be useful. However I shall stay as long as I can. Some one today said, 'How can you talk of the Prussians coming to Paris, Mademoiselle? They dare not.' I did not say so; but they came before!

18*th*. I saw the Imperials today going to the Bois. He, She, and It. The Empress is still a good looking woman though, of course, not the beauty she was when they went over to England, (in 1856 was it?), when I saw them at the Crystal Palace with the Queen and Prince Albert. Only 14 years ago! Then they were in the height of their glory, and the friendship with England at, and after the Crimean War gave Louis Napoléon a certain *cachet* of respectability. Since then how many wars, and yet we go on crying '*L'Empire, c'est la Paix*' and in the same breath, we cry '*à Berlin!*' The Austrian war, and the Italian campaigns have succeeded and Italy is united, or nearly so, and should the Government here require all its troops, those from Rome will be recalled; and then?

The *Lanterne* is most amusing reading now; I will send you a specimen. Rochefort says just what he likes and no one stops him. So likewise the ultra Radical papers. It seems today as if war were likely to be averted. Prussia is doing all she can apparently; but Bismark is wary and wise, and no one here is his equal. Who knows whether with the wisdom of the serpent and the cunning of the skilled diplomatist, he may not be so scheming that war, if declared, may be the act of France? For such a man, it may not be difficult to egg your enemy on, and by suave words to make the trusting world think you are his friend. Time alone will show, for the papers here tell us nothing; I only gather news from my *Times* and the Belgian newspapers which the master has.

19*th*. The Emperor is becoming more and more unpopular. When he drives in the Champs Elysées there is little cheering, and what there is is meant, they say, for the boy. He is a delicate looking little fellow, very like his mother in face. The Emperor is withal a kind man. I heard a story today which is probably a pure fiction, but is typical. He asked one of the Turcos on guard at the palace if he were happy in Paris. The man said, 'Yes, but he was so cold.' He had no gloves on. I thought all soldiers wore gloves? So the Emperor sent him some warm ones. Such are the little stories which make up the Imperial newspapers, as the scandals of Madame * * * and Monsieur * * * * * make up the *Figaro*. And all the time we are dying of impatience about this wretched war scare.

July 2nd. 'Salomé' is *médaillée* but not with the *Médaille d'Honneur*. I wonder why, for it is far and away, as a colour study, and for strength, *the* picture of the year; and as far as one can see Regnault is the most promising of all the younger men; but 'Salomé' is a small picture and the *M. d'H.* always goes to a big one. M. Tony Robert-Fleury's 'Derniers jours de Corinthe' is such—quantity rather than quality; and perhaps R. is too clever for the big-wigs. It does not always do to be too clever at the beginning of your career—you must be put back. Certainly those who know say that his studies of animals and of his Moroccan surroundings are most masterly, and being a *Prix de Rome* one would think would save him from being snubbed.

15th. War is declared! Certainly the Emperor is in the wrong as far as we know, which is not very far! And now he is popular again. Naturally it is a winning (or a losing) card to play as regards dynastic wisdom. We thought the whole dispute was patched up as the offending candidate to the Spanish Crown had been withdrawn. And now, lo! and behold! H. I. M. is not satisfied, and he has declared war. He being unpopular risks his last card—may it not be his last gasp! It is a base thing worthy of the family to thrust a country into war for nothing; not that the country wanted much thrusting! We are quite ready 'even to the last button upon the last man's gaiters'—though why the buttons should have been only recently sewn on is known only to Marshal Leboeuf and his *confrères*. The Liberals still rave against the deed, but the people have *all* turned their opinions inside out. War is always most popular in France as elsewhere, for at bottom, man is but a fighting animal in his heart of hearts, with a seemingly serious varnish of peacefulness, and until the bill comes in he loves to bluster and is not sorry to fight. I have just come from Duval; everyone is talking war, and Paris has forgotten poor 'Salomé' in her desire for a trip *à Berlin*. Just a few days' pleasure trip, '*Cela ne durera pas longtemps.*' Also, significantly, we sing the 'Marseillaise' and no one stops us; and we all shout in chorus, *à Berlin!* Moreover we carry red flags and want to wear red caps. Such is the last phase of the Empire, Monsieur Emile Ollivier's Liberalism. Whereunto will it lead?

It all came upon us today like a thunder clap. I went over to the rue St. Sulpice to see Madame Greata and stayed dinner, all the talk being, war or no war? About 9.80 a ragged regiment came along the street singing the 'Marseillaise,' waving red flags and chinese lanterns, dozens of young men and women on their way to Berlin. A little later I went round the corner to mount my Clichy-Odéon omnibus, and we rumbled along in our usual clumsy way until we arrived at the Boulevard, where we stuck fast. All Paris seemed to be congregated on that particular spot. Our friends with the flags and lanterns still shouting and singing, were picking up other delegates for the Berlin trip—it was a surging mass screaming in discordant keys, the grand old 'Marseillaise' which has endured a forced silence for some twenty years. What a fine melody it is (when sung in tune naturally, but just now enthusiasm is greater than our ear or our musical knowledge). We stuck in the crowd on the Boulevard unable to move for three quarters of an hour; but at last the cumbrous vehicle wriggled its way out, and we went up the hill. Arrived at the Avenue, the Concierge greeted me most cheerfully: '*Voilà, Mademoiselle, voilà la guerre en effet.*' But next morning my old servant presented another side of the picture as she opened the door wringing her hands: '*Ah! Mon Dieu, mon Dieu, comme c'est triste, la guerre!*' Her son had been killed in the assault of the Malakoff—'*Vous autres, vous avez été aussi à Sevastopol, n'est-ce pas?*' Experience is a wise teacher, but like a good example not always successful.

21*st*. Today I saw several regiments depart amidst much enthusiasm mingled with tears.

The troops march along between two hedges of motley crowds. Handkerchiefs are waven, women squabble as to who shall carry the men's rifles, children clutch the hands of fathers and brothers —every one sings, and shouts not a little, and one begins to feel that the 'Marseillaise' is somewhat *de trop*, if it be possible for Patriots to have too much of a good thing.

22d. In an omnibus today, a Zouave discussing the *mitrailleuse* with the conductor explained it to the admiring company thus: 'You just turn it round like a wheel, and Puff! it sweeps every one down!' The Zouave was as confident of our resources and readiness as Monsieur le Maréchal and the Turcos at the Palace gates. Besides, 'the Prussians have no *mitrailleuses*!' That was unanswerable. There is curious silence upon the part of the newspapers; I hope it be not ominous. H.I.M. is going to the front, and an ovation is expected.

28th. H.I.M. hath departed, but without the most minute ovation. The Garde Mobile has also gone, and likewise without an ovation—*au contraire*, with much lamentation and weeping of wives and mothers; and the temperature of the enthusiasm has fallen, not only because our voices are getting husky; but as 'All is well,' why call out the Garde Mobile? The fire waxes fainter, and folks begin to ask, 'Why this war?' Newspapers for news, give stories of old campaigns, and relate acts of bravery: 'Where our soldiers appear, the Prussians retire!' Another journal professes to find Prussian spies everywhere, even in the disguise of sheep's clothing—that of Sœurs de Charité! The ill-treatment of 'our brave troops' by the 'Barbarians' is a common theme. Meanwhile we meditate upon Imperial words of wisdom and comfort, as displayed upon white *affiches*.

Augt. 2nd. A battle at Saarbrück and the little Prince Imperial's 'Baptism of fire'; but I must wait for my *Times* newspaper for the particulars, and the *truth*!

August 5th. The Secret Treaty! Can it be true? If so, it seems as if Statesmen were liars of the first water, and not always polite ones.

6th. This has been a day of marvellous excitement. My *déjeuner* consisted of lamb and newspapers, or rather newspapers and lamb, for I devour the papers with more avidity than the meat. The *Liberté* says, 'Such a defeat was no defeat because followed by a victory'—no particulars. The Prussians call it 'a sanguinary battle, but a glorious victory'—so both nations are happy, and both are victorious! It is strange that the news arrived in London yesterday morning, whereas it was only *affiché* here late in the evening. Oh! those dreadful official *affiches* printed upon white paper in token of their purity! 'Although we were successful, the enemy remained in possession of the ground.' Or 'We succeeded in routing the enemy, but were unable to retain the position'—and so on. Possibly Paris may think now that the Germans are neither fools nor cowards, but as H.I.M. had the magnanimity to say, 'a noble and stubborn foe.'

And then the little meannesses of the mob! Seizing a banker named Hirsch yesterday because an *employé* made a remark in favour of Prussia; and so the police had to surround the house and write up: *Maison Française non Prussienne.* I expect it is a fact, that should a bad defeat take place the throne will collapse. If the enemy occupies Metz, the French will not accept any terms of peace, but will fall back upon Paris, with a siege as the result. Can it be possible? H.I.M. counted on a disunited Germany, and has now discovered what some of us who have travelled in Rhineland knew before—that however much the Rhenish folk may dislike Prussia, they hate France far more. I do nothing but read newspapers—work is hopeless. How can one paint without peace of mind? It is terrible seeing all the reserves going off to be killed. Ill-trained, bad shots, utterly useless except as targets for the enemy's guns. The waste of life is terrible. The last news is that the Prussians lost 80,000 or 100,000 men killed at the last battle[1] while our losses were only in four figures! One general was

[1] Woerth.—ED.

killed and another committed suicide! That alone proves it to have been a bad affair; and yet the Mobiles are said to fight like demons until it is hopeless—then they retire, or surrender, or—run. While meditating upon the sadness of defeat after defeat, which is a fact although the papers say nothing so unpleasant, in rushes Madame Caron: 'Such a splendid Victory! The Crown Prince taken prisoner and 25,000 men!' I feel faithless having read my *Times*, but looking out towards the Boulevard up go the flags, and all the shouting and singing begins over again only minus *à Berlin*. 'We must go out and get tickets for the Opera,' says G.; 'it will be like the old story of Rachel and the *Tricolor*, with Marie Sass in the place of the great tragedian.' So out we go. Crowds on the Boulevards, all the red flags and Liberty caps, and the lanterns which we thought were burnt out, have taken a return ticket. Marie Sass is espied in a *petite voiture*, and immediately she is made to stand up and sing the eternal ditty amidst peals of cheering and shouting. But five minutes later, the flags were being hauled down, 'by Emile Ollivier's order,' and the songs and cheers turned into curses and groans and cries of '*Nous sommes trahis*,' are heard all around. Groans take the place of the 'Marseillaise' and the joy on the people's faces is turned into anger. 'Don't speak,' said G.; 'they are attacking Germans, and they may think you are one.'

And at that moment a man was thrown down and would have been killed but for the Sergents de Ville. '*A bas les Prussiens, à bas l'Empereur, à bas* every one,' is the sort of feeling now. Alas! I fear the hope of a drawn battle is over, and defeat stares us in the face.

Sunday. Another white *affiche* stuck up admitting terrible defeats. MacMahon has been defeated, and Froissard has retreated—whereto we are not told; in fact Paris is treated as if it were a wayward child. Perhaps it is! Certainly there is a political reason for the reticence, and the Government's enemies assert, scarcely under their breath, that Madame la Régente is answerable for much, and that her opinion is diametrically opposed to MacMahon's;—the old error of the Home government overruling the man, and a capable man, on the spot. The poor little Prince figures no more at fire baptisms. How dramatic that was! Taking the heir to his 'Baptism of Fire'—and slightly cruel; he is a delicate boy and they say he was terribly frightened; but I should not have thought he would have been placed near enough to see the fighting. There is comfort at the end of the newest *affiche*: '*Mais tout n'est pas perdu.*' And to think that we have come to this after all our *blague*! If Metz falls 'they' will soon be here; and those who read Foreign papers feel pretty sure Metz will fall. It is a wonder our English papers are not stopped. De Jonghe also has

A SPINSTER AUNT

Belgian ones regularly. The Germans evidently have better guns, better soldiers, better discipline, more men and more power of endurance, a quality in which the French do not excel, and never did.

11*th*. I went to Neuilly to find that Edmond had been called out; he is a Garde mobile. The cook's brother has also gone and is in the camp of the enemy, being an Uhlan. Every one says, 'Will Metz hold out?' Will Metz falling mean peace, or a new *Coup d'Etat*? The whole thing seems hopeless now, but every one says, 'Oh, there is no fear; the Prussians cannot get to Paris.' I am not so sure. . . .

Another great excitement; we are put under martial law! What does that mean? I went out to make some calls, as I cannot work; besides, I wanted to gain information; but no one seems to know. Paris is always in a way under a military Governor, but it is supposed that he will be more active now. One's idea, one's only sensation is that we may all be strung up to the nearest lamp post—*à la lanterne* under a new dress. People are pouring into the city from the suburbs. Furniture and worldly goods, cattle, sheep, stores of all kinds. 'Then we really shall be invested?' 'Oh dear no; they will not dare to come to Paris, beautiful Paris'; but I heard today that the Louvre authorities are packing up the treasures which will be sent to Brest—the 'Venus de Milo' safe in her own trunk.

18th. All today the excitement has been intense; we are in 'a state of siege'; we must not utter 'seditious cries'; we rush about like restless spirits; all our pence go in newspapers, which give us no information. I went this afternoon to Dr.—out; then to the Bowdens—out; I wanted to see if I could borrow enough money to clear out in case of anything happening before my supplies arrive. At night I lie awake and think I hear the enemy's guns in the far distance; all is so quiet in the street now as if Paris were silently sobbing her life away. And I am getting tired of the endless *blague* of the papers. This is the sort of thing: 'If the Prussians have the audacity to advance upon our sacred soil (Paris, *bien entendu*), not one will leave it alive.' Very Victor Hugoish, and an appropriate sequel to *à Berlin* and 'Crossing the *Rhin Allemand* to-morrow' of one little month ago! What a contrast. 'The love of aggrandisement of the Prussians is insatiable; *ils voudraient la Venise et Trieste comme Kiel et Amsterdam*'—and so on. Were it not so ineffably sad and miserable, it would be comic. However, the reasoning public (a very small percentage of Paris) begins to see through the trump card of 'H.I.M. Napoléon-le-Petit,' and his dynasty is doomed. Will the French be completely crushed, or will the Great Powers step in before the beautiful city is destroyed? As an outsider one does not see why they should.

A SPINSTER AUNT

Quiet reigns on the Boulevards, and the state of siege means nothing more terrible than closing the gates at 10 P.M. in case a spy might slip in. Heaps of arrests have taken place lately, 'suspicious persons,' but the rest of us go on much as usual, and think no more of martial law terrors than of the ice at the North Pole. All is quiet; but it is just that quiet which kills. Last night I lay awake watching the little high-up window facing my bed, until I fancied a ladder was being placed in the garden below; and another little grain of nervousness would have disclosed the spike of a German helmet mounting the ladder step by step. I heard the distant guns—pure imagination. I got up and peeped through the window looking into the *Atelier* and I thought I saw an Uhlan and a woman supping—it was only the Rubens lady, Madame Venus, dancing in the moonlight. The railway whistles seem to be more numerous than usual, and one hears distant cries of the anti-Imperialists mixed up with the Patriots Marseillaising. 'Tis maddening; and as soon as I can, I shall depart. General Trochu is put upon the Defence Committee, to fortify Paris.

15*th.* My cheque has come, so you will soon have to read my journal in England.

16*th.* Today I trudged out to Hirsch the banker, but as ill-luck would have it, Hirsch' was one of the banks which have been closed—the name! but they are, I believe, Alsatians, which the unreasoning mob does not take into account when it throws stones at the windows. When I arrived at the Bourse, Sergents de ville were placed all round the bank. '*On ne passe pas.*' However, I begged hard and was permitted to pass round to the back door; but I was too late. '*On ferme à deux heures, Madame.*' How was I to know that? So, having nothing particular to do, I went upon an exploring expedition. I crossed the Pont de Carrousel and turned into the Rue du Bac, where I met crowds of angry visages. I recrossed the river by the Pont Royal; intending to pass through the Tuileries Gardens —closed; singing, hustling crowds at all the gates, and opposite, pouring into the court of the Corps Législatif, hundreds of *Députés*. '*A bas l'Empereur*' is muttered everywhere, and the most curious thing is the complete absence of Sergents de Ville, which looks bad, as one may be sure the secret police are correspondingly numerous and active. Seeing we were in for a thunderstorm, I ran round to the Faubourg St. Honoré and took refuge in a *Café*. No sooner was I within, than a crowd of blue and white Blouses ran down the street. '*Fermez, fermez,*' every one screamed, and up went the shutters; but '*à bas l'Empereur*' was sufficiently sonorous to be heard from behind the closed doors. Happily hailstones of considerable size descended to help the side of law and order, and the crowd, for the time being, dispersed.

17th. I have made up my mind to leave to-morrow or the next day, so went to the Embassy to get a pass; then to see my friends. Emma is going to stay through the siege—I wish I could. As she says, most of the Patriots are leaving; it may be very trying if the siege goes on for long, but it will be most useful to have some sensible women, for they are wanted very much. They (the B.'s) are taking in stores for 3 or 4 weeks. The last news is that MacMahon is to fall back upon Metz instead of coming to help Paris. Is that the idea of the clever Person at the Tuileries? MacMahon was wise; but dynastic reasons send him to the rat trap to help (?) Bazaine. They also talk of Trochu as a capable man to take MacMahon's place here. But all is rumour, and probably all news is false, except that the heights round the City are not to be fortified!!! Good news for the enemy!

18th. I am off and you will get this latter part by post with the Queen's head thereon. Adieu, la Belle France; may I soon be back in Paris, for I love it, and just now it has all my sympathy. At Duval's where I always breakfast, I said good-bye to the chief and dropped some pence into the box for Sick and Wounded. These boxes are put up everywhere. '*Adieu, Madame,* if you must go; *Mais croyez-moi, ce n'est pas nécessaire;*

tout s'arrangera. Les Prussiens n'arriveront jamais à Paris.' Such is the confidence of the ever buoyant French character! May Peace come soon, is my desire. On the boat I was dozing peacefully, my mind free of the Prussians and all their ways, when I heard my name shouted by the Steward. 'Why did you not reply sooner? here's your permit to leave France.' Why in the world should I be disturbed for a useless piece of paper, when I am practically upon English soil? There is no peace in this world, and yet we delude ourselves into thinking it an attainable necessity. How long will the War Fiend continue to disturb the land; how long will the eloquent words of John Bright be realised? 'The Angel of Death is amongst us; you may almost hear the beating of his wings.'

Good-bye, dear Mary; I am glad to be back in the dear old Den in peace and quiet—the quiet of a London Street!!! Your loving Jane who hopes soon to see you.

Sept. 5th. So you see, dear Mary, we may all sing '*Vive la République!*' You won't; but we do. Will it last? Of course your politicals say no, but the damage to Imperialism is so great that it cannot revive yet awhile, and as there are so many heirs to the French throne no one can say what may or may not happen; the first thing now is to save the country. 'How are the mighty fallen.' And what a strange career that of the

A SPINSTER AUNT

ex-Emperor. Beginning as an exile he ends (so far as the end goes) a prisoner. Paris, *i.e.* France, intends to fight to the bitter end—I admire her for that, though she may go farther and fare worse. One of my earliest recollections was the talk about Louis Napoléon returning to Paris. He had been living in London and all his goods were to be sold when he left. We wanted drawing-room curtains, and so my elders went to the sale to look at some, but they sold for too high a price. No words could ever be found strong enough for my Father to express his hatred of Imperialism and especially for Louis Napoléon's treachery; and as the Pater always said, he has not the greatness of his uncle. You know the Father was in Paris for a year after Waterloo looking after the wounded and studying in the French hospitals. He too loves France, and reads the war correspondent's letters with avidity. 'What a change in the care of the wounded; there is frightful suffering still on the battle field, but in 1815 wounded men were found on the ground eight days after the battle.'

I have written to M. Loutrel, a painter and a Republican, to congratulate him. He was a National Guard in '48 and afterwards, and told me the real reason, according to him, that the *Coup d'Etat* was such a success. The Government had sequestrated all the N. G.'s drums, and without the *rappel* they were unable to assemble. I wonder? One would think some other means of assemblage would have been found. But of course the whole plot was most cleverly worked out by Louis Napoléon's party, and the dastardly deed was effectually done. Monsieur Loutrel saw men, women, and children drop down like ninepins in the streets—and that was organised by the man who became the dear friend of Europe and especially of Great Britain.

    Good-bye dear Mary

        Ever your affectionate Cousin J.

[The following letter is not dated, but it must have been written during the winter of 1870-71; and as it refers to incidents connected with the Franco-German war, I place it here instead of in the following chapter.—ED.]

MY DEAR MARY

I am spending all my spare cash (tho' I have none!) on the Comédie Française company now established in London. A few people go into the stalls and a few poor French folk into the gallery, but otherwise the Londoners have not risen to the advantages of the situation. I saw Got the other day in 'L'Avare'—exquisitely played by the whole company, as a matter of course.

It is curious the slowness of the Londoners to appreciate good art when they can get it easily. In Paris English people pay heavily, or *font*

A SPINSTER AUNT

queue to get into the Français: here the house is half empty, almost as empty as the Lyceum was some years ago (in 1856, I think) when Ristori paid her first visit to London. We had tickets sent us night after night, and such was the fascination of her acting to me, that I beat up all sorts of strange people to go with me, although I knew not one word of Italian. Ristori's acting in 'Pia dei Tolomei' was heartrending, and my poor companion was the only person in the house with dry eyes.

There was a charming concert at St. James's Hall a few days ago, for the French Sick and Wounded Fund. Gounod, Faure, and Madame Viardot-Garcia who sang '*Che farò senza Euridici*,' sublimely. Her voice seems as fresh as when I heard her 'create' the part of 'Fides' in the 'Prophète' 20 years ago at Covent Garden. Faure sang '*Les Rameaux*,' a beautiful song composed by himself, the accompaniment being played by Gounod upon an harmonium. That was a delightful and unique pleasure.

CHAPTER XV

ACTORS AND ACTRESSES

[No date.—ED.]

DEAREST MOLLY

You said in a letter you envied me my theatre going. 'Tis true, I have seen a good deal. I saw the beautiful Shakespeare revivals of Charles Kean in 1857. The 'Midsummer's Night Dream' was beautifully got up. So was 'Richard II.' The Episode between the acts, of the Progress of Richard and Bolingbroke along Cheapside, was charming, and considering the smallness of the Princess' theatre, marvellous. Ellen Terry played a street boy jumping about upon a huge tub at the side of the street clapping her hands and shouting.

Mrs. Kean was excellent in 'Henry VIII.,' and perhaps Charles Kean was no worse as Wolsey than in any other part, but I never liked him and much preferred Phelps in that and other plays. His Sir Peter[1] was excellent. Mrs. Kean sang the music of Ariel behind the scenes in 'The Tempest.'

[1] Teazle in the *School for Scandal*.—ED.

A SPINSTER AUNT

Then I was present at one of Grisi's last performances in 1861, and Mario's, ten years later, (July, 1871) in 'La Favorita.' Poor Mario, he sang so flat, it was painful to listen to him. It is such a pity singers do not retire when their voices begin to play them unpleasant tricks, and stick to it—the retirement; Grisi had a good many 'last times.'

I heard 'Faust' in 1868 with the original Marguerite—Madame Cavalho—the best of a great many I have seen, including Mesdames Patti and Lucca. The part did not suit the former—it is too dreamy a character; whereas Patti in 'Il Barbiere' and 'Don Giovanni' (as Zerlina) are performances which may be called perfect.

I saw Madame Ristori many times in 1856, and only regret that young as I was, I was not taken to see Rachel. These things build up one's character and educate us; and I shall never cease to be thankful I saw so much when I was a mere child. People little think what impressions children get from seeing good art, dramatic and pictorial. Fechter was another fine actor, especially in the 'Duke's Motto' and such pieces; but I liked his Hamlet better than any one else's, except Rossi's. I saw the latter at Milan, and what impressed me so much was his tenderness to his mother in spite of her misdeeds. Most Hamlets are brutal to her, and of course she deserved such treatment; but at the same time being his mother, some sort of pity ought surely to be expressed? I know no Italian, but I understood far more of that performance than of many a one in English, in which the actors rant, and scream, and mouth their curiously accented words. But you must go to Paris to hear elocution on the stage and in the pulpit. If a French priest talks nonsense, which he frequently does, he clothes it in words and dresses it in gestures which make his sermon worth listening to. Beautiful language and a finely toned voice fascinate most folks. And still more are they factors upon the stage than in the pulpit.

'Zaïre'[1] is not a lively piece, but to hear Maubant and Sara Bernhardt recite the verse was a joy; and what an exquisite voice her's is! it stands out as one of the two *perfect* voices that I have heard in my life—the other being Dr. Liddon's.

I wonder how many Sir Peter Teazles I have seen? Once, when quite an infant, I saw old Farren; where and when I have forgotten.

Among Othellos, I rank as finest, Salvini; but he is a little too realistic in his parts—he literally *saws* his throat! I like him better in the 'Gladiator.' Tamagno in Verdi's 'Otello' is very grand. And what a voice he has! I heard him at the Lyceum with the La Scala company from Milan. I thought the roof would be blown off! One thing I resent

[1] By Voltaire.—ED.

in these modern times—the elaboration of scenery and accessories. Surely Charles Kean's Shaksperian revivals were sufficiently good in this respect. Addison somewhere in the *Spectator* ridicules this realistic tendency, and prophecies 'real water'; well, we had it in the 'Colleen Bawn'! We don't want to see the full moon rising in the same place as the retired sun; but there is a limit to magnificence upon the stage, and excessive details are apt to detract from the acting. In some cases this may be the object, so as to amuse the public who otherwise would be bored. But I rejoice to think that I saw at the Français, Delaunay the 'Misanthrope' sitting on the one real chair, with two others and a table painted on the drop within a foot of his back! I should like to see a Hamlet played in evening dress *à la* Garrick. If the acting were absolutely first rate one would not even see the white tie and swallow tails. If acting be really good, we are insensible to little accidents on the stage, as we are in real life.

Another kind of insensibility to details, I witnessed at Covent Garden one year, when Drury Lane was under the same management. It was a matinée of the Walküre. Two persons came in late and flopped about to find a seat in the dark. Presently they fumbled about with the programme and then whispered to each other to the annoyance of their neighbours. When the curtain came down, said one of these dames: 'Is this the " Great City " ? ' ' No, the " Walküre." ' ' But it's on the bill.' They had thought they were at Drury Lane! and 'wondered' why the 'Great City' was being sung!

Addison has some quaint remarks upon the stage in his time. He was no mean critic of ways dramatic and he complains vigorously of the symbolic accessories of his day. 'The ordinary method of making a hero, is to clap a huge plume of feathers upon his head, which rises so very high, that there is often a greater length from his chin to the top of his head, than to the sole of his foot. . . . This very much embarrasses the actor who is forced to hold his neck extremely stiff and steady all the while he speaks; and notwithstanding any anxieties which he pretends for his mistress, his country, or his friends, one may see by his action, that his greatest care and concern is to keep the plume of feathers from falling off his head.' The younger generation may see this sort of heroic Hamlet in Lawrence's portrait of 'John Kemble.' And are we not sometimes reminded in the best of acting-managers' theatres of Addison's 'broad sweeping train' which follows the Princess in all her motions, and finds 'constant employment for a boy who stands behind her to open and spread it to advantage.' . . . 'It is in my opinion, a very odd spectacle, to see a queen venting her passion, in disordered motions, and a little boy taking care all the while that they do not ruffle the tail of her gown.' Does not this remind us of the anxiety of the grand ladies attending Elsa at her marriage, lest their fulsome trains should catch upon the nails imperfectly driven home by the stage carpenters upon their hurriedly erected staircase? And cannot we endorse Addison's comment upon the train and boy when he says he 'must confess' that 'his eyes are wholly taken up with the page's part, and as for the queen, I am not so attentive to anything she speaks, as to the right adjusting of her train, lest it should trip up her heels, and incommode her, as she walks to and fro upon the stage.'

The Spectator recommends his countrymen to follow the example of the French stage, 'where the kings and queens always appear unattended and leave their guards behind the scenes. . . . I should likewise be glad if we imitated the French in banishing from our stage the noise of drums, trumpets, and huzzas, which is sometimes so very great that when there is a battle in the Haymarket theatre, we may hear it as far as Charing Cross.' How has realism attacked the supernatural? The device of the Ghost in 'Don Giovanni' taking long strides and pausing upon each foot is the traditional method; but this manner of human progression is also employed by the very vigorous knights of the Holy Grail, who are certainly not entirely spiritual beings. Addison says a 'spectre has very often saved a play although he has done nothing, but stalked across the stage or rose from a cleft in it, and sunk again without speaking one word.' But the spectral 'White Pilgrim' did not save the exquisite poetry of Herman Merivale from being a failure, (although its first exponent recited the lines with dignity and beauty of diction); possibly partly because the wheeled platform upon which the spectre travelled was too obviously a stage device.

For the moving of pity one modern method is quite Addisonian, 'the principal machine' still being 'the handkerchief. In our common tragedies, we should not know very often that the persons are in distress by anything they say, if they did not from time to time apply their handkerchiefs to their eyes. Far be it from me to think of banishing this instrument of sorrow from the stage. . . . all that I contend for . . . is that the actor's tongue should sympathize with his eyes.'

But our heroines have another wonderful invention for illustrating grief. Who discovered the institution of the one hairpin which upholds the lengthy locks—the 'principal machine' of feminine stage agony, the twin 'property' of the stage handkerchief? It surely cannot have been born out of realism, for who has ever seen a woman in real life prancing up and down a room with flowing locks? There is also danger in the fashion, for I remember once seeing Fedora's chignon drop off behind the couch and hang by one tiny tress, an accident which might have caused some tittering had it happened to a lesser artist than the 'divine Sara.'

Children are decidedly sure cards to play upon the stage. Do we not all (I am speaking of the semi-aged) remember Miss Bateman-Leah's little girl and the poor little babe who was thrown into the Foundling Hospital turn-about cradle during a snow storm, Janet Pride Celeste by name, if I mistake not. But 'a modern writer' unnamed by Addison, 'observing how this had took in other plays, being resolved to double the distress, brought a princess upon the stage with a little boy in one hand, and a girl in the other. This, too, had a good effect. A third poet being resolved to outwrite all his predecessors, a few years ago introduced three children with great success; and, as I am informed, a young gentleman, who is fully determined to break the most obdurate hearts, has a tragedy by him, where 'the first person that appears upon the stage is an afflicted widow in her mourning weeds, with half a dozen fatherless children attending her like those that usually hang about the figure of Charity. Thus, several incidents that are beautiful in a good writer, become ridiculous by falling into the hands of a bad one.'

And then as to stage butcherings. 'The French critics, who think these are grateful spectacles to us, take occasion from them to represent us a people that delight in blood, for we strew the stage with carcasses in the last scenes of a tragedy'; and we are bidden to observe the Greeks who did their slaughterings behind the scenes. 'Sophocles conducting a tragedy under the like delicate circumstances' (as Hamlet), 'made Orestes convey himself by a beautiful stratagem into his mother's apartment, with a resolution to kill her. But because such a spectacle would have been too shocking to the audience, this dreadful resolution is executed behind the scenes; the mother is heard calling out to her son for mercy: and the son answering her, that she showed no mercy to his father: after which she shrieks out that she is wounded, and by what follows we find out that she is slain.'

But are all deaths upon the stage to be avoided? Apparently not, as 'Horace's rule was that decency forbade the display of parricides or unnatural murders before the audience'; so we are happily justified in allowing our Camellia ladies, our Fedoras, our Adriennes, and many another to die before us in the full glare of gas lamps. 'At the same time,' Addison wishes to observe, 'that though the devoted persons of the tragedy were seldom slain before the audience, which had generally something ridiculous in it, their bodies were often produced after their death, which has always in it something melancholy or terrifying.' Truly so.

A SPINSTER AUNT

Are you well acquainted with the *Spectator*? I mean the old volumes; the articles are delightful reading, and as fresh as if they had been written yesterday, to say nothing of the style. Now a days style is rather considered good when it confuses thought—words seem to be used for that purpose, and paragraphs are pages long; the old *Spectators* did not require their readers to turn back, to read a passage six times; even then possibly remaining unenlightened. Words were used to elucidate thought, not to veil it.

Yes, I have seen a good deal of play acting in my time, and of first rate character; for instance a number of the French actors and actresses and singers during each of my sojourns in Paris. The Brohans were most finished actresses in such comedies as 'La Joie fait Peur,' with old Reynier. I could have seen Frédéric Lemaître, but Mlle. Vully advised me not to as he was *passé*—it was a return to the stage and reappearance in 'Robert Macaire.' But I did see Déjazet and a wonderful artist she was in her old age as the Duc de Richelieu. Croizette was also admirable; indeed all of those that I saw at the Français and the Vaudeville were wonderful artists: Pasca for instance, and Mme. Fargueil. And what a cast they had at the Vaudeville in those days.[1] Old Parade at the latter, and at the Variétés old Dupuis and Mme. Chaument. I should like you

[1] Probably 1868-70.—Ed.

to have heard her recite *Les deux Pigeons*! By the way, I think I remember Déjazet also reciting those verses.

[*Diary*. No date.—ED.] Trite but true it be that it is improving to see ourselves as other parties see us; and so an amusing account is sent me from the other side of the world purporting to be the views of a Colonial upon the inhabitants of these little islands in the North Sea.

We are 'proud' of being Englishmen (apparently the writer includes Scots and Irish in that word—Englishmen) I hope the others won't see it, for of course they, the six millions or so of Irishmen and Scotchmen, are far more important than the poor thirty or five and thirty millions of English. Of course it is a fact that the Colonies 'have nothing to learn from us.' We have Free Trade and good sanitation and all that, but it goes 'for nothing.' But Melbourne is I believe where we were fifty years ago as regards drainage and so on; and London is probably the healthiest city in the world; what of that? The workhouses are a 'disgrace.' Well, a better system might perhaps be invented, a sort of alms house; but surely a system which provides a home for worn out workers where they can sit on easy chairs and smoke, where they can go out of doors in non-uniform clothes, and where they have books, papers, decent food, games, and friends to visit them, cannot be so very bad.

A SPINSTER AUNT

It is a pity our poor folk have not the same worship of ancestors as the French and the Japanese. Certainly the reverence for the old parents in France is one of the most beautiful traits in the French character. How often one sees in Paris on a Sunday or Fête day, the old mother in some old world *coiffure* walking about the streets with a son in a top hat, and a daughter in the newest fashion of gown. Here at home, it sometimes happens that the old mother or father is left in hospital with a false address in order to get her or him shunted into the 'House.'

Our churches are only 'half full' and we are choked with 'vested interests, and hampered' when we desire reform. But other people say that Knights of Labour in America are ruining trade there, and certainly they are not unknown in our Colonies.

Then we have 'thousands of miserable children.' That certainly is a *crux*; but when the Colonies are populated from North to South, and from East to West, and the average family may be six or seven, and the father has no regular earnings beyond an average of 15/- a week, how will the Colonials get on? At present workers are few and wages are high. Here it is contrariwise: workers are many, and wages low.

'Our poor people are ill-fed'—alas! how true, but where can we buy meat at 8d. or 4d. per lb.? and how, in a city of 4 millions of people can we be as fine a race as in a sparsely populated country where I believe the largest town population is 150,000 or 200,000?

Then our Colonial friend is scandalized at our Sundays! and this just as we were beginning to feel proud of them! 'I have spent Sunday in the East End, in the North, and in the West End. But Sunday does not exist in London. It is a holiday simply. With us it is a day of rest; but that does not seem to be the case here.'

What is implied here? That we do not do our duty as Christians? If so, we certainly may plead guilty in spite of thousands of churches and chapels crammed to suffocation. We many of us wish that a larger percentage of the population fulfilled their duties as creatures paying homage to their Creator, even if they felt no comfort in prayer, no joy in thanksgiving. But is the population of any other city more openly religious? Do we find, in any country, that the worshippers are more than a tithe of the community? It is sad, but it is a fact, that numbers of well-meaning persons, to say nothing of the irreligious, vicious, degraded and ignorant, find no comfort in worship, and do not even regard it as a duty. And that being so, how can Sunday be better spent by such people than by improving their health, or in storing their minds with new contents, and in innocent recreation such as looking at pictures, and hearing music. Take the

A SPINSTER AUNT

East End. Churches are filled; the People's Palace is crammed. In the West we find the same. The Parks are full; the concert rooms are full; the trains and omnibuses are full. Yes—there is the fault, I presume, to our Colonial cousin. But how in the world are we to get away from the 'miserable hovels' in which we live, unless we take train or coach? The few must work, that the many may find recreation. That cannot be helped. One thing our Colonial Critic does not comment on. Is there another city in the world, where 3 or 4 millions of people of all classes, including the very lowest, where such a motley crowd as one sees in London on a festive occasion, can be kept in order by a handful of policemen? Surely that is something to be proud of.

Feby. 27, 1871

MY DEAR MARY

I have seen today one of the most glorious coaches conceivable, equal to those in the Grand Trianon—Mr. Speaker's on his way to St. Paul's for the Thanksgiving. As usual, when any procession is going along in front of the National Gallery, we students are allowed to stand on the paved court in front, which being somewhat above the level of the street, enables us to see over the heads of the crowd. The Procession was fine as such things generally are in the way of troops and carriages, but Mr. Speaker's eclipsed them all. I do not remember the coach ever parading London before. It is enormously heavy and was drawn by dray horses which resemble the old Flemish creatures of the coach's period. It is, of course, something after the style of the Queen's glass coach, which we have not seen since the Prince Consort's departure, and his Worship the Lord Mayor's; but it is a *vis-à-vis*, only holding two persons. By the way, so is the Lord Mayor's but his Sword Bearer and Mace-bearer sit upon stools looking out of the windows of the doors. I wonder if that be a modern innovation? Mr. Speaker's coach is smaller, and he and his Chaplain alone occupy it. He was arrayed in all his glory, bedecked in gorgeous robes and imposing wig. No, I must be wrong about the Chaplain, as I saw the mace; but the crowds dodge their heads about so, that it is difficult to see everything. The crowd was most enthusiastic.

28*th*. I could not send this last evening. The *Times* has another edition of its Moral Lesson to His Royal Highness, hoping that he will profit by the teaching of typhoid and turn over a new leaf. I wonder will he ever reign? There has been so much feeling about the Queen shutting herself up, and so many whisperings in certain quarters of the population, and in their newspapers about abdication and a republic, that there is no knowing what may or may not take place in the near future; but this terrible illness seems to have had the effect of turning the tide. Between ourselves it is not quite 'manners' to tell a man that 'if he follows the ways of his great-uncle, we shall not, etc. etc.' Yet that has been the tone of many a Journalist. They are so fond of preaching Virtue and Morals with big capitals; and with all the agony piled on and on, over and over again; and yet they crowd their pages with hideous immoralities. H.R.H. has a very difficult part to play; he takes the place of the Sovereign in all ornamental functions, and in many business matters; and yet has no power to use his own judgement or carry out his own ideas in matters of State. But probably he is all this time studying Statecraft, the results of which we may see later on; and one talent he reigns supreme in— that of always saying the right thing in the right place. Probably when he succeeds to the throne we shall see the results of years of calm reflection, (and all the moral lessons!!)

CHAPTER XVI

OBER-AMMERGAU

Sep. 1871

IN THE HOUSE OF S.S. MATTHEW AND JOHN.
(MATTHÄUS AND JOHANNES ZWINK.)

DEAR MARY

I am not going to describe the Passion Play as you can read all about it in the papers; but I will try and give you some real idea of the interest of this our pilgrimage.

We had to leave Ulm at 5 A.M. in the dawn, a lovely rose-pink effect, and as we had arrived in darkness the night before we saw nothing of the town. Arriving at Immenstadt we took a carriage, which after a delightful drive landed us at Reutte for the night. We lunched at Schatwald upon delicious pink trout, apparently the staple fare of the country. A lovely drive down a pass was lost to view by the darkness.

Reutte is a picturesque little town, and there we saw the first painted dwellings which abound all over this land. Some houses are ornamented with clauses from the Creed or verses from the Bible,

A SPINSTER AUNT

or pictures illustrative of Christian doctrine. It is quaint, and the villagers do it themselves. Might we not some of us adopt this line of business, instead of painting pictures which no one wants? Well done, it would improve our streets—but the advertisements on the hoardings perhaps are not encouraging in this matter. We had a charming coachman who took us all the way.

From Reutte we drove for hours through a pine forest after passing the beautiful Planensee, where we met the King's waggons with his *Batterie de Cuisine*; he is shooting somewhere about there.

Arriving here I called out to Dorothea (I was on the box), 'Is not that man under the umbrella like Edward?' 'Why, it *is* Edward.' And lo! having said he would not go, he had come over from St. Moritz for the last performance.

Our rooms are simplicity itself and large; there is a German here also, who is astonished at my early hour for retiring—8 P.M.; not at all astonishing after our hurried travelling and the excitement of the drama. I need scarcely say that, considering that the best German hotels only give one the bare necessaries of domestic comfort, the arrangements here are primitive, and the manners and customs of the natives those of early cave dwellers. Our washing basins are pie-dishes, our water jugs the size of the average cream jug, and we drink our coffee out of china rummers.[1] But the whole place is so imbued with the spirit of the play, the men are so thoroughly gentlemen—nature's gentlemen if you like, that one does not notice the shortcomings in civilization. For instance, I wanted to go over to Ettal, and I asked old Matthew if any one in the village could lend me a donkey, as it was too far to walk there and back. 'You could have Christ's ass; I am sure he would lend it to you,' was the answer, spoken in all simplicity. Needless to say I did not make that journey. It is one of the peculiarities at Ammergau that during the play year, the people call each other by their acting names.

And when Matthew brings out our coffee,—we sit on a bench by the doorway,—he offers it with a little bow which would not disgrace the most courtly of old-fashioned French gentlemen.

We have had the great chance of seeing the play twice, for on Monday morning guns went off at 7.45 denoting the King's arrival—he had not been all the summer—so every one rushed to the theatre but me! I was so tired, and the strain of 8 hours was so great, that I determined only to go for the second part; and I found that the latter (after the Garden of Gethsemane scene) was quite as impressive as the first part appeared on Sunday. The Crucifixion seemed then to fall

---

[1] Glasses upon stands formerly used for spirits and water, or punch. —ED.

short of my anticipations, but it was evidently only the result of my own worn-out condition.

The charm of the whole of the first part is wonderful. The entrance into Jerusalem, the people strewing palm branches; the plaintive music, an echo of Mozart; the dignity of Mayer's bearing; the parting with his mother; his tenderness towards her—all culminating in the Agony in the Garden, which was almost too intense to be borne. The Chorus too, their singing, especially of '*Ah! welch' ein Mensch!*' was delightful; and again, the dignity of the actors' and singers' movements—mere peasants be it remembered, was astonishing.

One part of the Passion I never realized before —the length of time spent in going to and fro, to Pilate and to Herod, and the various examinations of Our Blessed Lord.

A charming little picture was the coming of Peter and John down the side street, talking over the events of the day; and then soon afterwards St. Peter's denial and the sorrowful expression upon Mayer's face as he turned and looked upon Peter,—one of the most pathetic incidents in the drama. Another thing connected with the performance is that the impressiveness is so intense that one is not struck by the literal rendering of Jonah and the Whale, which is really very comic, also the cock-crowing, and so on. The peasants laugh, but nobody of less simplicity could possibly do so. On the Monday, the theatre being much less full, one could see the extraordinarily ugly and clumsy attire of the Bavarian peasants. Their sleeves are a yard across the shoulders, and their hips two yards I should think in circumference. And the crudeness of the colours of the stuff and handkerchiefs. I wanted to buy an umbrella and add to my impedimenta. Such colours! But I restrained my desire.

The king is a beautiful creature physically; one of the handsomest men I ever saw—but so full of art that he hates statecraft. Can one wonder?

We have had a quiet peaceful week since Monday when most people left. The Dean [1] and Lady Augusta were staying just opposite us, and we saw him tucked into his goloshes by his wife when the carriage came up for their departure —clogs and *sabots* would certainly be useful here for the mud is awful. There are no proper roads or paths; the houses are jotted about, and roads just cleared to lead to them. We did not see the terrors of the last piece of the way up to the village, until we left. Our man had a beautiful pair of thoroughbreds, of which he was very proud, but he hired two enormous cart horses to pull us up the hill: and going down was really awful, the inclination of the carriage being so great that we seemed to be sitting upon the driver's head! What would have happened if the

[1] Stanley.—ED.

horses had bolted? A terrible smash I fear, and no one left to tell the tale.

To see the Passion Play is an experience, or rather a privilege—the most marvellous sermon I ever heard; but the great charm is the mental atmosphere. Mayer walking about the fields with his book of devotions; the beautiful music heard from the meadows; the quiet God-fearing lives of the villagers; the reverence displayed at mass and so on. Another feature of the drama is the extraordinarily good acting from the secular and dramatic point of view; the part of Judas, for instance, was as fine a piece of acting as you would find on the best stage in any capital of Europe. Unfortunately it is to be feared that as time goes on the ideal performance may get vulgarized by visitors. Even now the same sort of Americans who chip off pieces of stone from our old churches as *souvenirs* are to be seen hustling about for the signatures of the principal performers. One such rushed into our house: 'Where is John? where is he? I must see him, I want him to sign his name in my book.'

The morning after the last performance, while we were putting on our hats, this same John (he played the Evangelist) came up the ladder into our room to wish us good bye. 'He was going up the mountain to fetch the cows.' We hardly knew him, for his hair which had been two years growing long, had already been cut.

RECOLLECTIONS OF

The Spinster (John's aunt and housekeeper) embraced me, and Matthew and the old mother almost wept. They are charming people, absolutely unconventional and true; and may they always remain so, is our prayer.

At Munich we went to the Opera; 'Rheingold.' We had been to museums and trudged about, and were dead tired. Result: Edward and D. went to sleep. Ada was supremely bored, and I confess to wishing that there might be a pause, or that I too could slumber—a confession I am ashamed to make—but remember we had been museum tramping all day. But no! the music went on for two hours with no break; and the only part I could lay hold of was the Rhine Maidens' music, which was very lovely; but Wagner wants much study.

At the Hofkirche on Sunday we heard some exquisite music, a full orchestra; also in a *Biergarten* one evening, a Classical concert, somewhat spoilt by the rattling of glasses and the smoking of pipes and cigars, but from a social point of view most interesting, for there were civilians not a few, and officers very many, accompanied by their wives and daughters. You know the Passion Play was stopped last year when the war began because so many of the men had to go to the front, but Mayer was exempted from service in consideration of the part he played—the Christus.

You will see that I am finishing this letter at

A SPINSTER AUNT

München, and I have just heard an opinion about the Passion Play which endorses mine; namely that Mr. Tom Taylor said the acting of the part of Judas was as fine as anything he had seen on any stage. Mr. T. you know is the dramatic critic, I think of the *Times*, and therefore his opinion is worth quoting; and besides, is it not delightful to find oneself in the same boat as a great critic? And now in the words of the Johnsons and Austins and Richardsons and lesser fry, Permit me to remain ever my dearest and most esteemed cousin, your most affectionate and loving kinswoman, JANE.

[No date.—ED.]

MY DEAR MARY

Have you ever asked yourself, if you have met strange folks in the train, what they can be socially? My experiences have been much the same, I suppose, as other people's, but really some of them (the experiences) are worth remembering.

The other day, being holiday time, I was travelling along the South Western from Salisbury. A young gentleman entered the carriage with his mama and sister, and he had no sooner sat down than he expressed himself thus: 'I find it a beastly bore that the summer holidays must be passed away from the sea because Father wants shooting.' Then chimed in the sister: 'And what a nuisance it is that the tennis court is not the full size.'

I wonder how such people could travel in Ruskin's way, a carriage and pair, with the luggage that is now necessary for the young: croquet and tennis implements; fishing rods and lines; golf, guns, musical instruments and trunks laden with the garments necessary for these sports, and other festivities. This and other reasons of course compel railway travelling; and how do the various travellers disport themselves, think you?

Observe the number of newspapers and magazines considered necessary—of the making thereof luckily for such young people there is no end. Off goes the train, and whatever may be the beauty of that part of God's earth through which he passes, the intelligent 19th Century youth fixing his eyes immovably upon some illustrated paper or magazine, imagines that he is gaining useful information of various kinds, quite oblivious of the fact, that even from the window of a railway carriage, a vast amount of really useful knowledge may be acquired as to the manner of cottage building and the making of hay-ricks in strange countries; and also as to the qualities of a variety of pills, mustards, and soaps manufactured in our native land and puffed in our railway stations. But there is another study which travellers may indulge in most profitably—man; I mean man in the generic sense. In London

A SPINSTER AUNT

when in the evening, men jump into the carriage laden with newspapers of various shades of pink and green, or white—(why not blue?)—one knows that without fail they will turn to the page devoted to 'Sport.' But in the country quite a different spirit prevails. The weather is commented on, the yield of hay is discussed, the corn, the roots, and so on; but the women's talk is naturally concerning domesticities. 'There now, Master Stodge, how be ye? Ye must ha' got a fine fortin' along wi' yere pore missus?' 'Lor no, Missus Perks, what wi' gettin' things for 'er when she came in, and a cartin' on 'er out, I aint much the better, poor old Meg. But I reckon I'll miss 'er o' evenin's when I come along 'ome.'

And then the curious folks one meets when compelled to travel by slow trains. What in the world can that woman be who takes you, a complete stranger, into her confidence at once; and as soon as the door is slammed, fires off a volley of information about her nearest relations and their most private doings. She arrives poppy-red and breathless. 'There, I knew 'ow it would be, and I told 'im so. All this tearin' about, and then 'ee misses the train, 'ee do, and the funeral's for 4 o'clock and the next train can't get there till half past; and to think as 'ee should be for showin' no respect to his wife's mother, nor nobody else. Oh, she war a good 'un, she war, and simple. *She* didn't want to be wreathed up in flowers, and didn't want to be pushed on no truck. Her would have,' says she, 'a polished coffin and a pall, and there's plenty in the village would carry she.'

Then there are the erratic travellers, one often meets them on the Continent, who take a ticket to some place across country, and never work out any connections; when they get to a junction, they ask the guard if they change. 'Yes, you change here right enough, but you can't go on for 3 hours.' 'Lor now, to think o' that; and my old man 'ee war for meettin' I by the two o'clock.'

Another class of traveller, generally a woman, begins to realise that she ought to get out of an omnibus when it is just beginning to move on; and yet, the angel on the footboard scarcely mutters an oath!

The window question of course brings out many peculiarities. Why should some of us suffer from stuffiness because another person hates fresh air? Or why should one set of folks be compelled to be stifled because the others can live in an oven? Ten people in a carriage, a baby, a cat, and a canary, the bird chirping more and more as the infant gives vent to crowing and inane ejaculations at the lamp; and then:—'*Would* you mind my putting up the window? I am *so* afraid baby may catch cold, as she's just got over the measles.' Or; 'I *hope* it's not incommoding you to have the window shut; but I'm *so* afraid of a draught.'

A SPINSTER AUNT

'Oh dear no, not at all,' answers the polite liar, in a condition of increasing agony.

Then there is the poor creature who craves for sympathy:—'If she had only known, *she* never would have married. After slaving for *him* all my life, to think that he should go and leave me with all them children and nothin' to keep them on!'

A war sometimes suggests curious remarks, as when an old lady, being told by a young girl knitting belts, that they were for Kitchener's Horse, asks 'what part of the horse they were for?'

Amongst selfish travellers, who excels the incoming man when some one remarks that the carriage is not a smoking one? The aggrieved expression upon his face betokens his contempt for persons who object to smoke and still more to its accompaniments!

But we must not forget the kindliness of some travellers—those who lend their wraps to the foolish, slightly clad women who travel with babies on a cold day; or those good Samaritans who amuse the hot and tired children upon a long dreary journey.

I once had a friend who professed to hate children, who said she could 'murder' any child who made a noise during the quiet movements of a Symphony; but why not rather 'murder' the idiot mother for taking her child to a concert?

RECOLLECTIONS OF

Well, this same friend of mine would keep a bread-and-jam-besmeared infant quiet during a long railway journey by cutting up a newspaper into a fleet of boats, and birds, and beasts innumerable of all shapes and sizes!

Another class of eccentric travellers are those who 'only take what they can carry'; and so they encumber the carriages and corridors with huge bags and holdalls, making it impossible to move—innocent persons who, bringing in a box half a yard high, 'think it will go very well under the seat.' Not it! it remains a stumbling block for the unwary throughout the entire journey, like the heavy bundles and boxes in the racks, their mission seems to be to act as moral blisters, for there is no better school for practising all the Christian and Pagan Virtues than travelling by train, tram, or boat.

But of all delightful fellow travellers, who can excel the lady and her daughters who had been so busy shopping in Venice, that they were obliged to omit seeing the 'Colleone' statue. 'Did it matter much? We are going away tomorrow by the 2 o'clock train. Of course if we get our shopping done in time, we could go along and see it before we start; but it is so far off. People told us it was the finest statue in Europe; but we have been all about Italy so long that we are rather tired of statues. But if you think we *really ought* to see it, we will try and go after we have got the bead necklaces and things; and you must remember there is another equestrian statue at Padua, and we are going there next. Won't that do?'

Or that delightful old soul who was going to Rome, and longed to see Hadrian's Villa, because she had been told 'that he was so kind to travellers.'

RECOLLECTIONS OF

CHAPTER XVII

PARIS

4th January 1872
BOULEVARD DE CLICHY, PARIS.

HERE I am once again, my dear Mary, in Paris, and I hope to stop for some years. L. and I came to the conclusion that we should like it now we have no particular ties in London, which I always hated, for there is no sun and less and less light every year.

It was a business turning out the old home where I was born! Such an accumulation of rubbish! Parcels of *Athenæums* since a period previous to my entry into this world, I think from the very beginning of the journal. I packed everything but the piano myself in skeleton cases, and all will go over to Paris by the good ship *Esther*. It is much less expensive than by railway. I came over alone, as L. is going to wait at her sister's until G. and I are properly settled in a flat. I left the evening before Christmas Eve, and almost missed my train by a ludicrous accident or incident. We had a parting tea—Robert, Ellen, and myself—in the dismantled drawing room. We sat on boxes as the men were carting off the remains of the furniture which was to be sold. The poor Den was pitiable to see. The Padre came in to say good bye, with a terrible *figure de circonstance*. Then came the time to start; the cab was at the door, and I put on my coat. Where was my bonnet? We hunted everywhere and found it not. Had it been carried off in a drawer? An express messenger was sent down to St. Martin's Lane, and happily it was found in one of the chests for sale. Here was a bad beginning.

G. met me in Paris and we hunted about and found this apartment. Nice large rooms and light. On Christmas Eve we went to the Midnight Mass at the Madeleine; it is not very devotional to see seven masses going on at once, and the behaviour of the people is not devout. They mostly go to spin out the time before the *Réveillon* suppers. Of course I do not mean the good folk; only the crowd. But it ought to be an ideal office. I will write again soon.

Y^r affec^{te} JEANNE.

January 18*th* 1872.   BOUL^D DE CLICHY.

DEAR MARY

I am not yet working for I wanted to see the horrible destruction done by the War and Commune. By the way, I did not tell you how I execrated the Germans when we stopped at Amiens and Creil, for their hideous spiked helmets were all along the line until we passed the latter place. And I noticed all the way so many little hillocks surmounted by a cross, where the poor men were buried—now getting covered by corn, but which for a long while will be evidences of the hideousness of war.

I have been to St. Cloud. What havoc! One sees a shattered house with a balcony hanging down, and in a room the remains of furniture, and perhaps a broken looking-glass upon the walls. But *on dit*, that the wreck of St. Cloud was caused by the French shells of Mt. Valérien falling short of Sèvres where the Germans were located. Here in Paris everywhere one goes are scaffoldings round the public buildings, and many *must* be pulled down. The Hôtel de Ville, the Tuileries, the Cour d'Escompte, St. Eustache, the Ste. Chapelle and heaps of other churches are all more or less damaged. The city is a wreck. Most of the buildings will be repaired, but I fear not the palaces, for dynastic reasons; though I imagine if the Prince Imperial or the Comte de Chambord are wanted, the fact of having no palace to live in will not keep either away. It is sad to see the city now; but I daresay by the end of the year, *tout sera rétabli* except the little Prince. Had Jules Favre not been a sentimental idealist, Paris would probably have been saved; but he wept over the capitulation, and Bismark let him keep the guns upon Montmartre to shell the city. Fancy trusting a Parisian mob under such conditions as defeat and starvation! Everything in the way of unnecessaries is to be had very cheap. Lovely furniture is sold for next to nothing at the Hotel Drouet, where I have invested in a Louis XVI. *commode* and a Dutch marquetry cabinet for the prices of ordinary modern things of the same kind; and I saw an entire suite of Louis XVI. *salon* chairs and a *canapé* go for 1000 fs. There were nine pieces altogether, white wood, covered with the most exquisitely designed pale grey-blue and white satin. Of course people sold their things before the siege, and now the dealers are trying to realize their purchases and they are ready to let things go for half their value—or less.

Your affectionate JEANNE.

May 1. 1873

DEAR MARY

I must just send you a letter about 'Le Bon Bock'[1]—every one is chattering and howling over it. For my part I find it vastly clever and intolerably vulgar. Some of this painter's things I like immensely, but of all the Impressionists, Dégas, to my mind is the best of the whole

[1] By Manet.—ED.

clique in spite of his endless ballet girls as subjects; but his colouring is very refined and beautiful. De Neuville's 'Dernières cartouches' is, like all his battle subjects, very touching. In the pictures of the moderns we have war depicted from the privates' point of view—the man who suffers most, and naturally, because the artists served during the war in the ranks, and many of their friends were killed. Consequently battle scenes abound and have become interesting. If you want to see what war is, look at De Neuville and Verestchagin—horrible, cruel, grim. If you want to see the so called glory, go to Versailles and look at Horace Vernet's Staff officers sitting on their beautiful chargers calmly surveying the battle, from a safe place. When one thinks of such a life as Regnault's being lost, such talent wasted (partly it must be admitted by his own fault, his silly bravado) it is appalling. Henner's 'General Chanzy' is *very* fine, one of the best, if not the best portrait in the Salon.

May 1874. PARIS

Just a word, dear Mary, about the Salon. The *clou* this year is a new painter's 'Grand-père.' Bastien-Lepage is the new and rising man. He is not exactly an Impressionist, nor is he exactly a Realist; but he has broken away from conventionalism, and is himself. His 'Grand-père' is alive and you cannot forget him.

We had, at the Studio today a great discussion upon luxury. There are several girls of the big world there, and of course many poor ones; and just now, as there is much poverty consequent upon the war, many people are talking upon the subject of not spending money upon luxuries. The difficulty is to know what is a luxury. 'Expensive unnecessaries,' said one, 'like pictures.' That caused a protest from those of us who wish to make painting our living, and so we called out, 'Strawberries at 50c. apiece.' Then some one else cried 'The rich spend money upon heaps of things they could do without.'

'Of course they do; but all these highpriced goods called luxuries help multitudes of poorer people to exist; and how would the world get on if every one lived the life of the Hermits of the Desert, or of St. Simon Stylites. Even he must have received gifts of bread and dates, which must have been made and grown by some one, and taken up to his column by a friend on a ladder, unless he had a crane and a basket. How could we get on if there were no industries but the absolutely necessary ones?'

'Ah! but, I am speaking of art and other things which are not mere industries.'

'Art! does not the making of a picture mean the making of a frame? the use of paints? and brushes? the sitting of models? and so on. And does not the making of frames, the grinding of colours, brush making, paper making, and divers other fabrications useful to artists—do not all these industries employ multitudes of people? If the rich men and women can afford it, the purchase of pictures, and jewellery, and beautiful stuffs for clothes is not luxury in a bad sense. It must do good to circulate money. If no one takes a cab, what becomes of the men of that useful calling; but that could also be called an unnecessary luxury, as the person could walk possibly, and to his own advantage, or go in an omnibus. But the cabman would suffer. I suppose keeping a carriage is a luxury if not absolutely a necessary; but the employment of coachman and grooms is useful, to say nothing of the industries connected with the keeping or breeding of horses. If a man puts down his carriage and gives the money he saves to a hospital, he possibly is the cause of his coachman being out of work, of his family being half starved, and of illness which succeeds want of work and worry. Surely it is better to help the man to live, than to give money to the hospital which will have to keep him in his sickness?'

'Ruskin proclaims against luxury.'

'Oh yes, but Ruskin's political economy is not immaculate. He is a good, though narrowminded art critic, and a most exquisite writer upon art—one may say he is a poet who sings in the most melodious prose; but his social ravings are most unpractical. For example; his railings against railways! If we travel we must not go by train—we must have a carriage. No doubt that is *the* way to travel; but in the old days, most of us would never have stirred from home; the Grand Tour was for the few, and blessed the man who had the money to do it. Now, of course, to a Ruskin, or a Duke, or an American millionaire the world is spoilt; but we do not, all of us possess a father who has made a fortune in business, and so must go by 2nd or 3d class trains, or not go at all. And I believe, in spite of Mr. Ruskin that a rich girl is quite justified in spending £20 upon a ball dress, for the making of that dress has supported many industrials, and done far more good than giving away three fourths in charity.'

'Good trade means work and wages; and it is far better to encourage work than to give doles. There is far too much of that in England, don't you think?'

So we all talked on and on; no one having any fixed opinion.

I shall finish this when I come home from the Salon. *P.S.*—Luxury may demoralise the individual? But then comes in, the greatest good for the greatest number. How difficult Social questions are to settle—Politics are nothing in comparison, and so often the doing good with the best intentions, turns to evil. I must leave off rambling on or I shall never arrive at the Palais de l'Industrie. . . .

. . . . .

There is a great 'Christ Crucifié' by Bonnat painted for one of the Law Courts or *Mairies*. You know the form of taking an oath here, and I suppose in all Roman Catholic countries, is to hold up one's hand before a Crucifix—a far more impressive action it looks than pretending to kiss a generally somewhat dirty Bible. The 'Christ' is a finely modelled figure, but it is no disparagement to modern art to say that it is not a Rubens nor a Velasquez. The background is possibly rather hot—it is a sort of burnt sienna, orange, and madder combination beloved by the painter in his portraits, and when this or any other combination of colours works in with the tones of the portrait, it is not disagreeable; but as a background to a nude figure it somewhat kills the flesh painting. If one compares the general effect of two pictures which have nothing in common, this 'Christ' by Bonnat and one of Henner's nudities, one sees at once how far more harmonious is the background scheme of the latter painter. Of all the French artists, the one which appeals to me most as a colourist is Baudry. His portraits live; they are as strong as Bonnat's but more refined, more subtle; unfortunately much of the best part of his life has been taken up by the Opera decorations which are sure to be ruined sooner or later by gas, and he is so conscientious, that he does every inch of the work himself. So it is said.

Ever your affecte. JEANNE.

[No date.—ED.]

DEAREST MARY.

We have most excited afternoons at the Cirque d'Hiver concerts, as Monsieur Pasdeloup is determined to push Wagner, and the crowd, mostly, is equally determined not to listen to his music. Of course it is only patriotism, so called, as the French could not possibly be so dense as to dislike the 'Tannhäuser' Overture and the 'Lohengrin' Prelude—it is mere national feeling against a German who was, certainly, most offensive towards France during the war; but such feelings ought not to come into our appreciation or depreciation of an artist's work. Last Sunday there was a tremendously noisy scene. All through the Lohengrin 'Prelude' there was a certain amount of mild protest and hissing, and at the end a perfect Babel of cheers and hisses. One set screamed '*encore*' or rather '*bis*'; the others hissed and 'boo-ed.' Needless to say we helped the cheerers. M. Pasdeloup tried to speak; then he wrung his hands. One saw his mouth move, but nothing was heard. This went on for five or six minutes. At last quiet was restored, and he then said 'he would repeat the "Prelude" at the end of the concert, and those who did not want to hear it could leave.' Much cheering and stamping of feet and banging of umbrellas followed this speech and all was peaceful until the end of the programme. Unfortunately a crowd of silly youths did not go out and when the orchestra began to play, we could not hear a note. More boos and hats thrown about, and sticks rapping the floor, and more minutes wasted. However the conductor laid down his baton and calmly sat down and waited for quiet and peace, which came at last, the objectors being ejected by the Sergents de Ville, and one may hope with some shame.

M. Pasdeloup is a wonderful man. At one of the concerts some people in the front of the stalls went out during a movement of a Symphony. The conductor stopped the band and turned round facing the delinquents, and there he stood until they were at the other side of the entrance door. After the cheering with which this action was received had subsided, he recommenced the movement. It would be well if English Conductors would copy Monsieur's excellent example, especially during their beloved oratorios. It is comic to contrast the reverential upstandings during the singing of the 'Hallelujah Chorus' at St. James' Hall, with the exceedingly irreverent processional stampede which takes place during the final chorus, 'Worthy is the Lamb.' We English are a strange people, and we temper our reverence with the not unnatural desire for a cab without delay—immediately, and before our neighbours can find one. Of course the difficulty of getting home is answerable for the anomaly, but really musical people would surely sacrifice their comfort to their reverence, especially when one thinks of the words? At the same time nothing to me is so wearisome as an Amen fugue, be it at the end of an Oratorio or of a Magnificat. Why go on endlessly singing a, a, a, a, a .... me, me, n, n, n, n, —— ?

Paris still disports itself in more or less handsome carriages, but of a sober colour. The Bois is every afternoon full of them and they seem to me to be better turned out than the London world's equipages. Of course the sky is clearer and consequently the clothes of the driven look more *chic*; but the coachmen with their fur tippets are an addition, and two or three Russian carriages, one with three horses, lend picturesqueness to the scene. By the way, do you know why the outer of the three beasts always keep their heads turned sharply to the right and left? They are strapped in that position! The S. P. C. A. ought to interfere; and people talk of the brutality of bearing reins! In the winter, when there is enough snow these Russians carriages turned into sleighs look charming. The horses fly along jingling their bells; the drivers are enveloped in fur—so are the masters and mistresses, and they all bear themselves, (the coachmen holding the reins in both hands) as if they were tearing along the Neva. I remember once seeing Prince Albert driving the Queen in a Russian sledge in Hyde Park. You know my father liked a walk in the Park, and it was amusing to be with him for he knew every one by sight. I remember years ago seeing Count d'Orsay in the highest of cravats and the tightest of strapped down trousers, like all those hideous portraits of the Orleans family on the upper story at Versailles. Rogers the poet we used to see, and the learned Prince Lucian Bonaparte who loved literature more than his relations. And then the Duke, and the Queen and Prince, with their boys arrayed in kilts. The Row was excessively pretty with ladies in Cavalier hats and long feathers, and sweeping habits almost touching the ground. The carriages too were worth looking at. Curricles and yellow chariots and family coaches—the simple brougham was all but unknown; and then the cabriolet called familiarly cab, with the small Tiger up behind was a very smart turn out for a fashionable man. Upon Drawing room days it was a sight to see the carriages and state coaches with a couple of servants up behind dressed gorgeously, in silk stockings, and cocked hats, and carrying gold headed sticks and bouquets. 'How are the mighty fallen!' But independence and comfort are worth the fall, though beauty and picturesqueness have departed therewith. This is a utilitarian age.

You asked me in one of your letters whether I had ever seen an election in the old rowdy days. Yes, I was once at Salisbury and sat on the hustings to hear the speeches and it certainly was not a very edifying entertainment—there was much howling and screaming, cat-calling, cock-crowing and all that sort of thing, with intervals of egg chucking, whether rotten or newly laid, I cannot say. And upon another occasion I saw John Stuart Mill addressing the crowd on the hustings, in Covent Garden market just outside St. Paul's church. That was a more seemly entertainment, probably the Westminster burghers had something better to do than to throw eggs or other missiles about. But there was a good deal of shouting and vulgar chaff and many noisy invitations to the candidate to 'speak up, old chap,' and 'don't smother your B—— or D—— voice'—not an unjust request though impolitely adjectived, for we could not hear a word of the worthy philosopher's address at the back of the crowd. He spoke with much impressiveness, but so inaudibly that the impressiveness did not impress his audience. However the newspapers next morning gave us a full report, which did as well or better!

RECOLLECTIONS OF

3rd May 1875

MY DEAR MARY

It is dawn. After a lovely starlit night, Venus and Jupiter doing the honours to the waning moon as she saunters along the southern sky, a peaceful fog is rising, while the Fowls of the Air are singing their praises in tuneful ditties. But we are sad, for our little Judy is no more. You remember her? How pretty and graceful and clever she was—but so nervous. I always think she must have been born during the War. The year we were at Sèvres during the Fête, when the fireworks began, she always crouched under the table trembling and moaning; likewise during thunder storms. She was a 10 franc doggie; we bought her of the servant at the Restaurant below, and were first attracted to her by seeing the cabmen running after her cracking their long whips —in play of course, but poor little Judy never saw the joke and cried piteously. Then when the servant went out the little creature was left alone in the 6th story room. Frequently she crept down and lay upon our door mat, and of course she was always invited to partake our hospitality, and so we became fast friends. She danced and loved music; and I grieve to say she did not appreciate Wagner; but when I played any thing by Chopin or Mozart she would get out of her basket and lie down under the piano. She also loved the ' Danse des Sylphes' as being a French doggie, she was bound to do. Happily she was not ill long. Yesterday when she went down with Rosalie to fetch the letters (she used to bring them up our four stories in her mouth) I noticed that she dropped them at the first landing, so I went down and carried her up. We sent for the Vet, who pronounced it to be cancer which I had suspected for a long while. '*C'est très grave, Madame, très grave.*' He gave us something to deaden the pain and prescribed Burgundy, but it was no use keeping the little dear alive to suffer. Up to now, she had had no pain; it came on quite suddenly. It was agonizing to see her, so we determined to let the Vet assist her in her journey to the place to which good doggies go; for surely it cannot be true that such love and affection end here? If their love dies out like the flame of a candle, why should the higher animals live for ever? We have souls, we say; but what is the soul? I presume it is our better nature—love, devotion, unselfishness, self-sacrifice, and duty personified; does not the dog possess all these qualities? . . .

Evening. We took our little friend to Sèvres in a basket this afternoon, to bury her in the woods in which she delighted to run about. Wee though she was, digging a hole large enough with a trowel in hard ground was a long business, and after a time, I espied a pair of eyes upon the top of a blue blouse eagerly watching us. Doubtless the man thought it a case of a new born babe being hidden away, which made me nervous. G. said I was foolish; nevertheless after some minutes she was not unwilling to go and explain the case. The man offered to help us, which he did very effectively; and then we laid her gently in the hole covered with leaves, a real babe in the wood, and sorrowed after more, unfortunately, than many a poor wastrel baby. Before we went home, I cut upon the beech tree above the little beastie: 'Little Judy, May 8, 1875. R.I.P.' 'How intensely silly' some folks would say; and 'profane' etc. etc. But I do not think you will! Good bye. Do you remember the child and dog in a big chair at the R.A.? Little Judy figured several times in pictures, and quite earned her living, as you know. She sat as well as the small Annie, and together they were most useful; but it is her affection not her usefulness which I shall miss. What shall we do without her? 'Have another,' says Common Sense; 'No more pets,' says Sentiment. I imagine no vows have so often been broken as the one everybody utters—'I shall never have another dog.' The following epitaph was composed to the memory of Judy and another little dog, her old friend who died the same week:

> 'Two little friends have passed away
> Friends of each other, and friends of men;
> Faithful, devoted, kindly and true
> What more could be written of me and you?'

A SPINSTER AUNT

I am afraid I often feel more sympathy with dogs than with members of my own race. If you meet a strange dog, he nearly always greets you with confidence if you speak kindly to him. The man or woman requires an introduction, even when they meet at a friend's house, which ought, one would think, to be a sufficient passport to respectability. Once, I remember being dragged by my sister to an At Home in a learned lady's house. 'It would be so interesting, for she knew everybody in the literary world.' Well, I went—not without misgivings. The room was crowded and a general buzz was going on like the hum of Brobdignagian Bees. I found it slow, not to say very slow; I knew nobody, and had I known any one, I could not have crossed the crowded room to get near that individual, for every one seemed occupied with everybody else. It was just the sort of entertainment which is dubbed *so* interesting—by the Inner Circle. I was not of that distinguished tribe, and so I stayed in the back room with two or three others of the Great Unknown. Presently a man arrived with his dog, a beauteous Russian hound, without whom he never went anywhere. He, the man, gravitated to his kind in the crowd; the hound lay down in front of the fire and composed himself to comfort, if not to sleep, feeling that nobody wanted him. I spoke a few words of sympathy—the dog lifted his head and surveyed me. He then sat up, and took a few very searching observations, and finally, being satisfied that I was not a bad sort, he advanced, wagged his tail profusely, leant his beautiful head upon my knees, and for the rest of the evening we conversed together, silently for the most part, but as old friends who are happy just to be near each other in the same room. This sad business, (I do not mean the At Home and the hound) has made me indifferent to the opening of the Salon, so I shall say Good night.

5th. I have just come from the Salon. There are of course many fine things—there always are, and equally of course all the battle painters receive much homage, and rightly, for they certainly touch our hearts with pathetic incidents of the late war. Detaille's 'Régiment qui passe,' recalls the days before the catastrophe. A picture by J. F. Laurens attracts much admiration—'L'Interdit'—it is, like all his work, tremendously strong. But the most beautiful, or one of the most beautiful pictures in the Exhibition is by the flower painter, Fantin-Latour,—a portrait group of 'Mr. and Mrs. Edwards.' It is not a blaze of colour, nor in any way a *tour de force*; but for rich subtle colour and characterization, it is a masterpiece. I admire some of the American painters so much, Harrison and Pierce, the former especially; his landscapes and sea things are charming. Also Hitchcock who paints 'Madonnas' after the modern religious manner, or rather a religious scheme which is in the spirit of the Italian Renaissance. Talking of Italy, can anything be more degraded than modern Italian art? (Of course I except a few Italians like de Nittis who are practically Frenchmen.) But the pure Italian stuff, especially what is politely called Sculpture, is beyond contempt.

RECOLLECTIONS OF

CHAPTER XVIII

BATH

[No date.—Ed.]

BATH. *November.*

DEAR MARY.

I came here with E. a few days ago. It is as you know a 'City of Palaces, a town of hills, and a hill of towns'; so says some one. I frankly admit, I am disappointed.

It is notorious that opinions upon persons and places are as diverse as Nature's own handiworks. This city of Bath, for example, is extolled by some persons as a perfect example of Palladian architecture—grand, noble, unique; whereas others see it as a medley of disjointed squares, streets, and crescents, and dingy and smoke-begrimed houses. Even in the 18th Centy. when it was in its prime, it was as much abused by Smollett as it was admired by Fanny Burney. Evelina found that 'the charming city answered all her expectations. The Crescent, the prospect from it, the elegant symmetry of the Circus' rejoiced her heart. True, the Parades want something of a 'more striking elegance than a mere broad pavement,' to satisfy her ideas, but the view 'affords a beautiful prospect and charming vista of Prior Park and the

A SPINSTER AUNT

river Avon.' No doubt Fanny is right, for the view must have been exquisite before the valley of the Avon was choked with houses. But what says Mr. Matthew Bramble[1] of the Circus? It is 'a pretty bauble looking like Vespasian's amphitheatre turned outside in. Had it a Colonnade like Covent Garden, the chairmen would have had shelter from the rain instead of being obliged to let their chairs soak from morning to night till they become like so many boxes of wet leather for the benefit of the gouty and rheumatic.' Evidently Mr. Bramble disliked Bath. Gay St. is so 'steep that in snowy weather you would go up or down it with the most imminent hazard of broken legs.' And then the smoke-blacked houses, the 'vapours which rise from the baths and rivers, the want of plan in the squares and crescents making them look like a wreck of streets disjointed by an earthquake, or as if some Gothic devil had stuffed them altogether in a bag, and left them to stand higgledy piggledy just as chance directed.' He made 'divers desperate leaps at the upper regions, but always fell backward into the vapour pit, where they gasped like Chinese gudgeons in the bottom of a punch bowl.'

I wish I could have seen the King's Bath in its glory; now it is most commonplace and even Evelina would not be shocked. She was 'amazed at the ladies. True, their heads were covered,

[1] *Humphrey Clinker*, by Smollett.—ED.

but the very idea of being seen in such a situation is indelicate.' This bath is described by Miss Lydia Melford[1] as a 'huge cistern. The ladies wear jackets and petticoats of brown linen, with chip hats, in which they fix their handkerchiefs to wipe their faces; but truly, whether it is owing to the steam which surrounds them, or the heat of the water, or the nature of the dress, they look so flushed, and so frightful, that I always turn my eyes the other way—My aunt, who says every person of fashion should make her appearance in the bath, as well as in the Abbey Church, contrived a cap with cherry ribbons to suit her complexion.' Another person wore a 'hat trimmed with blue,' and when she came out of the bath although she took 'assafoetida drops' she was 'fluttered all day.' Poor dear. Our old friend who disapproved of swimming was of this type of person, a contemporary, I dare say of Miss Melford's. I am afraid even in these days we look not a little frightful in the water, in spite of elegant costumes. Nothing can overcome the clinging of a wet garment, which is not beautiful, although the Greeks seem to have admired it, judging by their statues. Perhaps the Greeks were better made; they were nearer to Mother Eve than we are.

Bath society in Fanny's time was 'dismal'; she heard many 'melancholic ballads'; (we only hear

---

[1] *Humphrey Clinker.*—ED.

melancholic piano organs); 'we also hear street squalling,' says Fanny: 'Some ladies sing catches and nothing can be more ridiculous than a concert of this sort. Oh! such singing! worse squalling, more out of tune, and more execrable did she ever hear.' But one day she had a treat which possibly made up for the ladies' silly concerts, for the Bishop of Peterborough proposed 'a frolic,' and they all went to tea at the Vauxhall, or Ranelagh of Bath, the Spring Gardens. This, the present cricket ground, was 'low and damp . . . but they say, dancing when the air is moist, is recommended as an excellent cure for the rheumatism.' If it turns to wet, at present it is only foggy, I shall take to jigging by myself round the field. I should like to have seen the gardens when the 'frolic' was held, for it was prettily laid out and approached from the South Parade ferry, or from the old city ferry by the East Gate. There was a grotto, where Sheridan is said to have written his lines to 'Delia' otherwise Elizabeth Linley, his wife, the beautiful Mrs. Sheridan of Gainsborough. I should like also to have seen that Grotto—now one only sees dirty crowds and cricket balls.

Here is a verse of 'Delia':

' 'Then tell me, thou grotto of moss-cover'd stones,
    And tell me, the willow with leaves dripping dew,
  Did Delia seem vex'd when Horatio was gone?
  And did she confess her resentment to you?'

RECOLLECTIONS OF

It was from her father's house in the Crescent that Sheridan eloped with Miss Linley—a sedan chair conveying her to the post-chaise in waiting on the London Rd. Five years later, when Mrs. Sheridan was staying with her parents in Bath, the lovers wrote to each other in these trifling effusions. He, to her, thus:

'To LAURA.

'Near Avon's ridgy bank there grows
  A willow of no vulgar size,
That tree first heard poor Silvio's woes,
  And heard how bright were Laura's eyes,'

and ending:

'*Tis* Spring, sweet nymph, *but Laura is not here.*'

And she replies:

'To SILVIO.

'Soft flows the lay by Avon's sedgy side,
  While o'er its streams the drooping willow hung,
Beneath whose shadow Silvio fondly tried,
  To check the opening roses as they sprung.'

I am no judge nor lover of poetry, but if I may be allowed to say it, this seemeth to me to be sad trash. If I do find some verses I like, I am always told they are very minor poets such as Christina Rossetti and Adelaide Proctor; and here and there a scrap in a newspaper by a budding poet who never blooms, pleases me. Some of Shelley's also appeal to me; but there again they are his minor poems. The major effusions of most poets bore me not a little.

A SPINSTER AUNT

How we should have liked to see Gainsborough's Georgina in the flesh![1] 'She was lovely,' says Fanny, 'because in excellent spirits. Vivacity is so much her characteristic, that her style of beauty requires it indispensably; the beauty, indeed dies away with it. . . . The expression of her smiles is so sweet and has an ingenuousness and openness so singular that, taken in these moments, not the most rigid critic would deny the justice of her personal celebrity. She is quite gay, easy, and charming; indeed, the last epithet might have been coined for her.' She looks it all in her portrait.

The Master of the Ceremonies was even in these later days, 'a pretty little gentleman, so sweet, so fine, so civil, and polite,' that Miss Lydia Melford is quite overcome by his charming talk 'both in prose and verse' . . . 'and he is a great writer, and has got five tragedies ready for the stage.' And he ' squired my aunt and me to every part of Bath; which to be sure is an earthly paradise . . . the new buildings, Princes-row, Harlequin's-row, Bladud's-row, and twenty other rows, look like so many enchanted castles raised on hanging terraces,' like wicked Babylon. Alas, how we have degenerated; we have no 'pretty little gentlemen' to take us about, and 'no charming parties made, some to walk on South Parade,' as in the time of Nash.

[1] Duchess of Devonshire.—Ed.

RECOLLECTIONS OF

Bath is no longer what it was! Whose funeral could now be described as follows: 'The peasant discontinued his toil, the ox rested from the plough, all nature seemed to sympathize with the loss, and the muffled bells rang a peal of Bobs Major—People crowded on the housetops.' But this is mild by the side of one of the epitaphs: 'and which of us will earn such an epitaph as: A constellation of the Heavenly sphere—Venus, Cupid, and the Graces are commanded to weep, Bath shall never find such another.' Well, the times have changed and the present Nashs will have to take a lower seat in the world's history; and as to Lord Chesterfield's advice upon games we seem to do all we should not. 'A gentleman will not play at cribbage, all fours, or putt; or in sports of exercise, be seen at skittles, football, leap-frog, cricket, driving of coaches, etc. for he knows that such an imitation of the manners of the mob will indelibly stamp him with vulgarity.' To us it seems curious to put leap-frog and cricket side by side, and it may be possible to play the latter without 'vulgarity' in this 19th Century. But I suppose we are more serious; we do not 'trip away to chapel' and 'then take places for the play.' Nor do 'the Loves and Graces call' us 'to a little private ball.' If we have these things they do not come from Cupid and the Graces. But I dare say some of those I meet in the Pump room now might say they have had enough and to

A SPINSTER AUNT

spare of some of the things jumbled together by the rhymester:

> 'Paid bills, and musicians,
> Drugs, nurse, and physicians
> Balls, raffles, subscriptions, and chairs;
> Wigs, gowns, skins, and trimming
> Good books for the women,
> Plays, concerts, teas, negus, and pray'rs.'

In Jane Austen's time the fashionable parts of Bath were the Parades, the Orange Grove, the Abbey Yard, which were decorated with orange coloured ribbons. Queen Square had gone down in the world: 'Remember, Papa,' says one of 'Persuasion's' young ladies,—'none of your Queen Squares for us!' Where does fashion live in modern Bath?

CHAPTER XIX

MISS GARIBALDI

Diary. 1875. Of course 'we could never live without a dog.' Does not every one say that? and with less reason than I, for I have been a very short part of my life dogless. In my childhood there was Merry, an English terrier, and then dear little Nipper, a cousin of Merry's. Nipper went everywhere with us, even to Cambridge when I was about three years old, in the phaeton. She and I were packed in the hood. That was the only time I have seen a real mail coach with guard and coachman in scarlet, like the penny postmen—the twopenny postmen wore blue. The coach was glowing in light as it passed us one evening, the guard trumpeting its arrival: Her Majesty's Mail painted in large letters upon it.

After Nipper we had a wastrel, Topsy; she followed me to school one day, and said, 'please befriend me.' So we did; and she was a loving creature, but fickle. I could have endorsed François Coppée's sentiments in 'Le chien perdu'; but Topsy disappeared, I know not where or how.

A SPINSTER AUNT

'Quel regard! long, craintif, tout chargé de caresse,
Touchant comme un regard de pauvre ou de maîtresse,
Mais sans espoir pourtant . . .
Si vous arrêtez, il s'arrête, et, timide,
Agite, faiblement sa queue au poil humide
Sachant bien que son sort en vous est débattu,
Il semble dire :—Allons, emmène-moi, veux-tu ?
On est ému. . . .'

Do not most of us succumb to pity and fellow-feeling for yet another undesirable? In the case of poor Topsy we echoed the poet who wrote:

'Poor little mongrel, you've only one friend
That cares to pat you, or take you up ;—
And when that comedy comes to an end
Who will think of you, ugly pup?'

. . . . . .

So I hope some day, as I sit by the fire,
And this flickering lamp at last goes out ;
Your poor little flame with mine will expire
In the darkness we know so little about.
Pup, by that wag of the tail you say
That all your wishes with mine agree—

. . . . . .

Then why did she disappear? and echo answers why? and the verses are not quite appropriate though charming. After Topsy, Sid who was lost, and Jack whose independence led him away from a happy home and safety. Then dear Lily, and Judy; and now Baldi. There were also two or three stray people who stepped in, and ungratefully departed after a few good meals; or possibly they did not like the surrounding humans, or their quarters. They seemed grateful, but 'we would rather go elsewhere'; and luckily they went before they were much loved.

Baldi, as we call her, is a half-crown dog, and like the little Judy, she came from the home of a vendor of strong drinks. She first made herself manifest by creeping under the fence of a certain Wiltshire garden, and racing round and round it with the puppy owner of that same garden, one Gretschen, the Dachshund. We tried over and over again to catch Baldi, but neither diplomacy nor bribery had any effect upon her, her ruling passion being evidently an inordinate love of freedom; and so, when at last we succeeded in inducing the innkeeper to part with the puppy, we determined to rename her after some one who recalled liberty and freedom. Her old name was Lisbeth. Of course she ought to have had a feminine name, but none suggests itself which seems to be quite appropriate, and so we are obliged to adopt the surname of the man whose watchword was liberty, and whose career showed an almost complete absence of self aggrandisement —Giuseppe Garibaldi.

'What's in a name?' Do we acquire qualities which certain names represent to our minds? If that be true, naming a child is a serious matter. Some one once said that 'we cannot be too careful in the choice of our parents.' Surely the selection of a name requires equal care?

A SPINSTER AUNT

Certainly Baldi is an example of a non-self-seeker, for when her own particular friend goes out, she lies for hours curled up in the great arm chair gazing intently at the door. And in all those unselfish little ways in which the average dog proves itself the superior of the average man, or the domestic cat, she is vastly above her fellows. Do the above superior creatures disturb themselves willingly, and leave their pipes, or their fishbones, in order to welcome their friends? The dog, however, does so gladly. Even when sick or dying, it will forget its sufferings, and endeavour to wag its tail ever so feebly; and if, in its weakness, that effort should be impossible, will not its glazing eyes give you one last look which shows forth the wealth of love and devotion still overflowing in its failing little heart?

Baldi's appendage, by courtesy called a tail, is a mere tuft, not even the most consummate flatterer could call it a tail, but it is most expressive in its movements; and it must be borne in mind, that although tail moving in all animals seems to be as easy as speech is to man, yet it shows no little talent to express love, sympathy, joy, sorrow, and laughter by the gentle swaying to and fro of a two inch tuft.

Little Baldi is a dog of character; indeed I may say all my canine friends have been noted for this special quality, probably by reason of the mixed character of their ancestry. Does it not stand to reason that a pedigree is really only a form of degeneration, inasmuch as the same class of fool is being constantly reproduced; whereas with a variety of ancestors, there is a chance of inheriting a variety of follies, which, amalgamated, may evolve themselves into a form of genius. Hence we find that most of the world's greatest men have been of obscure birth, and consequently of a parentage made up of a variety of characteristics which have nothing in common. Why then should we desire pedigree in our dogs when it really means the multiplying of certain qualities over and over again, until they become so subdivided that they are unrecognisable? Why, again, should we be so eager to surround ourselves with perfectly beautiful animal forms, when our own minds and bodies leave so much to be desired?

From the point of beauty Baldi has no pedigree —she is sufficiently plebeian, as I have said, to be a dog of character, but she lacks intellectuality. She is not like Judy, apt to learn, but in her own uneducated manner she is exceedingly wise; and unlike many of her superiors, she knows her own mind. Thus on her first arrival, having been unmuzzled and unchained, she took refuge from her new masters under a table and duly snarled and snapped—London had, at present, no charms for her. But a little mild chastisement promptly and gently administered with a fan, duly produced love, coupled, for a very short time, with fear, and then perfect harmony was installed between us in all our ways and desires.

A few days after her arrival in London, I took her to the other side of the Regent's Park to bide in Kent Terrace during my sojourn in the country. I conveyed her by train to Baker St. The next day she was taken into the Water Garden and unchained. Thereupon she rushed off, and was found a few minutes later upon our door-step half a mile away. How she found her way home, whether by the park or by the Marylebone Rd., remains a mystery. Did she follow, above ground, the evil odour of the Underground railway? It is impossible to say; but it shows considerable sagacity to have found her way from Hanover Gate to Cambridge Gate on foot, when she had gone the greater part of the distance in the opposite direction by train.

Another instance of the small person's sagacity was her repeated efforts one day to attract my attention when suffering from some discomfort in her mouth. For three days she followed me about everywhere, looking piteously into my face. 'How stupid you are,' she seemed to say, 'don't you see how uncomfortable I am? why don't you help me?' I did see, for she constantly twitched her head about by day, and at night she jumped in and out of her basket and paced the room so incessantly, that I could not sleep. At last it occurred to me that the poor little creature might be suffering from toothache, so I inspected her mouth, and I found a double tooth detached from the gum, and the pointed fang sticking into her cheek. She could not get it out with her tongue, and I had no proper weapon, so I bethought me of a button hook which acted excellently well; and when the operation was over, the never failing little tongue poured forth its owner's thanks upon the amateur dentist's hand. . . .

We are frequently told that animals have no reasoning powers, but my experience points to the opposite conclusion. I once knew a horse which, meeting with an accident in passing through a *porte-cochère* leading into an inner courtyard in Paris, refused absolutely to enter the passage again; but he had no objection to passing in by another entrance at the opposite side of the court. His memory was good. And my own dogs afford many examples of reasoning power, particularly little Baldi. . . . When we left London last March I took a furnished house near Christchurch for three months. The servants, very old friends, are strangers to the dog, so my lady would not let me move out of her sight without much pain and grief to the neighbours as well as to herself. She even followed me into church when she had the chance. But the day our furniture arrived and was placed in the new house, we lost her for a time, and then Miss Baldi was discovered after much running about and searching between the two houses, coiled up on her own particular easy chair in the attic of this new house. There she felt the ineffable pleasure of being at home after four months' sojourn in a strange land. But this fear of strangers has its inconveniences, for once, when after the death of her own particular friend, we went for a couple of months to Honfleur, I was obliged to give up the pleasure of a two days' excursion to Caen and Bayeux because the little beastie objected to being left at home without me. It was doubtless, some folks will say, shockingly weak on my part; but if a young person howls like a bear, and goes on howling incessantly, what in the world are you to do? I once knew a dog who had to accompany his mistress to East-End slums, drawing-classes, and country mansions, because once, when left alone, it fasted for 48 hours. This sort of devotion may be very flattering, but it is also extremely embarrassing.

Baldi is a white curly haired person with black ears and saddle à la Judy; in fact a repetition, physically, of the Judy dog, but with a difference. Baldi's black patches are larger, her legs are longer, her hair is less silky and much more curly—'like a little lamb,' as the children say; and her tail, as I have explained, is no tail, but a mere tuft some two inches in length—a very expressive tuft, all the same, but devoid of the beauty attached to Mademoiselle Judy's long feathery appendage. Some people call Baldi a truffle dog.... Our little pet has a companion in Thomas the cat. They began their earthly sojourn about the same time, Tom being given to us when Baldi was about 10 months old. At first, Pussy, with the want of confidence inherent in the cat tribe, arched his small back, spit, stuck out his claws, and showed by his general behaviour, his Pagan nature; but frequent saucers of milk for common use produced a more fraternal state of affairs, and at last the tiny kitten allowed himself to be perambulated about the house in Baldi's mouth,—the dog practically mothered the kitten, proving once more the fact so well known to all real friends of animals, that to compare the unhappy conditions under which some married folks live, to the lives of the domestic cat and dog, is false, and libellous to the four-footers. To lead a 'cat and dog life' means that the husband snarls, and the wife puts up her back and hisses with a venomous tongue— or *vice versa*. But as a matter of fact this unpleasant behaviour only exists between animals who are strangers upon the Queen's highways. Such creatures as Baldi and Thomas, living under the same roof, are as affectionate to one another as the most loving of married people, perpetual lovers like Mr. and Mrs. Garrick. When young our two little people played together uproariously

A SPINSTER AUNT

and always kissed when they first met in the morning; and if, later on, the play became of shorter duration, it was the fault of the puss cat, whose temper is not angelic, and being some sizes larger than his companion, and rough in his manner, his claws occasionally caught in Baldi's hair, with most disastrous consequences. But they remained excellent friends up to the end of their common life, when we retired to rural surroundings, and were obliged to leave Mr. Thomas Pusscatt in London with his dearest friend, our cook.

Baldi like all people of character, has a will. In a man or woman, this is called firmness; in a child, a dog, a cat, a horse, cow, sheep, or pig, it is designated obstinacy; yet there is much family likeness between the two qualities, especially when firmness is strongly developed by grandmothers, aunts, uncles, and cabinet ministers, or by elderly pillars of the Church—laymen, spinsters, widows, and such like. Even those who may be likened unto the outside walls and buttresses of the edifice, are not always free from this virtue. But there is this difference between the two qualities; obstinacy may, in the interest of its possessor, be chastised; but even with gentle speech it is difficult to circumvent firmness; and to smite its owner with a fan would be considered unseemly.

But if somewhat obstinate the little dog is not of a jealous temperament. There was at the top of our house in London a semi-circular balcony which we dignified by the name of the *loggia*. There we cultivated a few fuchsias and Virginia creepers, which flourished wondrously, and which are still a marvel in their country home after 12 years of London smoke. The *loggia* was a delightful place in summer, with just room enough for four small seats, and from it we gazed at many a glorious sunset over the park. In winter it was the meeting place of thirty or forty birds who were duly fed on crumbs and lumps of fat bacon.

Of these creatures, my wild, though tamed, friends, Baldi was not the least jealous, nor were the birds afraid of the dog, and many have been the summer evenings of delightful twilight which we passed together upon that Regent's Park *loggia*—the birds picking up crumbs upon the balustrade, and Baldi snoozing upon her mat.

Like all her fellows when kindly treated, Miss B. reciprocates the devotion lavished upon her, and when one of her friends, an old servant, died, never again would she enter her room; but she had a greater loss later on. Her own particular mistress who walked her about the Park daily, became ill, and the dog, having been through the experience of a prolonged illness ending in complete disappearance, would not stay in the room with her sick mistress. But when the end came, she went about the house searching for what she never could find; and for 6 months at least, she

A SPINSTER AUNT

went into the room every morning, to take a look round. If the door were shut, she asked me to open it. She would then trot up to the bed and return crestfallen. 'No, she is not there,' she seemed to say. And the remarkable part of the story is that she never carries out the same tactics when I temporarily go away; experience tells her that my absences are not preceded by illness.

Baldi's latter days are as happy as peace and contentment, added to the devotion of three willing slaves, can make them. She has daily walks over moorland, and strollings through sweet-scented pine-woods. If she does not admire the rich colouring of the heather and bracken-covered hills, the beautiful reddish purple of the budding silver birches, the brilliant autumn tints of young beeches and mountain ash, and the exquisitely tender blues and greys of water and sky, it is not her fault. She was not born with the artistic temperament which Judy possessed, and all my training has ended in complete failure. To imagine the Judy dog diligently licking off the bearskin head-gear of a little water-colour drummer boy, because she found sweetness in a concoction of brown and purple madder, would be an impossibility. Nor could Judy have sat down upon a wet sketch, or even a dry one. But poor little Baldi is completely void of all artistic feeling by nature, and education and training give her none; for she has always been my constant companion in divers sketching expeditions, and she lies patiently curled up at my feet for hours, without, however, imbibing a grain of art culture. If education will not change the leopard's spots, neither will it give stripes to the horse—which proverb is no reflection upon the intellect of Miss Baldi. The little lady is lucky in her canine as in her human friendships, her most devoted admirer amongst four-footers being a certain high-class gentleman of Scotch birth, one Mr. Matthew, who very frequently visits our garden.

The wild birds are even friendly and hop about on the grass regardless of her presence, for loving peace herself, she leaves others in peace. May her end also be peace—a peace long deferred.

A SPINSTER AUNT

CHAPTER XX

BAYREUTH

[No date. Probably 1882, as 'Parsifal' was finished in that year.—ED.]

My dear Mary

At last I have the desire of my heart, or one of the many desires; viz. I am off to Bayreuth to hear 'Parsifal.' . . .

Left Leipzig in morning early. Arrived B. in time for lunch. Such a crowd, but found a Restauration where they kindly permitted me to sit down at the *table d'hôte*. Tongues many wagging in various languages, German over-topping all in power. My German has left me, I mean the sense of the words I hear; they seem familiar but I do not know the meaning thereof. '*Ja wohl*,' '*Gewiss*,' '*Geehrtes Fräulein*,' '*Gott bewahr*,' '*Mein lieber Herr*,' and the Bavarian '*Jor, Jor*,' '*Es ist heiss*,' and so on, are the only sort of words I understand.

We had several courses of foods, ending with the only good feature of a German meal, the pudding things. Rusks fried and bathed in juice with cherries sitting on the top of them, and a variety of cakes with coffee. But as I wanted to get off to see the town, I grudged the time spent in dining. I did not wish to be like the Germans in the *Farmacia* at the Florence Certosa, who remained so long sipping *Chartreuse* that they had to lose the opportunity of seeing the exquisite Donatello tombs. However, as all things necessary come to an end sooner or later, so did that dinner at the friendly Gasthof.

Out I went, and so did every one else; and there was a general scampering all over the town to see the sights good Wagnerians ought to see, and all the relics they ought to worship. As I did not desire so to worship, I wandered round the town peacefully, away from the crowd which to me was distracting. I know nothing more so than human babble added to the cracking of whips.

At last the time came to go into the theatre. My seat was right in the centre. It is a wonderful place. Nothing but stalls divided down the centre and five entrances on each side, so the building is emptied in a few minutes. No one is admitted after the music has begun. Excellent rule. Darkness except on the stage; another excellent idea. Suppose any one fainted? Everybody is too much impressed for that; or they are not emotional; or peradventure they are bored, most of them, and therefore not inclined to be ill.

A SPINSTER AUNT

However, some of us are not bored; but still, is not the first act somewhat '*langweilig*'—tell it not in Germany; but I did feel the first act to be stagey. The procession of Knights so slow of step, and so sonorous of voice, was to me (I should say it with bated breath if there were any one to hear) rather uninteresting and *long*. When the end came, I made my way out to a garden which suggested refreshment of body and coffee. Presently three girls arrived and also ordered coffee, and then we chatted and found we had mutual friends in London. Where do you ever go without meeting some one who knows somebody you know? It makes one wonder where all the millions are who are supposed to inhabit the land, for we all apparently keep turning round and round in a prescribed circle. We talked and discussed; one of the three was evidently æsthetic, and probably a Wagner worshipper pure and simple. She was dressed in what was, years ago, described as the 'greenery-yellowey Grosvenor Gallery' style. The others were ordinary human beings, luckily matter of fact, for one of them looked at her watch.

'Good Gracious! the time is up—they must have begun.'

'Surely not; your watch is wrong. We heard no silver trumpets.'

'We shall be shut out.' And here the Æsthete began to suppress tears.

'Let us go and try.'

'Certainly, and I shall use my best German and extra best smile to the door keeper.'

Off we went. Arrived at my door (I do not know where the others sat), I began: '*Ach! sie haben angefangen.*'

'*Sie können nicht hinein gehen, Fräulein.*'

'*Ach! bitte, mein Herr.*'

'*Es ist verboten.*'

I felt my heart sink into my feet, and could only repeat, '*Bitte, bitte,*' but the door remained closed, and I was in despair. However this being a desperate case, I put all my bad German together, and the more I heard the Flower maidens singing, the more I smole my best smile. . . . It succeeded.

'*Sie müssen kein Lärm machen. Sie dürfen nur auf der Treppe stehen bleiben.*'

'*Ja, Ja. Ich danke Ihnen vielmal,*' and I put a little coin in his hand. Then I crept up the stairs, fearsome of stumbling in the dark, and stood entranced by the beauty of scenery and music; but we had missed all the Klingsor part.

Presently I felt a large hand take hold of my arm and pull me up. I went up three or four stairs. Then another hand took hold of my other arm, led me a few inches, and then pressed me down into the last seat of the row. There I stayed, unable to see who my benefactor was.

A SPINSTER AUNT

The second act is exquisite, but one does not like to see a fat German as Kundry acting Mary Magdalen. It was Frau Materna, somewhat too elderly, but a magnificent actress. Herr Gudehus was Parsifal. That scene of the washing of the feet is very poetic, but it wants such people as the Ober-Ammergauers to act such parts. The German actress does not do; in fact no professional actress would do. When the curtain closed in I saw my benefactor, a most kindly, big German; and I thanked him profusely—it was really a most kindly act.

Then I met my friends again, and we struggled to the dining room, there to find that we ought to have taken tickets in the morning. There was not a vacant space; but by dint of waiting in a crowd, and edging my way up to the *buffet*, I contrived to seize upon four sandwiches, so called in Germany—rolls cut in half, buttered, and a lump of meat or fowl placed between the bread. I passed these on to my friends, and mercifully we succeeded in getting near the coffee *buffet*—beer was more in requisition.

The pause between the 2d and 3d act is longer than that between the 1st and 2d—otherwise I do not know how we should have got through our sandwiches—and *we were very hungry*. If one had a knife, even only a penknife to cut the meat; but having got through some of the bread, the upper part, the problem was how to manage the meat? One gulp would upset one's digestion, and fingering and tearing it like a wild animal —let me descend the curtain at this point. As to finding any one to take our money, it was impossible, but seeing a heap of silver coins on a counter I threw some on the top and so increased the pyramid to my best ability.

The third act is a repetition of the first with additions. The end is beautiful—the children's voices and the descent of the Dove; but taking it altogether I should prefer Parsifal done in a Concert Hall.

I returned in the night, leaving at 10 o'clock. An express took me to some junction where I waited a couple of hours for a slow train which landed me at Leipzig at 6 A.M. next day, exactly twenty-four hours after my departure; and four hours of 'Parsifal' added to ten or twelve of train is slightly tiring; not a bad example of endurance for art's sake. But had I turned into a comfortable bed, I should not have slept after the excitement.

---

20 April 188 ?

Herewith, dear Mary, a copy of an envelope just arrived. While staying in Essex, I wrote to a friend who misdirected her answer, and after many days the letter was returned to her. Being a curiosity she sent it on to me. She directed the

A SPINSTER AUNT

envelope to Parkhurst instead of Parkeston, and no Essex; so the letter was sent to the Isle of Wight. On one side, scribbled over the Parkhurst in red ink was: '*Not I. of W. Try London N.*' On the seal side, '*Not Parkhurst Rd., Holloway, N.*,' and '*Retd. from H.M. Prison Holloway, and not known there.*' That is information, which, being my cousin, you may not be sorry to receive.

[Here the letters end abruptly, and the remaining leaves of the Diary are a blank.—ED.]

Printed in the USA
CPSIA information can be obtained
at www.ICGtesting.com
LVHW021643090923
757421LV00009B/1204